Books by *Eugene Rachlis*

Peter Stuyvesant and His New York (CO-AUTHOR)
Indians of the Plains
The Story of the U. S. Coast Guard
They Came to Kill
The Voyages of Henry Hudson

The LAND LORDS

The
LAND

LORDS

Eugene Rachlis &

John E. Marquusee

Random House New York

Grateful acknowledgment is extended for permission to quote material from the following: *The Legendary Mizners,* by Alva Johnston, published by Farrar, Straus & Cudahy, Inc.; *Business Week; The Yale Review; Modern Architecture,* published by Horizon Press, Inc.; *The New York Times,* reprinted with permission; *Fortune Magazine,* 1930, 1947, 1952, 1960; *A Child of the Century,* copyright 1954 by Ben Hecht, by permission of Simon and Schuster, Inc.; *Time,* July 3, 1950, copyright 1950 by Time Inc.; *Dodsworth,* by Sinclair Lewis, published by Harcourt, Brace & World, Inc.; *New York Herald Tribune,* 1931, 1933, 1934; *New York World Telegram,* 1933; *Atlantic Monthly,* copyright 1951, 1952 by William Zeckendorf.

FIRST PRINTING

© *Copyright, 1963, by Eugene Rachlis and John E. Marqusee*

All rights reserved under International and Pan-American Copyright Conventions. Published in New York by Random House, Inc., and simultaneously in Toronto, Canada, by Random House of Canada, Limited.

Library of Congress Catalog Card Number: 63–8337

MANUFACTURED IN THE UNITED STATES OF AMERICA BY KINGSPORT PRESS, INC., KINGSPORT, TENN.

DESIGN BY TERE LOPRETE

22875

*To all the men who have developed the space
in which Americans live.*

Contents

1   John Jacob Astor and the Pastures of Manhattan   3
     "Buy the acre, sell the lot."

2   The Land Gamblers: Visionaries and Victims   31
     "Verily, the people are mad."

3   The Van Sweringen Brothers and the Discovery of Suburbia   60
     *"My favorite authors are Rand and Mc-
Nally."*

4   Flagler, Florida and Fantasy   87
     "Just follow the crowd."

5   Abraham Kazan vs. the Slums of New York   131
     "We'll never get the job done."

6   The White-Collar Cities of Fred F. French   164
     *"Manhattan Island must be recon-
structed."*

7   Harry Black, the Man Who Built Skyscrapers   194
        "Bigger and bigger."

8   The Levitts and Their Towns   228
        *"Ninety-nine per cent of the people pray
        for us."*

9   William   Zeckendorf's   Many-Splendored
    Cities   257
        *"I'd rather be alive at 18 per cent than
        dead at the prime rate."*

    Photographs   *following page*   180

    Notes and Acknowledgments   297

(*x*)

The LAND LORDS

"Buy the acre, sell the lot."

I

John Jacob Astor
and the
Pastures of Manhattan

Shortly before his death in 1848, John Jacob Astor, who was then the richest man in the United States and one of the half-dozen richest in the world, recalled a youthful oversight. "Could I begin again," he told a friend, "knowing what I now know, and had money to invest, I would buy every foot of land on the island of Manhattan." Since, at the time, Astor was by far the largest property owner on Manhattan (some of his contemporaries believed he did own every foot of it), the statement was not one of those bootless reflections on missed opportunities with which people often torment themselves. It was simply Astor's way of confirming the soundness of his instincts about real estate. For nearly fifty years Astor had bought goat farms, empty lots, swampy marshes and other parcels of Manhattan land lying beyond New York's city limits. The city, hardly more than a village when Astor started gathering property, was concentrated at the foot of the island; country homes and estates were maintained in what is now Greenwich Village, and working farms to the north of that. New York grew, as Astor anticipated, and the value of his land multiplied, bringing him enormous profits from rentals and occasional sales. Astor kept buying land in the path of the city's expansion, and watched the city and his profits continue to grow. However pleasing the ownership of every foot of Manhattan Island would have been to Astor's ego and bank account, he did not need them to prove that he was the outstanding real estate operator of his day.

Astor's success was based on his ability to see a given piece of land, not for what it was, but for what it could be. Even before the completion of the Erie Canal in 1825, which spurred New York's first great population and building boom, Astor knew that the underdeveloped land he held would be needed for homes, offices, shops and factories. In retrospect, Astor took fewer risks than some of his successors; New York could expand in only one direction. Nevertheless, it was as much an act of faith as of sound business judgment for him to invest on a large scale in what was, after all, useless land.

The great American real estate operators who followed Astor have been guided, as he was, by the principle of buying land for its potential use. Unlike Astor, however, they could not always be certain about the direction of a city's or a region's growth. As a result they have had to learn to influence the direction of that growth. When they succeeded in this they had an impact on the lives of their contemporaries and often on future generations as well. The successes came from putting land to uses Astor could not have prophesied. Suburbs—from high-priced imitations of country estates to the homogenized packages which are stacked around so many of our cities—have risen from all but deserted fields and flourishing potato farms. Low-cost apartments and skyscrapers have replaced meanly used land—slums and run-down industrial areas. Fabulous resort cities have been built on mosquito-infested swamps. And in the process men have gambled money and reputations—their own and other people's—on the proposition that the American land was due for a change in the direction they had foreseen.

John Jacob Astor would have had no difficulty in recognizing the methods of his successors. Chances are, though, that he would be appalled that the return on investment had been so sharply reduced since his own time. Although most of America's real estate operators always had profit clearly in view, none sought it with such single-mindedness as Astor. From the time he left Germany at the age of sixteen, there was within him an unrelenting drive to acquire wealth. Along the way, he also created a myth about himself, and certainly helped establish the American rags-to-riches tradition which reached its apogee in the works of Horatio Alger. By the time he was known as "The Landlord of New York," the story of his life and his business dealings, frequently spiced by invented details, was a model for Americans and would-be Americans. The possibility that anyone at all could find in America what Astor found there was implicit in a book of advice for potential immigrants published while he was still alive. *Wiley and Putnam's Emigrant's Guide* cited him in 1845 as a foreigner who had made good, and concluded that "there are few such specimens in any country of the bold and enterprising merchant, the honest man, the unassuming gentleman, as John Jacob Astor." In the United States itself, where the sententious aphorisms of Benjamin Franklin were already gospel to many on the basis of phrases like "time is money" and "little strokes fell great oaks," Astor's success was in the best tradition of *Poor Richard*. Horatio Alger, who was fourteen years old when Astor died and was thus exposed to the legend at an impressionable age, had only to spin variations on the actual facts and add a dollop of Franklin to create an array of fictional heroes whose application of the proper virtues always made them their fortunes. Like the young men in Alger's books, Astor was hard-working, honest by the business standards of his day, modest in his manner and dress, and undeniably thrifty.

The facts of his early life might well have applied to hundreds of young Europeans who came to regard America as the land of opportunity. He was born in the village of Waldorf, near Heidelberg, on July 17, 1763, the fifth child of a butcher whose name, in the loose spelling of the period, was either Aschtor, Ashdoor or Ashdor. His mother died when he was four, and his father remarried soon after. The family was poor, and all of Astor's older brothers and sisters had left home by the time he was fourteen and became an apprentice in his father's shop. One brother, George, manufactured musical instruments in London; another, Henry, was a butcher in New York. Although it has never been verified, early biographers described John Jacob as an unhappy youth suffering under a cruel stepmother and a drunken father. Whatever the incentive, after two years at the butcher's trade, Astor imitated his brothers. According to the myth, he left Waldorf with a knapsack over his shoulder, walked to the Rhine (which was actually not very far away), worked his way to Rotterdam on a barge, and had enough money left over to buy a ticket to cross the English Channel. It also has been written that at the village limits he paused and vowed to himself "to be honest, to be industrious and never to gamble." Depending on definitions, he was to keep this pledge more or less, whether or not he actually made it.

(6)

London was not Astor's goal. Letters from Henry indicated that more opportunity for enterprise existed in New York. But the American Revolution was in progress and Astor had to make do with what London offered. He worked in his brother's factory, saved his money and, after a fashion, learned English. He was never to master the language despite four years in England and sixty-three in America; he always spoke it with a crude accent and wrote it in phonetics which were closer to his German pronunciation than to English. In 1783, when the peace treaty between the United States and Great Britain had been signed, John Jacob was ready for the most important step in his life. Of the fifteen guineas he had saved in London, he paid five for passage and five for seven flutes from his brother's factory, which he planned to sell at a profit—the first indication America was to have that Astor understood the value of negotiable merchandise. The remaining five guineas were to hold him until he got started. His ship, the *North Carolina*, left Bristol in November and entered ice-packed Chesapeake Bay in January. Only one day out of Baltimore, the ship was held fast. Some of the passengers walked to shore over the solid ice. Not Astor, who was always quick to recognize a bargain as well as his legal rights. Since he was entitled to food and lodging until the trip was actually completed, he remained aboard, eating regularly, if not too well. When, at last, it seemed that the ship's rations were running low, he departed. By his own account, he arrived in Baltimore on March 24 or 25, 1784. Astor was then a few months shy of twenty-one, and ready to conquer the New World.

In mid-April he was in New York, a town of 23,000 nestled on lower Manhattan, still carrying the marks of its Dutch beginnings and, of course, the recent war. His brother Henry had just married and was moderately prosperous. Whether he had a job for John Jacob is not known, but it is unlikely that the young man had come from Waldorf just to trade butcher's blocks. His first job was equally unpromising, however; he peddled bread, cookies and cake on the streets of New York for George Dieterich, a German baker, at whose home he also found a temporary room. Although he did not carry his bakery tray very long, Astor was not permitted to forget the experience. Many years later, his sister Catherine, who felt that his wealth had gone to his head, was overheard to remark, "Jacob was nothing but a baker boy, and sold bread and cake." By fall, Astor had placed his musical instruments for sale, and was employed by Robert Bowne, a Quaker furrier. Bowne was to be the last boss John Jacob Astor ever had. Within a year, Astor had learned what he needed to know about the fur trade, and with the foresight he was to show in most business matters thereafter, he decided that there was money to be made in skins and pelts.

Astor could not have chosen better. In Upstate New York and in Canada, Indians had furs to trade for the cheapest of trinkets, gunpowder and guns, blankets, tobacco or alcohol. And in New York City, London and the cities of continental Europe there was an insatiable demand for the hides of beaver, muskrat, raccoon, bear and fox. Fur trading was not easy work, as Astor was to learn. Long trips from the city to the back country, carrying a heavy pack and sleeping on cold and damp ground, were just the first steps in getting furs ready for sale. After that came the beating of the foul-smelling skins and baling them, an arduous job, for sale in a highly competitive market.

Astor did not plunge into the fur trade at once, but carefully tested it while maintaining a shop of musical instruments and supplies. His inventory came from his brother George in London; his capital from his own savings, a loan from his brother Henry and a dowry from his wife. Astor, like so many of his fictional counterparts in Horatio Alger, held that a good wife was essential to business success, especially if she were endowed with money, social connections and business skill. Sarah Todd had these qualities when Astor married her on September 19, 1785. He moved into his mother-in-law's home (Sarah's father had been dead for fifteen years) and by the following spring had converted part of it into a store containing "an elegant assortment of Musical Instruments, such as piano fortes, spinnets, piano-forte guitars, the best of violins, German flutes, clarinets, hautboys, fifes, the best Roman violin strings, and all other kinds of strings, music books and paper, and every other article in the music line." All of it, Astor announced in his first newspaper advertisement, was for sale "on very low terms for cash." But there was never any question that the musical line was a form of insurance; Sarah Todd Astor tended store while John Jacob took the road to Indian territory and pre-eminence in the fur business.

Within three years the music business was secondary to furs, and although the Astors sold instruments for some time to come they were never an important source of income. In addition to his own hard work—Astor's energy and willingness to endure extreme physical privation were marveled at by colleagues and competitors alike—his success in furs was also due to his ingratiating personality. He got along well with the Indians and the important fur wholesalers in Montreal, his two major sources of supply. Under English law, Canadian furs had to be shipped to England before they could be sold elsewhere. This restriction caused capital to be tied up longer than Astor might have liked, and added to his transportation costs, but the profits were still measured at a thousand per cent, a nice round figure which appealed to Astor until he learned to increase it.

On May 18, 1789, Astor took part of these profits and between fur trips made his first investment in Manhattan real estate. He bought from his brother Henry two lots and four half-lots on the Bowery Road and Elizabeth Street; the price was "forty seven pounds current money of the State of New York." Three months later he bought two adjoining lots from James Bolmer, an innkeeper. These cost him £250, presumably because they contained more or better buildings than the ones he bought from his brother. The next year, his growing fur business forced him to leave his mother-in-law's home and buy a store of his own. One at 40 Little Dock Street cost him fifty pounds, and also brought him mention in the city directory for the first time as "Astor, John J. furr trader." At the end of 1790 he bought another lot, and early in 1791 a half-lot. These were the last land purchases he was to make in the city for ten years, and do not give the slightest hint of the land hunger he was later to appease so voraciously. Their real significance is that after less than seven years in the United States, Astor, not yet twenty-eight, had £347 ($7,000) to invest, a substantial sum for the time. He was off to a good start.

What followed, and with remarkable speed, made this impressive beginning appear inconsequential. In 1796, soon after the U. S. and Great Britain signed the Jay Treaty, in which the British agreed to withdraw from their military posts in the Old Northwest, Astor told a friend, "Now I will make my fortune in the fur trade." One provision in the treaty revoked the requirement that Canadian furs be sent to England before resale. Astor's agents immediately swarmed into the rich fur territory around the Great Lakes; his buyers, and occasionally Astor himself, covered the

Montreal fur market. The pelts were shipped directly to New York or to Europe. Profits soared, and made possible even larger volume and larger profits. Trade goods in the quantities in which he now needed them were bought in London at reduced prices, so that Astor could afford to make better deals with the Indians than his competitors. As his supply of cash increased, Astor enlarged his stock; his shop now carried a line of guns, ammunition, English woolens, Chinese tea and fine silks. By 1800 he was worth some $250,000, had moved to a larger shop, and had bought a home on Broadway, the city's most fashionable residential street.

He was now thirty-seven and in the front rank among New York merchants. A less ambitious man might have stopped there, perhaps to consolidate his gains so as to provide for a secure future. Instead, as if the start of the new century were a personal signal to him, John Jacob Astor stepped up his tempo, not only in the fur trade, but soon in the two other activities which were to multiply his fortune by a hundred—trade with China and real estate.

Astor's imagination may have soared beyond the ken of his contemporaries, but his real estate purchases were also made possible by a steady source of cash that few of them could match. Most of it came from the China trade. In the early nineteenth century China represented an enormous, and comparatively untapped, market for furs, and no one in the United States was better equipped to fill that demand than Astor. The Chinese also paid well for ginseng, a medicinal herb which grew in Upstate New York, where Astor's fur agents could obtain it easily. The Chinese admired sandalwood, which was available in Hawaii, and in time Astor's ships controlled nearly the entire supply. Furs, ginseng, sandalwood, cotton cloth, dyestuffs and wine were carried to Canton, first on ships in which Astor was part owner, later on those he owned outright. On the return voyage they brought the teas, silks, spices and chinaware which American and European merchants eagerly bought. As always, part of the profits went for trade goods in London. These were delivered to Astor's fur buyers, and the process started again. It was easy to believe that Astor had become, as James Gordon Bennett said in the *New York Herald*, "a self-invented money-making machine."

Bennett's phrase was more colorful than accurate. In those days, at least, machines were not capable of starting themselves. One of Astor's most glorious triumphs was, aside from its profits, proof that, however efficient his machine, it was run by a man with ingenuity. He showed both qualities in 1808, when the embargo on foreign trade which Thomas Jefferson had imposed was becoming unbearable to East Coast merchants. There was nothing they could do about it, though, except petition their congressmen or the President himself. To Astor the situation represented a challenge he could not resist.

Astor started with Samuel Latham Mitchill, a Democratic senator from New York, a professor of natural history at the College of Physicians and Surgeons, and a friend of Jefferson's. According to a perceptive contemporary, Mitchill was "distinguished for scientific and literary requirements" but "strangely deficient in that useful commodity called common sense." On July 12, 1808, he wrote a letter to the President introducing its bearer, "Punqua Wingchong, a Chinese merchant," who had completed his business after nine months in New York and, despite the embargo, was "desirous of returning to Canton, where the affairs of his family and particularly the funeral obsequies of his grandfather, require his solemn attention." He was now in Washington, said Mitchill, "to solicit the means of departure, in some way or other, to China; but he feels at the same time a strong desire to see the Chief Executive officer of the United States."

Punqua Wingchong and the President did not meet; as Astor knew, Jefferson had left Washington for Monticello not long before Mitchill wrote to him. Wingchong did the next best thing; he enclosed Mitchill's letter with one of his own to the President. Jefferson's reaction was prompted by national interest and personal sympathy; he immediately wrote Albert Gallatin, his Secretary of the Treasury, recommending that Wingchong's request for a ship be granted. It was a case of national comity, Jefferson said, in addition to which the favor "may be the means of making our nation known advantageously at the source of power to which it is otherwise difficult to convey information." The chance to establish American good will in China outweighed the effect of a single exception to the embargo; and, he added, it was obviously so singular a case that "it can lead to no embarrassment as a precedent." Jefferson made sure Gallatin would comply by enclosing a blank passport and instructions to "direct all the necessary details."

On August 3, Gallatin sent Jefferson's passport to the collector of the Port of New York, described the special situation, and outlined certain conditions which had to be met by the ship which carried Wingchong, who by now was being referred to as a mandarin. Considering that an embargo was in effect, Gallatin was remarkably generous. Wingchong and his attendants could take, in addition to baggage and personal effects, their property "of about forty five thousand dollars . . . either in specie, or in furs, cochineal [a dye], ginseng, or any other . . . merchandise at his choice." Wingchong, Gallatin said, had already made arrangements for his voyage home "with the owner of the ship *Beaver* of 427 tons." Soon after he wrote to New York,

Gallatin informed Jefferson that he had "transacted the Chinese Mandarin business to his satisfaction & he will sail in a few days." Almost at once, though, Gallatin had his suspicions. He knew that the *Beaver* belonged to Astor.

After forty-eight troubled hours, Gallatin wrote the President again, this time to say that if he had had any choice in the matter he would have hesitated. "I apprehend," he said, "that there is some speculation at bottom." Jefferson disagreed; the potential diplomatic results were great, and even "likely to bring lasting advantage to our merchants." The only merchant who was to derive a lasting advantage from the President's gullibility was at that moment preparing the *Beaver* for sea. As Astor urged his crew to speed, word spread from the docks of New York to Philadelphia and Boston. The voyage could not have been kept a secret under any conditions. Except for coastal vessels, Astor's was the only activity on the waterfront.

Astor's competitors reacted as expected. A group of Philadelphia merchants wrote Gallatin angrily denouncing Wingchong as "an imposter, and an insignificant instrument in the hands of others." Some of them had been to China and recognized him as a "petty shopkeeper" from Canton. The opposition Federalist press used the story to club the administration. Wingchong was variously identified as "a common Chinese dock loafer," "a Chinaman picked up in the park," and by some as not even Chinese at all, but a Lascar sailor or "an Indian dressed up in silk and adorned with a peacock fan," his props having been supplied by John Jacob Astor. By the time Gallatin feebly answered the Philadelphia merchants and even Jefferson felt that the *Beaver* "should be detained," Astor's ship was outward bound.

She returned to New York on June 1, 1809, with a full cargo of teas, silks, spices and chinaware. Since she was the first ship from China in more than a year, her goods were worth a good deal more than in ordinary times, and Astor cleared some $200,000 on the single voyage.

Although he was not to manage as satisfying a coup again, Astor continued to do well in the China trade until he got out of it in 1825. From it, and from the American Fur Company, he drew the money with which he made his first large real estate investments. He had proposed the fur company in 1808 as a government-sanctioned operation to promote the national interest and benefit all American citizens. In fact, reported an early biographer, tongue in cheek, his plan was "to concentrate the western fur trade in the hands of only such American citizens as had been born in Waldorf, Germany, in 1763, and had arrived in the United States from London in the spring of 1784." Except for the intrusion of the War of 1812, during which he lost the lucrative western fur posts he called Astoria, Astor's plan was nearly fulfilled. His own sound knowledge of the business and the ruthlessness of his traders—stirring up the Indians to attack the mountain men who preferred to deal with the Rocky Mountain Fur Company, illegally manufacturing and selling liquor to the Indians—gave him an eminence just short of monopoly in America and supremacy in the London and Canton markets.

All told, Astor spent nearly fifty profitable years in the fur trade, but it is an ironic commentary that when he sought to be memorialized in print he subsidized Washington Irving, then America's outstanding author, to write the story of Astoria, the major failure. No such setback marred his years in the China trade or in real estate. His earnings from the land made it possible for him to buy even more land, which in turn created more earnings with which to do it all again. Even his contemporaries who thought that only death itself could stop the Astor spiral did not really understand what he was accomplishing. "Indeed," a biographer said, "he could now die, and his descendants could sleep for a hundred years, and still the House of Astor, founded on the rock of Manhattan, would prevail against all enemies."

Although John Jacob Astor had been active in real estate since 1800, he did not devote himself exclusively to Manhattan land until 1834, when, at seventy-one, he sold the American Fur Company. The shock of his wife's death that year had affected his health, and he did not feel up to the complicated maneuvering required to run a fur empire. His family and friends were concerned about the physical change in him. In 1794, when he sat for two portraits by Gilbert Stuart, he had been a good-looking, athletic man of thirty-one, above medium height, broad-shouldered and obviously in excellent health. A portrait painted in his fifties shows a corpulent body, stubby arms and legs, heavy cheeks and a double chin. In 1834, Philip Hone, a prominent New Yorker who saw Astor often, noted in his diary that "his health is declining. He appears feeble and sickly." Health aside—he lived fourteen years after that diary entry—Astor was perceptive enough to see that the fur market was shrinking, just as he had known ten years earlier that the China trade was becoming more competitive and less lucrative than when he had been able to fool the President of the United States. What is more, he had thrived on intense personal involvement in his affairs, and he knew he would enjoy dealing in the land in his immediate vicinity.

Manhattan was booming. Since the opening of the Erie Canal in 1825, New York had attained the importance its citizens had anticipated when they celebrated with joyous land and water parades "the meeting of the waters." In that year alone five hundred new business houses had opened in the city. They went up so fast that collapses of finished structures were common; when one brick building came down during a thunderstorm it was found that the walls were only a brick and a half thick at the base and practically no mortar had been used. Although most of the island north of what is now Union Square still consisted of privately owned farms, the New York and Harlem Railroad had by 1834 been completed as far as Yorkville, and horse-drawn cars were carrying passengers there for 12½ cents. In the urban part of the city the population was pushing 250,000, nearly ten times what it had been when Astor arrived fifty years earlier. There was urgent need for houses, shops and factories, and, of course, for the land on which to put them. The earlier residents and the wealthy had long since provided for themselves; in 1834 Henry Brevoort built a magnificent home, for many years one of the city's finest, at the corner of Fifth Avenue and Ninth Street. But newcomers had to shove and bid against each other to find choice properties for homes or businesses in the heart of the city.

Astor was not surprised. He had anticipated a surge and, if anything, may have been too pessimistic. Ever since he first bought on Manhattan he had had two convictions which guided all his subsequent buying, selling and leasing of land, and which apparently evaded other moneyed men of his time: New York, with its natural harbor and access to the interior, had to grow; and on the island of Manhattan there was no place to go but north. Astor bought north of the city's business and residential districts—and waited for the population to follow him.

His theory and practice of real estate was no secret. One story, although probably apocryphal, was, like most of the legends about Astor in his lifetime, accepted as true. In

(17)

its best-known version, Astor had sold a lot near Wall Street for $8,000. The buyer was confident that he was one of the few men in New York who ever outwitted Astor in a business deal. When the papers were signed, he could not resist gloating. "Why, Mr. Astor," he said, "in a few years this lot will be worth $12,000." "Very true," Astor is supposed to have replied. "But with this $8,000 I will buy eighty lots above Canal Street. By the time your lot is worth $12,000, my eighty lots will be worth $80,000." And this, the story concludes, proved to be the case.

Astor's profits in real estate did come from transactions similar enough to this one to give it an element of credibility. The story is also useful in that it helps counter a long standing myth that Astor never sold his properties, but held on to them as their rental income climbed higher and higher. It is more likely that the phrase attributed to him—"Buy the acre, sell the lot"—expressed his attitude. Nevertheless, between sales, rental income was an important source of Astor money. In fact, his first major investment in Manhattan real estate was based on rental property which he did not own but held on long-term lease from Trinity Church. Trinity was one of the largest landowners on Manhattan, but the state legislature, to which the church represented Tory aristocracy, had limited its income to $12,000 a year. Even this seemed too generous to the Democrats in Albany, and early in 1797 they appointed a committee to investigate the church's financial affairs. The chairman of the committee was Aaron Burr, who was amazingly adept at finding ways to make money, a skill he may have developed because of the speed with which he spent it. The investigation was not carried out, possibly because in May, Burr became leaseholder of 465 lots in Greenwich Village owned by Trinity for which he paid an annual rent of $269. The lease had been given originally for ninety-nine years to Abraham Mortier, a Loyalist, and still had sixty-nine years of potential profit when Burr received it. Burr seems to have considered rental income too slow for his needs. He took out a $38,000 mortgage on his lease. By 1803, while he was Vice-President of the United States, he had fallen behind on his payments and, as always, needed money. Astor was the logical source. That year Astor bought the lease to 241 of the Trinity lots for $62,500 in cash plus responsibility for Burr's mortgage. He paid it off the next year for some $42,000 and, as Burr's need for cash remained constant, continued to buy additional sections of the lease from time to time. One purchase of $8,000 was made a month after Burr had killed Alexander Hamilton in their famous pistol duel.

Burr's financial problems were a boon to Astor, who subleased the lots at a profit. Tenants were responsible for all taxes, assessments or duties on their rented property. The ground rent, less than a dollar a lot per year, was paid to Trinity by Astor. Improvements made on the lots by tenants—buildings, fences, sidewalks, swamp-filling, hill leveling—reverted to Astor at the end of the sublease, although on some subleases he agreed to pay a fair price for buildings left by the tenants. Whatever the conditions, Astor couldn't lose. Property values increased, and when sub leases expired Astor renewed them at higher rentals and for shorter periods. In the ten years before he died, rentals alone—from the Trinity lands and other property—brought him more than $1,250,000.

While negotiating with Burr for the Trinity-Mortier lease, Astor was also working on the details of one of his most important purchases, the seventy-acre Eden farm which lay beyond the city limits. It ran from Bloomingdale Road (now part of Broadway) west to the Hudson River between what are now Forty-second and Forty-sixth streets.

Astor probably did not expect any immediate profit from this purchase, but it was a bargain he could not overlook. Mecdef Eden had inherited the land in 1797 but, according to contemporary gossip, had "frittered away" his money. In 1801, the property was ordered sold by the Court of Chancery. Astor and a friend bought it for $25,000, but not long afterward Astor bought most of his partner's share. Eventually, these acres which bordered on what was to become Times Square cost Astor $9,000 more; heirs of Eden required that much to relinquish any claims they might make on the land. Astor's descendants would reap the rewards of his foresight—these blocks, which include most of the city's theater district, the New York Times Building and the Astor Hotel among others, are among the most valuable in the whole city—but Astor himself did not go entirely profitless from the parcel. He sold twelve acres for $7,000, a fifth of what he paid for seventy, and leased twenty-one more to a farmer for seven years at $800 a year. Although these were smaller profits than Astor ordinarily liked, he must have been fascinated by the area. A few years later, when the Cosine farm, running from Broadway to the Hudson—from present-day Fifty-third to Fifty-seventh streets—was made available in another forced sale, he bought it for $23,000.

More immediate profits came from property nearer the city's limits than the Eden and Cosine farms. Greenwich Village, in which Astor held an interest by virtue of his Trinity Church lease, was directly in the line of the city's growth in the early 1800's; nearly five hundred acres of Village land was owned by George Clinton, former governor of New York and successor to Aaron Burr as Vice-President of the United States. Like Burr, Clinton often lacked money. In 1805 he sold half his property to Astor for $75,000. This amounted to 243 lots, at an average price of $300 a lot.

Astor met the demands of a growing city by selling thirty-two of the lots for more than a thousand dollars each in the next few years. This kind of return was appealing, and after Clinton died in 1812, Astor bought more of his land from the executors of the estate, as well as other Greenwich Village property from Trinity Church.

During his early period in real estate, Astor's purchases reflected the fortunes of his China ships and his fur trade. During the War of 1812, for instance, he bought very little. When the war ended, and the price of goods went up, he made substantial investments. For the next five years most of his capital went into building the American Fur Company, but he did not overlook available bargains in land. So-called water lots—land on Manhattan's river banks, under water at high tide—were being granted by the city for ridiculously low sums, on condition that they be filled in. For $32.50 per year for each lot, Astor acquired more than a dozen. Later, he petitioned for reductions in rent or remissions for thirty years, and usually won. He was slow in filling in his lots, and their stench brought complaints from citizens who considered them a public nuisance, but when he did, they became valuable additions to his earlier holdings. From 1834 until his death, however, he did not need either his China or fur earnings to finance his real estate. Income from rent alone more than covered his purchases of Manhattan land during that time.

When Astor turned his full attention to real estate, he also started construction of a hotel at the northwest corner of Broadway and Vesey Street; he called it the Park, but it was never referred to as anything but the Astor House, the name it eventually adopted formally. It was the only construction, except for his own homes, that Astor ever undertook. Philip Hone, who lived near its site, called it a *palais royal* which he guessed cost Astor between $500,000 and

$600,000. Despite the dust and rubbish which offended him during the period of demolition of existing houses, Hone felt that "the establishment will be a great public advantage, and the edifice an ornament to the city, and for centuries to come will serve, as it was probably intended, as a monument to its wealthy proprietor." It was six stories high, its front of blue Quincy granite, had "three hundred rooms each furnished with black walnut," and seventeen bathrooms, although Astor's original plans had called for ten. The additional ones were the suggestion of men to whom Astor leased the building, and he did not object to their extravagance as long as they paid for it. Astor also rented out the eighteen shops on the ground floor. During Astor's lifetime the hotel was by all odds the center for Manhattan's social life. He himself, however, saw none of its income. Before work had even started on it he conveyed it, "for one Spanish milled dollar," to his son William, who presumably received the $20,000 to $30,000 a year income it supplied. This was not the high return on investment that Astor usually enjoyed. Chances are he built the hotel for pride rather than profit.

A year after the hotel opened its doors, the country was plunged into the Panic of 1837. "Here in the city of New York," Philip Hone wrote, "trade is stagnant. Local stocks are lower than ever; real estate is unsalable at any price; rents have fallen and are not punctually paid, and taxes have increased most ruinously. The pressure is severe enough upon the owners of houses and stores who are out of debt, but if the property is mortgaged and the seven per cent interest must be regularly paid, God help the owners." While others may have required divine intervention, Astor was secure in ready capital, few debts and many credits. Although he himself did not foreclose many mortgages— simply because he did not hold many—he was able to purchase at exceedingly low prices from owners who needed cash. His average annual purchases of Manhattan land toward the end of his life amounted to $60,000. But in this period they rose to $160,000, and in 1838 to $224,000, as he gathered farms in Harlem, radish patches in the Lower East Side and odd lots scattered throughout the island. Invariably, everything he bought was a bargain, although once, when he won seven lots for a bid of $5,650, the Court of Chancery required that he pay $1,500 more as a bonus.

If he ever reflected on his choice of Manhattan as his area for real estate investment, Astor could find little to regret. His only disappointments in land were outside the city. On his earliest trips upstate and to Canada seeking furs, he had bought some lots, but they gave him neither great satisfaction nor profit. Once he bought several parcels in Canada for some £850, which he sold within two years for £1,060, a profit of nearly 25 per cent, small as measured by the returns in the fur trade. The buyer was Astor's brother George, who was in London and had not seen the property. When George died in 1813, his widow received a note from Astor assuring her that the property was worth between £1,500 and £2,000. But in 1836, when George Astor's executors were still trying to sell it, there were no buyers, and the property which had cost George about a pound per acre was being valued at two shillings sixpence per acre, about one-eighth the original price.

The speculative nature of wilderness and rural land was clear to John Jacob Astor quite early in his career, and aside from properties he picked up in payment for debts, he rarely looked beyond the city. One major exception to this practice started full of promise, and Astor entered it with great anticipation as well as all the ingenuity he had displayed in arranging the odyssey of Punqua Wingchong. This

(23)

one was even more carefully plotted, if only because a larger cast of characters was involved. In 1697, King William III had granted one Adolph Philipse enormous tracts in what are now Putnam and Dutchess counties, New York. In 1754, Mary Philipse inherited 50,000 acres of the original grant. Four years later she married Major Roger Morris, a British Loyalist; a family tradition says that she did so after turning down a marriage proposal from George Washington, then a colonel in the Virginia militia. In 1799, with the Morris family in England, the New York legislature ordered the property confiscated. A few years later the state broke up the property and sold it, mostly to farmers. The same thing had happened to other Tory holdings, and it is likely the matter would have ended there except for Astor.

Astor learned in 1809 that New York State had overlooked a significant fact. Under their marriage settlement, Mary and Roger Morris had only a life interest in the property. By the terms of the American-British peace treaty, the state's confiscation could apply only to the Morrises' life interest; when they died, their children were entitled not only to the land, but to the improvements which had been made on it. Major Morris was already dead, and Mrs. Morris was seventy-nine years old. Applying his own actuarial tables, Astor saw a swift and happy ending to this story. He had just realized his huge profits from the *Beaver* voyage, and he quickly negotiated with the three surviving Morris children to obtain their rights to the confiscated property as soon as their mother died. It would have been hard for them to resist Astor's offer. He paid them £20,000 (about $100,000) in cash; their alternative was a long and expensive suit on behalf of their claims and, because of the family's Tory history, no guarantee of results. Astor, for his part, had only to await the death of an old lady.

Mrs. Morris's refusal to die as readily as Astor had anticipated was the first, and probably the most irritating, of a number of inconveniences he was to face in this venture. Until she was gone, he could not evict the present occupants of the land, or seek redress from the state. Pending that, though, there were other things he could do. For one, because he thought it would be impolitic to petition the state as an individual, he sold parts of his claim to men who shared his vision. He was thus able to represent himself as acting in behalf of a group of citizens. He also realized a hundred per cent profit by selling one-fourth of his interest for $50,000. (Later, he managed to buy back most of what he sold, and in the end held all but a small part of the claim.) In 1813, when Mrs. Morris was eighty-three, and still annoyingly alive, Astor decided not to wait any longer. He formally notified the state that the group he represented was willing to settle its claims for $300,000; the sum, he said, was about half what the estate was worth, and would probably do no more than let him and his public-spirited partners break even. The state, however seriously it took Astor's plea, did not feel it incumbent to act during the lifetime of Mrs. Morris, and made no move. In 1819, Mrs. Morris was still up and about. On the assumption that she really couldn't last much longer, Astor raised his claim once more. His price was ostensibly the same as before, except that with interest for the waiting years, it now meant a payment by the state of $415,000. The claim was discussed at sessions of the legislature, but still without action. Finally, at the age of ninety-five, and sixteen years after Astor had predicted her early demise, Mrs. Morris died.

The state could no longer evade Astor's case. It took two more years, but in 1827 a complicated bill was passed which, in essence, provided that Astor would receive $450,000 in 5 per cent state stocks if he won his case in court. Astor had been preparing for just such legal proceedings for longer than he cared to think about, and he had a half-dozen of New York's finest lawyers working for him. The state attorney general responded by adding to his staff Daniel Webster and Martin Van Buren, who was ten years away from the presidency of the United States. Although there were technical questions, such as the wording of the original Morris marriage settlement, the case came down to Astor's legal right, as opposed to his moral right, to take the land from the people who had bought it in good faith, had lived on it and had developed it.

Webster, with the rolling phrases of the natural orator, argued the moral case. "It is a claim for lands," he said, "not in their wild and forest state, but for lands the intrinsic value of which is mingled with the labor expended upon them. . . . The individual who now claims it has not succeeded to it by inheritance; he has not attained it, as he did that vast wealth which no one less envies him than I do, by fair and honest exertions in commercial enterprise, but by speculation, by purchasing the forlorn hopes of the heirs of a family driven from their country by a bill of attainder. By the defendants, on the contrary, the lands . . . are held as a patrimony. They have labored for years to improve them. The rugged hills had grown green under their cultivation before a question was raised as to the integrity of their titles."

Astor's lawyers knew better than to compete with Webster on an emotional level. Thomas Addis Emmett summed up the Astor position in a single sentence: "Mr. Astor bought this property confiding in the justice of the State of New York, firmly believing that in the litigation of his claim his right would be maintained."

The jury found for Astor, and the state legislature prepared to make good on its promise to him. There were more delays, however, and public protests, before the state finally paid. The most violent objection came from Edmond Charles (Citizen) Genet, the former French diplomat who became a naturalized American. Genet published a pamphlet, quoting the proper authorities, which stated that Astor had no right to the lands, and the state no right to pay his claims. But it was public knowledge that Astor had some years earlier foreclosed several of Genet's mortgages; Genet's arguments, however learned, were dismissed as attempts at vengeance. In 1832, twenty-three years after Astor paid the Morris heirs $100,000 for their claim, he received the $450,000 in state stock, plus $110,000 in cash, which represented the interest due him from the time the legislature had first acted on his behalf. A student of Astor's financial affairs calculated his expenses in the Morris suit at about $50,000, plus the $40,000 due people who had invested in his claim. This left Astor with a return of some 350 per cent on his original investment, or about 15 per cent a year, not much compared to what Manhattan real estate was earning for him by then. Although he would still receive $22,500 a year in interest as long as he held the state stocks, Astor was not impressed by the total financial results. "I had much trouble and little profit by this transaction, though people think I made a fortune by it," he wrote his son-in-law.

Before he considered the Morris case closed, Astor caught the state of New York in one final error, and quickly filed a claim for its remedy. The stock certificates he had been issued called for interest to be paid on the first Monday in January, April, July and October. The original agreement had been that interest would be paid on the first *day* of those months. This meant a loss, however tiny, when the first did not fall on a Monday; and Astor never did like to settle for less than his legal due.

Exacting his due, no matter what the circumstances, was characteristic of Astor from his ice-locked landing in the United States until his death. In his last years his feebleness was pathetic, but his money sense never faltered. Hone, who dined with him one evening in 1844, noted that Astor "sat at the dinner table with his head down upon his breast, saying very little, and in a voice almost unintelligible . . . a servant behind him to guide the victuals which he was eating, and to watch him as an infant is watched." The analogy with infancy was apt. Not long afterward, Astor was being fed at a woman's breast, the only nourishment he could take, and for exercise he was gently tossed in a blanket every day. But his mind, Hone observed, was "good, his observation acute, and he seems to know everything that is going on." One day, according to James Parton, a younger contemporary who wrote the first biography of Astor, the eighty-four-year-old man was being tossed in the blanket when his agent called to report his receipts from the Astor rent rolls. From the middle of his blanket, Astor called, "Has Mrs.——paid that rent yet?" The agent had to admit she had not, and in fact could not, because she had had some misfortunes, and he pleaded with Astor to give her more time. "No, no," said Astor, "I tell you she can pay it, and she will pay it. You don't go the right way to work with her." The agent left, and mentioned the matter to Astor's son. Young Astor sympathized with the agent's problem, counted out the proper sum, and told the agent to give it to the old man as if it had come from the woman. "There," said Astor, when he had the money, "I told you she would pay it if you went the right way to work with her."

Even if the story cannot be documented it is the kind which Parton and other New Yorkers of the period believed about Astor. When he died on March 29, 1848, at the age of eighty-four, *Harper's Magazine* commented that "to get all that he could and to keep nearly all that he got—those were the laws of his being." Horace Mann, the educator, was even more bitter in denouncing him as one who had hoarded "wealth for the base love of wealth, hugging to his breast, in his dying hour, the memory of his gold and not of his Redeemer." When Astor's will was made public, his critics were even more articulate. Nearly all of his fortune, which ran between $20,000,000 and $30,000,000, was left to his second son, William Backhouse. Astor believed strongly in the principle of primogeniture, but had to temper it; the greatest personal tragedy in his life was his eldest son, John Jacob, Jr., who was born in 1791, and although he lived to seventy-six, was mentally incompetent from early childhood. Dorothea, Astor's second daughter, also outlived him; two of his four sons and one of his four daughters had died in infancy, and two daughters had died as adults. Bequests of varying amounts and properties were distributed for the care of John Jacob, Jr., to Dorothea, to grandchildren and other relatives, and about $500,000— from one-fortieth to one-sixtieth of the estate—was left for philanthropy. Of this, $400,000 was to establish a reference library, which was done in 1854; the Astor Library was for years the largest in the country and was eventually incorporated in the New York Public Library.

The library bequest, although enormous compared to the $25,000 left to the Association for the Relief of Respectable Aged Indigent Females and $5,000 to the Society for the Relief of Half Orphans and Destitute Children, failed to move James Gordon Bennett, whose *New York Herald* ran the entire text of the will on page one, an unprecedented bit of journalistic enterprise. Bennett suggested that "one half of [Astor's] immense property—ten millions at least— belonged to the people of the City of New York. During the last fifty years of the life of John Jacob Astor, his property has been augmented and increased in value by the aggregate intelligence, industry, enterprise and commerce of New York, fully to the amount of half its value." The other ten or so millions, Bennett said, was "quite enough for any reasonable person, of any rank in this country."

Bennett's arithmetic, while reflecting his own democratic views, was essentially a criticism of the age in which he and Astor lived, rather than of Astor himself. Unlike others of the new mercantile class, Astor never took part in illegitimate speculation or gambled in stocks. He did not have to; he had only to trust his sense of business timing, to know when to get in and out of the fur and China trade and when, above all, to get in and stay in Manhattan real estate. There is no question that the "aggregate intelligence, industry, enterprise and commerce of New York" multiplied the value of Astor's lands (and would continue to do so until the present, to amounts Bennett would be hard put to imagine). But Astor, from the time he envisioned a prosperous city on the farms and swamps he bought, had counted on just those factors—not apparent to anybody else when he started out—to justify his seeming madness as intelligent investment. As far as he was concerned, the millions he accumulated were no more than his due.

"Verily, the people are mad."

2

The Land Gamblers:
Visionaries and Victims

Of the innumerable get-rich-quick projects, both honest and
otherwise, that have had their heyday in the United States,
few have had greater appeal or flourished longer than land
speculation. In one form or another Americans have gambled in land since Colonial times. This is understandable
enough; for most of our history millions of cheap, and often
free, acres have beckoned to be populated, farmed or
mined. It was not hard to believe that large profits might
accrue to those who bought choice land early, created a demand for it, and sold out fast. Dealing in land this way is
roughly comparable to another American institution: a
poker game in which the deuces, treys, one-eyed jacks and
jokers are wild. Because card values and odds are so distorted in this kind of contest, intelligent gamblers stick to
the less dramatic, even homely, virtues of straight draw or
stud poker. In much the same way, experienced real estate
men prefer the slower, but more reliable, profits which derive from the development and improvement of their holdings. Nevertheless, some fairly astute men, among them

George Washington, to use an early example, have taken fliers in land speculation. Like others since, he was disappointed in the results, because, as he wrote a friend, "I have found distant property in land more pregnant of perplexities than profit." Although perplexities have always abounded, American land speculation has had its vigorous periods; at one point in the early years of the new republic it attained the characteristics of a national craze, a kind of predecessor to mah-jongg, crossword puzzles, hula hoops and yo-yos. "Were I to characterize the United States," wrote William Priest, an English musician who toured the country in 1796, "it would be by the appellation of the land of speculations."

Starting soon after the end of the Revolution, just about everyone who could afford it—and many who could not—owned a deed, often to property he had never seen, or a share in a land company of whose activities he knew nothing. Land companies were formed as the quickest way to raise money to buy large tracts, but many operators preferred to work alone or in partnership with just one or two other men. In all cases, the goal was the same: quick turnover. Those who managed to achieve this did make money. One of the most prominent speculators, Thomas Pickering, a war veteran turned politician and businessman, had picked up thousands of acres in Pennsylvania for about a shilling an acre and sold them later for nearly two dollars an acre to an association which in turn planned to sell them for even more. Pickering, evidently a sharp man for business, was himself a member of the association, thus standing to profit again if things went well.

Many of Pickering's holdings, as well as those of other speculators, came from the purchase of military land warrants. Several states had rewarded their war veterans with parcels of public land. These were negotiable and readily sold by veterans who did not plan to work them. Speculators bought them up wholesale and thus accumulated large sections which were considered more salable than small lots. In time, shady operators discovered they could sell the same warrant many times over, especially if the transactions were made in different states, and at a distance from the actual property. Many purchasers of these warrants arrived to take up residence on land which was already occupied.

The land fever caused many men, otherwise prudent, to plunge before they looked. "The best of New England capitalists and business men," a student of the period wrote, "placed hundreds of thousands of dollars in schemes they had never investigated and did not take the trouble to explore." In a typical example, this lack of caution caused one man to buy 100,000 acres from another who did not have title to them. A group in Connecticut bought deeds to 300,-000 acres in western Virginia before making a survey; when they got around to doing so, the parcel was short some 165,000 acres. Nor were other Americans considered the only potential land buyers. Speculators spent a good deal of effort trying to sell European capitalists on these fresh outlets for investment. Some sales were made abroad, many of which were legitimate. But a few men indulged in what they called "dodging," making a sale in Europe before they had actually bought the land in the United States, and counting on the down payment to take care of that matter on their return. In one way or another, some speculators did get rich. However, the Duke de la Rochefoucauld-Liancourt, who closely followed these goings-on while he was living in the United States, wrote that "though land speculations have given rise to great fortunes in America, they have also been the cause of total financial ruin and disastrous bankruptcy."

The evidence should have been clear to others besides Rochefoucauld. By 1800, after a run of about ten years, the first land speculation craze ended. Most of the companies had collapsed and a good deal of the land on which so many people put so much hope had gone back to the states for nonpayment of taxes or to cover debts. In Boston, Hartford, New York and Philadelphia, the major centers of speculation, debtors' prisons were operating at capacity. Robert Morris, the financier of the Revolution, was one of the most zealous of the postwar land speculators. As a result of some bad guesses, he spent many years in Philadelphia's Prune Street Prison, which he called "the hotel with the grated doors," and died, according to a contemporary, "lean, low-spirited and poor." John Nicholson, a brilliant, if misguided, young man who was one of Morris's partners, died in a nearby cell at the age of forty owing some $12,-000,000.

In view of the basic flaw in the kind of speculation that went on, it is surprising that anyone made money. There was just too much land available, and, as is true of any commodity under similar circumstances, prices remained low. Most speculators sought to sell to the wealthy, who could afford to hold large tracts as a long-term investment which would pay off during the inevitable expansion of the country. Some had to sell smaller parcels to individuals or groups who actually wanted a place to settle. But there were not enough customers of either type. While hustling for customers, the speculators had to pay taxes and cover other expenses. In time-honored fashion many communities taxed absentee owners higher than they did their own citizens. The other expenses were identical to those which dealers in real estate usually face, but which come higher to speculators: interest on loans—7 per cent was standard —salesmen and, precociously enough, press agents.

Except for the language, the publicity the early land speculators used was remarkably similar to that considered *de rigueur* today: ghost-written testimonials by prominent citizens—judges, congressmen, lawyers; and persuasion by intellectual and emotional arguments invariably emphasizing the health, wealth and welfare which would accrue to the fortunate purchaser. If exaggeration crept in now and then it was, of course, part of the game. Notes made by Priest of a speech he heard in a tavern while traveling from New York to Boston indicate that sales pitches may be one of man's immutable creations. One of his companions, Priest noted, took "every opportunity of singing forth the praises of New Virginia," a tract west of the Alleghenies. His "harangue," Priest said, to "New Englanders . . . staring with their mouths open," went something like this: "My Indian corn grows twelve to thirteen feet high . . . as to the climate, there is no comparison; this cursed cold northwest wind loses all its severity before it reaches us; our winters are so mild that our cattle require no fodder, but range the woods all winter; and our summers are more moderate than on your side of the Allegheny."

Similar claims were often made in print and distributed in Europe as well as America. As a rule, the titles of promotional tracts were rather dull—"View of the United States," "Guide to the Wilderness," "Description of Ohio" and "Observations on the Present Situation of American Landed Property" were some of them—but the contents more than made up for this shortcoming. American land provided "the means of employing money to greater advantage and . . . more obviously secure than has occurred at any former period in any country in the world," said one of them. Others pointed out the beauties of the land, the ridiculously small taxes, and the great numbers of settlers waiting to pay high prices once the tracts were broken up.

(35)

One Englishman saw the entire effort as a plot by Americans to ruin Great Britain, which he considered "their mother country." The French minister to the United States called the speculators "vile deceivers" and published letters in France attacking Robert Morris and others. These were comparatively mild words. When, after a period of relative quiet in the early nineteenth century, trading in land again became a national mania, criticism was expressed more directly. In its issue of May 9, 1835, *Niles Register,* an influential national weekly published in Baltimore, carried the headline "SPECULATION! SPECULATION!! SPECULATION!!!" over a roundup of news items from various cities. "Verily," the paper concluded, "the people are mad."

Yet the madness persisted. In the 1830's, the example of John Jacob Astor in New York was dazzling enough to hide the fact that he invested in city land, paid cash, improved the properties or insisted that his lessees do so, and found a steady return in renting. With the notable exception of his unexpectedly extended bout with New York State over the Morris land, Astor was not a gambler in the accepted sense; he liked a sure thing too much. Those who saw only that he got rich in real estate were inclined to take chances Astor would have considered unsound. Many applied his guiding principle of preceding a likely surge of population, but Manhattan, because of its size and shape, was a logical place for his system, while his imitators had to test it on the country at large.

Some guessed right, of course. Washington, D. C., became choice pickings for speculators soon after it was selected as the nation's capital. So did Ohio; as thousands of immigrants by-passed the Atlantic coast and moved into what was then called "the Old Northwest," the speculators were waiting for them. Throughout the nineteenth century, the land operators moved west with the country, developing new techniques, improving the old, and establishing patterns for speculation which have, with minor variations, become standard, even for such twentieth-century phenomena as the Florida boom.

The resale of large tracts for speedy profits having proved impractical, nineteenth-century speculators turned to "town jobbing." This is an Americanism for buying land on a likely new town site and selling lots at inflated prices. The only possible hitch was that new settlers might perversely choose a location not owned by the town jobber. The active town jobber had, therefore, to advertise the desirability of his site. Since this was a highly competitive business and large investments had been made, often in the form of bribes to get the site in the first place, town jobbers often were somewhat overenthusiastic. An English traveler described a typical sales campaign in his diary. "A speculator makes out a plan of a city with its streets, squares and avenues, quays and wharves, public buildings and monuments," he wrote. "The streets are lotted, the houses numbered, and the squares called after Franklin and Washington. The city itself has some fine name, perhaps Troy or Antioch. [Actually, most speculators immodestly named the towns after themselves.] This is engraved and forthwith advertised and hung up in as many steamboats and hotels as the speculator's interest may command. All this time the city is a mere vision. Its very site is on the fork of some river in the far West, 500 miles beyond civilization, probably under water or surrounded by dense forests and impassable swamps. Emigrants have been repeatedly defrauded out of their money by transactions so extremely gross as hardly to be credited."

The extent of the speculation was succinctly summed up by Michael Chevalier, a French economist, in *Society,*

Manners and Politics in the United States, which he wrote in 1839 after a lengthy visit. "The amateurs in the land at the north dispute with each other the acquisition of the valuable timberlands of that region," he said. "At the southern extremity, the Mississippi swamps and the Alabama and the Red River cotton lands are the subject of competition, and in the West, the corn fields and pastures of Illinois and Michigan. The unparalleled growth of some new towns has turned the heads of the nation, and there is a general rush upon all points advantageously situated; as if, before ten years, three or four Londons, as many Parises, and a dozen Liverpools were about to display their streets and edifices. . . . Pestilential marshes and naked precipices of rock have been bought and sold for this purpose. In Louisiana, the quagmires, the bottomless haunts of alligators, the lakes and cypress swamps, with ten feet of water or slime, and in the North, the bed of the Hudson, with twenty, thirty or fifty feet of water, have found numerous purchasers."

Not all of those who lost money in paper cities were capable of the revenge that Charles Dickens took when his own land gamble failed. Along with many Englishmen he had invested in the Cairo City and Canal Company, the creation of a notorious town jobber named Darius B. Holbrook. Cairo's problem was that it was under water a good part of the year, which offset its natural advantage of lying at the junction of the Mississippi and Ohio Rivers. Holbrook felt that he could overcome this drawback with "dikes, canals, levees and embankments." These would take money, but the amount Holbrook required was not likely to be raised if a true picture of Cairo were painted. He did what came naturally to town jobbers; he commissioned large lithographs of a thriving city and had them widely distributed, especially in Europe. In a short time, he sold $2,000,000 worth of Cairo City bonds in London alone.

As was so often the case, the bond buyers heard nothing for years. Dickens, who was not a wealthy man, had put up more than he could afford to lose. In 1842, he made a tour of the United States, but it seems likely that what he wanted most out of his visit was a look at Cairo. He got it, and it resulted in some bitter prose. "On ground so flat and low and marshy that at certain seasons of the year it is inundated to the housetops," Dickens wrote, "lies a breeding place of fever, ague and death, vaunted in England as a mine of Golden Hope, and speculated in, on the faith of monstrous representations, to many people's ruin. A dismal swamp, on which the half-built houses rot away; cleared here and there for the space of a few yards, and teeming with rank unwholesome vegetation, in whose baleful shade the wretched wanderers who are tempted hither, droop and die, and lay their bones; the hateful Mississippi circling and eddying before it, and turning off upon its southern course, a slimy monster hideous to behold; a hot-bed of disease, an ugly sepulchre, a grave uncheered by any gleam of promise; a place without one single quality, in earth or air or water, to commend it; such is this dismal Cairo."

The experience prejudiced Dickens against the United States and colored all his comments about the country. He got some satisfaction—and perhaps some of his losses back—by writing the novel *Martin Chuzzlewit* in which Cairo is thinly disguised as Eden, and the land jobbers not disguised at all. It was satire of a high order, but it is not likely that the butts of it bothered to read the book; they were too busy drawing maps of new cities.

During the years before the Panic of 1837, town jobbers bought government land which was offered at public auction by national land offices. In time, these sales became so frenetic that the phrase "doing a land-office business" was coined, and has remained in popular usage, to describe bustling business activity. Between 1831 and 1837, some 52,000,000 acres of public lands were sold for close to $66,000,000. Until 1836 buyers paid for their land with notes issued by "wildcat" banks. That year President Andrew Jackson ordered that only hard currency be accepted. With "rag money" no longer useful, the speculators, who rarely had gold or silver, stopped buying land, and in many cases had to return to the government what they had already purchased. Land-office business came to a halt, and the mania for speculation abated, although only temporarily.

Government land was not the only basis for speculation during the period before the crash. In staid New England, the offering of Maine timberland brought a similar surge of irrational buying and selling. Hugh McCulloch, a Maine banker, called it "the wildest speculation that ever prevailed in any part of the United States," an exaggeration in view of what went on elsewhere. "Brokers offices were opened in Bangor, which were crowded from morning till night, and frequently far into the night, by buyers and sellers," McCulloch wrote. "Not one in fifty knew anything about the lands he was buying, nor did he care to know so long as he could sell at a profit. . . . The same lands were sold over and over again until lands which had been bought for a few cents were sold for half as many dollars. As is always the case . . . inexperienced men became speculators, dishonesty was in the ascendant." The dishonesty was so universal, in fact, that when a man was later sued for defaulting on payment for land his defense was simply that the speculation in Maine was "so tainted with fraud, deception, cheating, lying and swindling, that the very term had become proverbial for these vices." The jury found for him.

In the depression which followed the Panic of 1837 it would have been hard for a jury not to be sympathetic with those who had been taken. By then, even the phrase "town lot" was opprobrious to all but a few, among them men like John Jacob Astor, who could afford to buy lots at depressed prices, knowing that when the depression was over their value would rise. But for every Astor who bought during this period, there were thousands who could not. Years afterward, as new land booms drove prices up again, stories of missed opportunities were as common as shares in land companies had once been, and often as extravagant in their claims. Some did have their own special quality of poignancy, though, like that of a Philadelphian who worked in Texas as a young man. "I bought 40,000 acres," he recalled, "which cost me ten cents an acre. When the title was made out, the parties from whom I bought the land, on discovering that I was still a minor, declined to complete the title or refund the money." That in itself was distressing enough for a youngster trying to make his way. But the full extent of the loss came years later, when, older now, and back in Philadelphia, the man realized that the city of Fort Worth was built on his lost property.

Real estate speculation having in a sense grown with the United States itself, it is not surprising that the most ambitious land schemes coincided with the nation's greatest period of expansion. In both speculation and expansion railroads were an important element. Before the Civil War railroad builders had already seen that there were potentially more profits in land than in transportation. Property values had to increase in towns and cities with railroad stations, and the men who owned that property, especially if they also owned the railroad which determined where the stations would be placed, had to make profits. It was as simple as Mark Twain and Charles Dudley Warner described it in *The Gilded Age, a Tale of Today:* "Mr. Bigler's plan this time, about which he talked loudly . . . was the building of the Tunkhannock, Rattlesnake and Youngwomenstown railroad. . . . The plan of operations was very simple. 'We'll buy the lands,' he explained, 'on long time, backed by the notes of good men; and then mortgage them for money enough to get the road well on. Then get the towns on the line to issue their bonds for stock. . . . We can then sell the rest of the stock on the prospect of the business of the road . . . and also sell the lands at a big advance, on the strength of the road.'"

By the time the federal government was encouraging the building of transcontinental railroads, Mr. Bigler's formula came in for a major improvement. Railroad men no longer had to buy land; a munificent government gave it to them. There were no major objections to this at first. Using the vast public acreage as an incentive to the creation of canals or other public utilities had been federal policy since the establishment of the government. It was not until the amounts of free land reached scandalous proportions that criticism began. The pattern was set by the Illinois Central Railroad Company, which in 1850 was granted alternate sections of land running to six miles on each side of its proposed tracks. The government's theory was basically sound; by retaining alternate sections—each a square mile in size —it also stood to benefit when land values increased. Still, the prize was a big one, and competition for the charter to build the Illinois Central was bitter. Abraham Lincoln, then a young lawyer, tried to win it for a group of westerners, but lost to Robert Rantoul, Jr., who represented an association of New York and Boston capitalists. (Twelve years later, Rantoul's son visited Lincoln at the White House; the President recalled the incident and laughed as he said, "Your father beat me, your father beat me.") All told, the Illinois Central was given some 2,600,000 acres; most of the acreage not used for right-of-way was sold at $5 to $25 an acre depending on proximity to stations and lines. Public land away from the railroad was then selling at $1.25 an acre, with few buyers. The English novelist, Anthony Trollope, who visited the United States during the Civil War, said, "Railroad companies were in fact companies combined for the purchase of land . . . looking to increase the value of it fivefold by the opening of the railroad."

The Illinois Central achievement inspired other men who did not know an engine from a caboose, but who owned property which would benefit by a rail line, to petition their Congressmen with fervor, logic and cash bribes. The possibility of the situation's getting out of hand was recognized fairly early, and even Horace Greeley, whose position on the American West may be the best known in history, did not think "hiring or bribing capitalists to construct railroads" was the proper approach. Nevertheless, the land was there, it was idle, and it was the cheapest form of subsidy the government could provide. When the Union Pacific was approved as the first transcontinental line in the early 1860's it was granted, in addition to a liberal construction loan, alternate sections running ten miles on each side of its tracks, a total of 12,000,000 acres. If there were those who thought this excessive, there were others, usually more influential, who thought otherwise. A railroad spanning the continent was the new symbol of an expanding America. Money was no object and the public lands even less so. "I don't begrudge them," said Senator Henry Wilson of Massachusetts in an impassioned speech defending his support of the railroad. By the time a charter was given to the Northern Pacific in 1864, the Senate did not even bother to record the vote by which the line was handed 47,000,000 acres, an area larger than the six New England states.

By virtue of its scale, the story of the Northern Pacific is almost a caricature of American land speculation. The land the railroad had at its disposal was not only the largest grant in American history, it was managed by one of the financial geniuses of the nineteenth century, Jay Cooke, whose banking house sold millions of dollars' worth of government bonds during the Civil War. Cooke had a talent for handling men and publicity as well as money, qualities which by all odds should have made him a successful land speculator.

The charter for the Northern Pacific had been issued in 1864 to Josiah Perham, a Bostonian who had his first fling at land speculation during the frenzy over Maine timberlands. Perham brought a number of prominent men into his venture, which he incorporated as "Josiah Perham's People's Pacific Railroad," and started to sell stock. But with the Civil War still on, few Americans were eager to take a risk even though $100 shares required only $10 in cash. English capitalists were even more reluctant to tie up money in what appeared to be a long-range prospect at best. Perham's charter had called for him to start construction within two years and to lay a minimum of fifty miles of track a year. In 1866, Perham petitioned Congress for an extension of his deadline for starting. He was given until 1868, and later, when he still did not have enough money, until 1870.

In 1869, Perham's associates decided he was not the ideal promoter, and turned to Cooke, the nation's outstanding fund raiser. Cooke had a few years earlier bought rich pine land around Duluth, Minnesota. In 1868 he had made a trip to inspect his holdings—some 19,000 acres—and returned with visions for the development of Duluth, then hardly a village. Cooke saw a great port and city where a half-dozen poorly built homes stood. He undertook to sell bonds issued by the Lake Superior and Mississippi Railroad which had as its goal the linking of the river and the lake. By using publicity techniques he had developed during the Civil War, he succeeded. At about the time he was most enthusiastic about the future of the area around Lake Superior, and business in government securities had dropped off, the opportunity to bail out Northern Pacific was presented to him. It fitted perfectly with Cooke's plans to develop Duluth, and he responded with enthusiasm.

He signed a preliminary agreement with Northern Pacific and organized a surveying party to make sure it was worth going into; even at his most optimistic Cooke was a careful man. His group consisted of bankers, engineers and journalists. General William T. Sherman had warned Cooke that much of the area was "as bad as God ever made or anybody can scare up this side of Africa," but Cooke's engineer, Milnor W. Roberts, saw dollar signs. "The immense landed property of the company . . . in connection with valuable town sites and water powers will ultimately be worth more than the entire cost of the railroad," he wrote Cooke. Samuel Wilkerson, an old Cooke hand considered by his contemporaries as a "universal journalistic genius," wrote letters which later became the basis for the international campaign to sell Northern Pacific bonds and land. His image, the opposite of Sherman's, was of "a vast wilderness waiting like a rich heiress to be appropriated and enjoyed." By the time he reached Puget Sound, Wilkerson could not be denied. "There is nothing on the American con-

tinent equal to it," he wrote Cooke. "Such timber—such soil
—such orchards—such fish—such climate—such coal—
such harbors—such rivers. There is no end to the possibilities of wealth here. . . . The soil sustains a growth of saw-
ing firs and cedars 200 feet high. . . . Salmon are not
caught here, they are pitchforked out of the streams. Jay,
we have got the biggest thing on earth. Our enterprise is an
inexhaustible gold mine. There is no mistake about it."

Since Cooke planned to rely on Wilkerson to mount the
publicity drive, it was just as well that the enthusiasm was
genuine. One of Cooke's friends said he had heard that
"Sam has found orange groves and monkeys on that route."
Wilkerson's descriptions, and the shape of the Northern Pacific route and its adjoining land from Lake Superior to Puget Sound, which was soon to be one of the best-known
maps in the country, produced the phrase "Jay Cooke's Banana Belt" to describe the banker's empire. Neither derision
nor the reluctance of some of his more conservative associates deterred Cooke. He had been buying Northern Pacific
stock at twelve to fifteen cents on the dollar, and was now
ready to start building a railroad and selling land. By all the
logic of the speculative mind Cooke could not help ending
up with a profitable line, valuable real estate along the way,
and dynamic growth for Duluth, where he was busily buying town lots by the thousands.

The stakes were big in Cooke's game; as a result the
chips represented large sums by any standard. His immediate task was to raise $5,600,000 to build the line from Du-
luth to the Red River. Of this, $5,000,000 was for bonds
backed by the company's land, the rest for capital stock. To
attract this kind of money, and even more later, Cooke held
out the promise of land profits. He established the Lake
Superior and Puget Sound Company, which became the
Northern Pacific's wholly owned land company. Subscribers

to Cooke's pool were encouraged to buy heavily, but in practice a popular purchase was the $56,000 package. In this —which by some complicated arithmetic represented three twenty-fifths of a one-twelfth interest—the buyer received $50,000 worth of Northern Pacific bonds, $6,000 in Northern Pacific stock, $12,000 in Lake Superior and Puget Sound stock, and $600 in Western Land Association stock. This last represented holdings in Duluth itself, thus providing a sort of ultimate bonus to Cooke's customers.

Cooke's campaign to raise money was carried out in two major steps. First he sought the support of prominent men, not just for their contribution, but for their value as living testimonials when he started his second phase: soliciting from the public at large. The first phase opened on a note of snobbism. The impression was spread that only a select few were being invited to join Cooke's pool, and as membership took on the attributes of a status symbol, some of the country's leading citizens hurried to make their donations. Among them was Schuyler Colfax, Vice-President of the United States, as well as governors, congressmen and judges. Cooke was also aware that some people whose names would add luster to his roll could not afford the ante; he carried on his own account bonds for Salmon P. Chase, Chief Justice of the United States. Others, like Henry Ward Beecher, the prominent minister, and Horace Greeley were put down for $15,000 and $20,000 respectively with some vague understanding about when and how they would pay. Beecher's gratitude was direct; a series of articles on the glories of the northwest by Sam Wilkerson ran in his newspaper, *Christian Union*. Philadelphia and Washington journalists were also rewarded, but to a smaller degree, and President Grant's private secretary, General Horace Porter, accepted Cooke's offer of bonds "with alacrity." Noticeably absent from Cooke's subscribers were New York capitalists;

like their European counterparts, they were skeptical of
railroads in unpopulated areas and they were suspicious of
the prose which Wilkerson and his colleagues turned out on
behalf of Cooke and the Northern Pacific. One of Cooke's
partners, H. C. Fahnestock, did not like "the fact that capitalists of the larger sort do not take to the scheme."

But Cooke did not need them. By January 24, 1870,
the $5,600,000 had been entirely subscribed and requests
to buy more bonds were still coming in. On February 15,
Cooke received a telegram from his chief engineer in Duluth. "Ground broken on Northern Pacific Railroad today," it
read. "One hundred men at work. Hurrah for the great enterprise. . . . Shall push the work vigorously." Town officials rose to the occasion, and the leading speaker at the
ceremonies predicted that the new railroad would not only
make Duluth great but would be the means of "eventually
compelling the annexation of Canada to the United States."
Cooke himself is not on record about such imperialist ambitions; he was probably happy enough contemplating the
returns promised by his glorious start.

Cooke did have one major problem, though—cash.
Subscribers to his pool were permitted to pay on the installment plan, in ten monthly payments, starting March 1870.
As a result, Cooke did not have the money to maintain the
building pace he felt necessary to justify his gamble. The
cash was available in the United States Treasury, of course,
and to this Cooke now turned his attention. It did not matter that the original charter to the Northern Pacific omitted
a government subsidy because of the size of the land grant.
Cooke's influence in Washington reached into the House
and Senate, the Supreme Court and the White House. His
"whirlwind lobby," as one student of the period called it, was
outstanding, even in a period when lobbying was practiced
by masters.

Cooke began with a handwritten memorandum listing the reasons why government aid was necessary to the Northern Pacific. He reminded the government of its duty to build the West and to encourage immigration to those empty lands; he invoked the Indians—the railroads would bring civilization as well as soldiers and supplies to the open ranges; he pointed out how the government's odd sections of land would increase in value along with what was given the railroad; he cited the value of minerals which were to be found along the railroad's route, and how the government would benefit by the production of gold, silver and iron. Just in case sweet reasonableness could not carry the day, Cooke spread shares in the Northern Pacific pool or made loans without collateral to congressmen whose votes were needed. Thus, the Speaker of the House of Representatives, James G. Blaine, who had earlier identified himself with Cooke's opposition, spoke heartily in favor of the Northern Pacific after he received a loan from Cooke's Washington office. Other Congressmen found Cooke a "generous friend." Nor did Cooke forget that bills did not become law until signed by the President. He sent a fishing rod and creel to Grant's son Jesse, and although undoubtedly pleased at a note of thanks in a childish hand, found more value in the President's own reaction of delight. Whereupon Cooke invited Grant and his son on a fishing expedition, to which they eagerly came. It is also likely that the President's name on several notes held by Cooke had something to do with Grant's support. Throughout the fight Grant was, in the words of Jay Cooke's brother, Henry, as "firm as a rock." In the course of the debate, the President personally sent word to congressmen that he favored helping the Northern Pacific.

Despite Cooke's bribes and arguments and presidential support, there was a hard core of opposition. One of his key lieutenants, Ignatius Donnelly, saw early "that the present Congress would rather give land than money." In the face of this, Cooke made it clear he would settle for a congressional resolution authorizing a mortgage on the land already granted to the Northern Pacific, and enlarging the land grant in certain areas. This was almost as good as actual money to Cooke and it placated the Congress. The resolution was passed by the Senate, 40 to 11, on April 21, 1870, and by the House, 107 to 85, on May 26. When word of the House vote was telegraphed to Duluth, the price of real estate in that city instantly increased by 10 per cent. The *Philadelphia Ledger* saw the bill as another in a list of "huge robberies of the public domain," and carried on a strong campaign against it, but this merely caused Cooke to spread some money in the offices of the *Philadelphia Evening Bulletin* and the *Washington Chronicle*. Soon there were editorials rebutting the opposition. On May 30, President Grant was scheduled to meet with his Cabinet to discuss the resolution. Rumors were strong that many members were opposed to it. That morning, Grant dropped in on Henry Cooke in the company's Washington office to assure him that all was well. Henry found Grant's position almost heroic. "He stood up against a tremendous pressure," he wrote Jay Cooke. Grant, of course, signed the measure; it is not surprising that some two years later Henry recommended to Jay that "for obvious reasons" he destroy a note of Grant's held by the company. On July 1, 1870, Cooke mortgaged the Northern Pacific's lands, and was ready to start building a railroad and improving the value of his land.

As the tracks moved slowly toward the Red River, Cooke continued his campaign to sell more bonds. These represented immediate benefits; the money would support construction of the road, and Cooke's banking house received a fee of 12 per cent on each sale. He started the selling campaign in Europe, in spite of previous setbacks there, by sending a highly paid agent to cultivate banking houses, the press and royalty, with instructions not to stint on spending money where it would help the most. As usual, there were bribes for the press, lavish entertainment and skillful publicity schemes. Cooke proposed that the French Bourse send three of its members to investigate the Northern Pacific route at his expense; he invited Bismarck to visit, and received a diplomatic reply, which, although negative, was grist for the publicity mill.

Unfortunately for Cooke, opposition at home was affecting sales in Europe. Rival banking houses led the attack, and were helped by sympathetic newspapers, especially the influential *Philadelphia Ledger,* which continued the anti-Cooke line it had taken during the congressional debate. Cooke's money poured into other papers which supported him; his friends tried to argue with the owner of the *Ledger,* and Cooke himself threatened to "establish a penny paper equal to the *Ledger,* reducing the expense of advertising fifty per cent." Most important, though, was the fact that the important London *Times* had an exchange agreement with the *Ledger* whereby it ran many of the articles which appeared in the Philadelphia paper. This was detrimental to the sale of bonds in England, until Cooke's European agent had a heart-to-heart talk with the financial editor of the *Times.* No one knows what words or other inducements passed between the two men, but Cooke soon received assurances that "a man who has saved 400,000 pounds sterling on his salary as editor of the *Times,* and lived like a prince all the time, understands the art of getting along." But this victory was not enough; the depressing effect of the Franco-Prussian War and earlier sad experiences of Europeans with American railroads were too much to overcome. Cooke realized that Europe was not the source of money he had anticipated. The bonds would have to be sold in the United States.

Because so much money was used for bribes and so many bonds held for influential men, there can be no exact count of Jay Cooke's expenses in promoting Northern Pacific bonds. However, by April 1871, Cooke's books showed $100,000 spent for advertising and $40,000 for maps and documents. A year later the figure reached $350,000. Even these figures—and they represent only direct payments— were out of proportion to what the sales of bonds brought in. What Cooke and his investors were looking toward was the sale of the lands, of course. But they were caught in the speculator's perpetual vicious circle: bonds had to be sold to build the railroad, which would enhance the value of the land, which had to be sold to retire the bonds—after which, the leftover land would provide the fabulous profits. If the company was extremely lucky the railroad might show a profit, too, but this was never a prime consideration. Cooke estimated that the sale of 287,000 acres a year—which was less than 1 per cent of the Northern Pacific's land grant —at only four dollars an acre would pay off the company's bonded debts. Cooke decided to break the circle in his own way. He would continue to push the sale of bonds, but he would also sell and colonize the lands. The result was the most ambitious land sales campaign in the history of American real estate.

Cooke loosed a fresh propaganda barrage in the United States and established land offices in England, Germany, Holland and the Scandinavian countries. "We will seek to gather into localities," he wrote a friend, "communities of emigrants, taking some from every class and sending them out in a body to establish a town or village of their own, transferring the name of their former residence to the new locality. . . . The same idea . . . will be extended to

(52)

Great Britain and all parts of Europe. Our idea is to carry the lands to the very firesides of the people . . . and give them the choice of a change of residence." In attempting to achieve this Cooke came up with some amazing ideas, including liberal credit terms for land buyers and a sort of predecessor to prefabricated housing. Each Northern Pacific land office had models of houses which were offered to potential immigrants at $200 to $1,000 depending on size. Cooke felt that such houses could be easily built "in the lumber country around our road in Minnesota, by machinery and from the same pattern, all ready to be put up." Furthermore, he said, the railroads would convey the pre-cut lumber to the owner's site and the house "can be erected in a day."

The encouragement of Europeans to colonize the West was not altogether novel; the other land-grant railroads had made some efforts in that direction, and in fact President Grant supported the idea. But it remained for Cooke to bring to it the public relations talents which had worked so well for him in the past. Maps and documents were published in the languages of the countries whose people he sought, and were widely distributed. The managers of steamship lines and European railways were cultivated and urged to reduce their fares for Northern Pacific émigrés. Money was efficiently distributed, as always, to the press, to influential men, to benevolent societies and to religious organizations to gain their support. The promotional material also had a familiar ring: Minnesota and Montana had a climate capable of healing any illness, what illness existed in this favored land was limited to the aftereffects of over-indulgence, a natural result of the hearty appetite which was created by the invigorating atmosphere.

Despite the crusading fervor with which Cooke's men carried out their assignment, only in Scandinavia was there real success. The introduction of labor-saving machinery in Norway, Sweden and Denmark had caused serious unemployment. Acting on this knowledge, Cooke's agents persuaded influential ministers to become leaders of mass migrations. Clergymen in all three countries cooperated and helped to organize colonies for the New World. But in Prussia and France, then at war, Cooke ran into the opposition of officials who did not want able-bodied young men leaving their countries. And in England, John Lothrop Motley, the noted historian who was then American Minister, refused to help. He saw no reason "to lug in the legation in indorsing the private land speculations of Jay Cooke."

Meanwhile, the campaign was not neglected in the United States. Groups of Civil War veterans were organized to help spur the westward movement. Major George B. Hibbard, himself a veteran, was made "Commissioner of Immigration for the Northern Pacific." He visited posts of the Grand Army of the Republic throughout New England and New York State, was present at each reunion, and formed new societies where none existed before. One result of Hibbard's energy was to bring about an act of Congress which doubled from 80 to 160 acres the amount of free government land Civil War veterans could take in the sections near the railroads. While this did not sell Northern Pacific land, it did have the effect of increasing population, which was second best. Some of Cooke's other techniques helped sales. Potential buyers could examine the land in person; the cost of their ticket on the Northern Pacific would be deducted from the purchase price. When the land was bought, free transportation was provided for the new owner and his family on the Northern Pacific and reduced fares on the Eastern railroads. Once arrived in Minnesota, the immigrants were received at large reception houses where they stayed until their own homes were ready. Food was supplied at cost and medical care was free.

Duluth boomed, and not even Cooke's reception houses were sufficient to house the newcomers. "The people just came flocking in," wrote one resident. "In a few months there were two or three thousand people added to the population. There was no place to put them. There was not a hotel in the place, and every family had taken in as many as it could accommodate. . . . They lived in tents; they put up the rudest kinds of shacks . . . until they could erect houses. As fast as the sides and roof of a building were completed, and before doors or windows could be supplied, the place would be rented out for lodgings. The owner would take a piece of chalk and mark off the floor space sufficient for a man to lie down, number the place and rent it out." Duluth seemed to warrant the prediction of Dr. Thomas Foster, its earliest booster, that with the coming of the Northern Pacific it would be the "Zenith City of the Unsalted Seas."

Despite the flow of immigrants, and despite the claims and predictions, there hovered over the Northern Pacific and its lands the more realistic prospect of failure. The bonds were just not selling fast enough. If it had not been for Cooke's prestige there might not have been any sales at all. In March 1872 Cooke himself lost his usual optimism. It appeared that sales that month would not run to much more than $400,000, "about as much as will pay accumulated interest." And for the first time, too, he seemed to be aware of the country's reaction to his zealous sales campaign. "We are denounced as swindlers, our roads, route and lands ditto, not only in England but Canada, and by secret circulars all around," he wrote a friend.

It was true that ridicule of Cooke had become a popular pastime. The phrase "Banana Belt" was by now a common joke. A New York broker wrote a parody of a Northern Pacific advertisement which got almost as much circulation as the original. N.P. bonds, the broker's version read, were available at "your nearest Bank or Banker, Butcher or Baker, Apple-woman or Peanut-man, Paper-vendor or Billposter." It referred potential buyers to a map which carried "a correct census of the inhabitants, including Indians, foxes, muskrats, white bears, black bears, grizzly bears, polar bears, Wall-street bears, bisons, stationary herds of roving buffaloes . . . grasshoppers and wheatfields." As for the land grant, it was larger than the "nine" New England States, "with the Northern part of European Russia, all of France, except Alsace and Lorraine, Turkey, a portion of New Jersey, and Coney Island added." Or, the writer continued, as large as the "two states of Delaware combined." With the railroad going through this vast expanse, he added, the price of lots "could only be estimated by multiplying the present value of Broadway lots by six, and adding the cost of the new site for the capital, west of the Mississippi." What is more, branch lines will be built "Eastward, Westward, Northward, and 'Sou-Sou-West by Southward,' stopping at all the important points on both Hemi-spheres going and returning, so as to drain the entire known world, and render valueless all the other railroads on the face of the Globe."

Laughter may be good for the soul, but it is notoriously unfavorable to the sale of bonds. The ridicule on Wall Street was matched in Congress, and reached a ready audience. J. Proctor Knott, a congressman from Kentucky, threw his barbs with the help of a map issued by the Northern Pacific. "Duluth," said Knott, "was a name for which souls had panted for years as the hart panteth for the water brooks. The symmetry and perfection of our planetary system would be incomplete without it. I see it represented on this map that Duluth is situated exactly halfway between the latitudes of Paris and Venice, so that gentlemen who have inhaled the exhilarating airs of the one, or basked in the golden sunlight of the other, may see at a glance that Duluth must be a place of untold delights, a terrestrial paradise fanned by the balmy zephyrs of an eternal spring, clothed in the gorgeous sheen of ever blooming flowers and vocal with the silvery melody of nature's choicest songsters."

The spate of jokes was the price Cooke paid for his methods. Even his most devoted biographer conceded that the reaction was natural. "The people" wrote E. P. Oberholtzer, "were so full of isothermal lines, comparative latitudes and glowing facts about climates, crops and distances from New York, Liverpool and Shanghai, of new cities set in concentric circles upon the map of the American Northwest that they were ready to enjoy the flowing satire." But the effect on the sale of bonds and land was no joke to Jay Cooke and Company as disaster threatened his great project.

Nevertheless, Cooke continued to push his plans. Duluth grew, other cities were established, and the railroad continued to move slowly westward. By June 1873 it had reached the Missouri River at Bismarck, so named to encourage German colonists to come to Minnesota and Dakota. Even though construction was well behind schedule, it was quite an achievement in view of Cooke's problems.

It was to be the last one he could boast. By then, Europe was definitely written off as a source of funds; an American railway bond, "even if signed by an angel of Heaven would not sell," reported a traveler in Germany. In the United States, despite the reelection of Grant in 1872, to the pleasure of the business community, money was scarce for any purpose, and interest rates were rising. The public airing of scandals in connection with the Union Pacific gave all railroads a bad name. By the end of the summer of 1873, banks were calling in loans faster than borrowers could pay. On September 8, the New York Warehouse and Security Company, which bought and sold railroads, suspended operations. Five days later, another New York bank followed, and rumors spread through Wall Street. On September 18, after a delightful evening of playing host to President Grant, Jay Cooke closed the doors of his Philadelphia bank. In New York and Washington his partners were doing the same. The House of Jay Cooke and Company had too much useless collateral—the bonds and stocks of the Northern Pacific.

The ensuing crash sent the United States reeling into a deep economic depression. Banks collapsed, railroads failed, stocks fell 30 to 40 points, until finally the Stock Exchange itself was closed, "to save the entire Street from ruin," its vice-chairman explained. And in Duluth "it was as though the very heavens had fallen," one man wrote. "From the giddy heights of a veritable boom, Duluth fell into a very slough of despondency. Real estate values went down, down, down, until offers at a discount of fifty per cent under former prices found no takers." Work was stopped on the Northern Pacific, of course, and the resulting unemployment had its effect on local merchants. Those who had enough money after closing shop quickly left town. In a few years the city's population dropped from 5,000 to 2,500. Along the incomplete lines of the railroad, communities which had foreseen a glorious future became ghost towns, soon to collapse beneath the pressures of the prairie winds.

Jay Cooke, who for a while held the largest single parcel of privately owned land in the United States, but could not bring about the big pay-off for himself, lived to see others profit on it. The Northern Pacific was reorganized in 1875, with the original land grant intact. Its new managers followed Cooke's plans of encouraging immigrants, and this time there was a rush from war-weary Europe. Europeans came by the thousands, and land prices boomed. In 1881 the railroad passed into the hands of Henry Villard, who had been an immigration agent for Cooke. Within a year Villard had 831 agents of his own in the United States and Europe, and land sales justified that number. But Cooke, who died in 1905, did not live to see how high the stakes rose in the poker game he had started. In 1917 the Northern Pacific reported to the Interstate Commerce Commission that gross receipts from its land sales were more than $136,000,000—and it still held thousands of unsold acres. The railroad, when it was finally built, cost $70,000,000.

Although Cooke did not attain anywhere near that amount of money, he did not leave the game as badly as many speculators. He managed to hold onto his real estate in Duluth. When the railroad finally connected the city to the Pacific Coast it grew again, and so did Cooke's holdings. The sale of his Duluth land was all that kept him solvent the last years of his life. For his faith in its future, Duluth also rewarded Jay Cooke, or at least his memory, with a statue. Few land speculators have ever achieved such recognition.

"My favorite authors are

Rand and McNally."

3

The Van Sweringen Brothers
and the
Discovery of Suburbia

Sinclair Lewis, whose camera eye so often caught American images in exact focus, once gave his readers a look at the changes in the land beyond Main Street. "To the North of Zenith, among wooded hills above the Chaloosa River," he wrote in *Dodsworth,* which was published in 1929, "there was being laid out one of the astonishing suburbs which have appeared in America since 1910. So far as possible, the builders kept the beauties of forest and hills and rivers; the roads were not to be broad straight gashes butting their way through hills, but winding byways, very inviting . . . if one could only kill off the motorists. Here, masked among trees and gardens, were springing up astonishing houses." To Sam Dodsworth, the businessman hero of the novel, "there was something slightly ridiculous about mixing up Spain and Devon and Norway and Algiers and transplanting them to the sandy hills of a Midwestern town, where of late the Yankees had trapped the Indians . . . but it was all a fantastic play to him, very gay and bright after the solemn responsibilities and the disapproving mansard roofs of the older residential avenues of Zenith. Here, at least, he reflected, was all the color and irregularity he had gone abroad to seek . . ."

The play that Sinclair Lewis, through Sam Dodsworth, found so fantastic and which had indeed become ubiquitous by 1910, actually made its appearance some twenty-three years earlier in Cincinnati. There, in 1887, the modern suburb, based on the artful subdivision of land and easy credit terms, was born. A young man named William Elmer Harmon cut a section of land called Branch Hill into twenty-five-foot-wide building lots, and offered them for sale at twenty-five dollars each. Buyers were required to take two or three adjoining lots, but purchases could be made with a down payment of two dollars per lot and installments of twenty-five cents per week per lot. Harmon, who started his business career as a salesman for a northern Ohio nursery, also promised to provide shade in front of each lot in the form of "the handsomest tree indigenous in America." And, as if this weren't enough, his first advertisement noted that the round-trip commuter fare from Branch Hill to downtown Cincinnati, a distance of twenty miles by railroad, was seven dollars a month. Given these conditions, it is not surprising that Harmon did exceedingly well; in his first year he cleared more than $15,000 on an investment of $3,000. Harmon's example inspired others, too many others as far as he was concerned, and when the competition in Cincinnati became too great he moved to Boston, and eventually to New York. There, in the tradition of John Jacob Astor, he invested in the direction of the population movement. The building of a subway system made it clear to him that Brook-

lyn real estate had to increase in value. He bought, Brooklyn
land did go up, and Harmon became a wealthy man and a
generous philanthropist. Before his death, his company, the
Harmon National Real Estate Company, was involved in as
many as 240 projects at a time. But in view of the place
suburbs have taken in American life since Harmon's initial
offering in Branch Hill, none of his later achievements can
match the significance of his first.

The idea of the suburb goes back to antiquity; communities were established beyond the city limits of thirteenth-
century Florence to provide homes for the wealthy who
wished to live away from the dirt and traffic in which they
worked. In colonial and post-Revolutionary America, the
rich often had country estates to go with their town houses.
But it was not until the growth of the railroads, and the development of commuter lines, that the modern suburb—or
the subdivision, as it was most often called—as pioneered
by Harmon, was possible. Despite Harmon's promotion of
Branch Hills as "the best chance ever offered in America for
a poor man to acquire good property," it became pretty clear
to early subdividers that there were more opportunities for
profits among the rich. They were the ones who could afford
to leave the city, and to whom the combination of town and
country house within commuting distance of work would
have strong appeal. The "astonishing suburbs" that Sinclair
Lewis noted owed a great deal to Harmon, of course, but it
is a debt comparable to that of Messrs Rolls and Royce to
Henry Ford. Early developers borrowed Harmon's ideas for
a small down payment, installment credit and the planting
of shade trees, but they also created zoning laws and architectural restrictions, and returned to the Florentine concept
of the suburb as a homesite for the rich.

By the time Lewis wrote *Dodsworth*, names like Forest
Hills, outside New York City; the Country Club District,

outside Kansas City; Lake Forest, outside Chicago; and Shaker Heights, outside Cleveland, were synonymous with suburbia, and with a class of residents with higher incomes than those of city dwellers. These developments had much in common: outsize building lots, landscaping to provide beauty and privacy, parks, tennis courts, golf courses, often ponds and lakes. Architecturally, even though owners had some freedom in the design of their homes, roughly the same proportion of traditional styles appeared in all the suburbs. Certain minimums were established for the building of houses, and some developers insisted on seeing designs before they were carried out. Since most suburban home owners tended toward conservative tastes these restrictions were rarely necessary; they derived from the reactions of a developer outside Baltimore who was confronted with an especially eccentric house put up by a property owner, and promptly established the practice, used ever since, of incorporating architectural standards in land sale contracts. For their own part, the developers of these communities were more concerned with establishing an ambiance which would lure potential residents than they were with architecture. In addition to winding roads and acres of grass, open lots were standard, reflecting both a desire to simulate rural conditions and to continue the American tradition of neighborliness.

The outstanding achievement in this special use of the land was Shaker Heights, the personal creation of a pair of bachelor brothers from Cleveland, Oris P. and Mantis J. Van Sweringen. Architectural writers and city planners have called Shaker Heights "the most spectacular" of the early American suburbs, and the one "that probably surpasses anything of like nature in the United States." A tenth-grader who lived there in 1961, when Shaker Heights was celebrating its fiftieth anniversary, called it "truly an ideal community" in an essay entitled "Shaker Heights Is All That is American"; it won first prize in a contest sponsored by a local newspaper. Students of American business rate Shaker Heights very highly because it was, in effect, the laboratory where the Van Sweringen brothers developed financial skills which enabled them to take over the country's major railroads and an important section of downtown Cleveland with practically no money of their own. Historians recall it as North Union, the residence, between 1822 and 1889, of members of the celibate religious sect who were called Shakers because of the frenetic dances which were part of their prayer meetings. And, inevitably, modern market researchers have applied their own dipsticks, discovering, among other things, that Shaker Heights families have "more possessions to call their own than the average family in the United States," that 99 per cent of them own washing machines, 84 per cent have dishwashers, 83 per cent have stereo or monaural high-fidelity systems or tape recorders, 81 per cent clothes dryers, 81 per cent garbage disposal units, and 58 per cent home freezers; that 90 per cent serve alcoholic beverages at home, 71 per cent cook with wine and 32 per cent use gourmet and specialty foods; that 97 per cent own a car and 68 per cent own two or more; that 67 per cent took vacations in the United States in 1960 and 14 per cent went abroad; that the median total family income is $27,150 and the median current market value of their property is $53,000.

None of the judgments, measurements, or historical curiosity would have surprised the Van Sweringen brothers, although it is not likely they would have submitted to the questions of a market researcher and certainly not to a study of their financial affairs. From the time Oris Paxton, the elder, and Mantis James, two years younger, ran errands, sold newspapers and lighted street lamps in the Cleveland of the 1890's they impressed employers with their ability to carry figures in their head. Although they were known to keep books in the course of amassing an intricate business empire, they never discussed their financial affairs except with bankers, and then only under duress. After they died, a past president of the Guaranty Company of New York testified before a Senate Committee that a syndicate headed by his firm sold a $30,000,000 issue of five-year, six–per cent gold notes to finance the development of some Van Sweringen real estate holdings, and that he did not take the precaution of examining the Van Sweringen balance sheets. Subsequently, as a result of the market decline, all but a few of the notes were retired at fifty cents on the dollar, causing a loss to holders of some $15,000,000. The banker's performance amazed Senator Burton K. Wheeler, chairman of the committee. "Even a hick lawyer from the sagebrush like me," he said, "would know better than that. You come out to Montana and do business that way, and we'll take your clothes—just the way the Van Sweringens got those dollars."

Besides a natural inclination to keep their business affairs to themselves, the Van Sweringens had an aversion to any kind of public exposure. Once, an official of their company hired an experienced public relations man without their knowledge. In a few weeks of energetic activity he managed to arrange for the placement of fifteen articles and shorter items about the Van Sweringens in magazines and newspapers, and sent them a note outlining his coup. The reply was a single sentence: "Better let sleeping dogs lie." When a public celebration was held for the opening of their Cleveland Union Terminal Building, with some 2,500 guests invited to honor the Van Sweringens, the brothers stayed home and listened to the program on the radio. Some of their friends attributed this avoidance of publicity to shyness, others to their business sense. One of the brothers, no one is quite sure which, used to tell the story of the old farmer who was asked by a group of boys whether they could use part of his field for a baseball diamond. After a long pause, the farmer drawled, "Well, I've said a lot of things that cost me money, but I can't recall the time when I lost anything by keeping my mouth shut."

The Van Sweringens, or the Vans, as most of Cleveland called them after they were established, kept their mouths shut, except presumably when they discussed matters with each other, but despite the tenor of the story, they were not unsympathetic to boys. Among the features they laid out for Shaker Heights were public parks and playing fields. These could well have been prompted as much by the memories of their own deprivation when they were youngsters as by their innate sense of what would sell suburban property. The Vans were born in Wooster, Ohio, a farm community about fifty miles southwest of Cleveland. When Oris was four and Mantis two their mother died. The Sweringens, as they were then known, comprising their father, an older brother and two older sisters, moved to Cleveland. With the two elder males at work, the two youngsters were raised by their sisters, who, on their way to spinsterhood, discouraged normal boyhood activity. The boys "were kept pretty well wrapped up, like precious bric-à-brac, in cotton wadding," a biographer has said of this period, and it may explain much of their adult reticence and their failure to marry. Controls over them became even stricter when their father died ten years after they came to Cleveland and Herbert, the older brother, ruled the family. Schooling for the young Sweringens ended at the eighth grade. Oris found work as a clerk, and when Mantis was ready for employment two years later got him a messenger's job in the same office. No one recalls seeing them separated from then until their deaths.

After five years of working together for someone else they decided to try to make good on their own. In 1900, following a brief ownership of a bicycle rental and repair shop, they took their first tentative step in real estate by acquiring a twenty-four-hour option on a piece of Cleveland property, which they sold at a $100 profit. A few weeks later they did the same thing with another property. This quick turnover was the strongest argument for a career the two young men had ever heard. Oris Paxton and Mantis James Sweringen, twenty-one and nineteen respectively, were embarked on the real estate business.

Except for its name, everything about Shaker Heights can be traced back to the two brothers. Although the religious sect whose name it carries was formally the United Society of Believers in the Second Coming of Christ, its followers were never called anything but Shakers in the United States from the time, in 1774, when they organized their first colony in Watervliet, New York. Eventually, nineteen colonies were established in the United States, including one some four miles east of Cleveland, on the property of a Western Reserve land grant inherited by a Shaker. In time the Shaker property expanded to fourteen hundred acres, but the Shaker colony itself was diminishing in size. Since strict celibacy was one of the sect's tenets it had to rely on recruiting. In 1888, twenty-seven aging members of what had once been a thriving three hundred on land they liked to call "The Valley of God's Pleasure," and which Clevelanders called Shaker Heights, moved to the dwindling Shaker colonies elsewhere. (Two still existed in 1961 —one at Canterbury, New Hampshire, and another at Sabbathday Lake, near Portland, Maine, with twenty-five

Shaker residents.) The fourteen hundred acres near Cleveland were rented at first and then sold for $316,000 to a Buffalo syndicate which cut a few roads, laid out some lots and put them on the market. By 1900 the land was grown over with weeds and brush, and it was appraised at $240,-000. After three real estate agencies gave up trying to sell it, its owners were not at all happy about their possession or its prospects.

At the turn of the century Cleveland was in the midst of a boom. Its shipyards were the busiest on the Great Lakes. Shipbuilding, shipping at the waterfront and heavy industry inland were bringing the city fresh wealth and people. The value and number of its products had more than doubled, the work force had increased more than two and a half times and capital investment and wages had more than tripled in a short span at the end of the nineteenth century. It had become an important rail center, and as raw materials were hauled in and finished goods sent out, fortunes were made. Some were based on oil and tied to John D. Rockefeller's Standard Oil Company which made Cleveland its headquarters, and thus the oil capital of the world. Some were made in iron ore, coal and blast furnaces; the M. A. Hanna Company, run by Mark Hanna, who was later to run the Republican Party, was formed in 1885 and was at once a major company. Whatever the source, there were Clevelanders with money, and an appetite for the things money could buy. Luxurious housing was inevitably one of their objects.

The Sweringen brothers in 1900 were still a long way from sharing Cleveland's prosperity, but the means by which they were to take their place among the city's—and eventually the nation's—most wealthy and powerful citizens was there. As boys, they had escaped their sisters' discipline from time to time by wandering in the abandoned fields of Shaker Heights. They did not then have a vision of a luxurious suburban development, however appealing such a notion later became to their romantic contemporaries. In fact, they did not do anything about this land until 1905, following a distressing experience in real estate. After their first successes, they had taken a number of lots on what is now Cook Avenue, but were unable to sell them. A foreclosure judgment was entered against them, and was maintained for two years. During that time they bought and sold under their sisters' names, and by 1904 managed to settle the judgment. When they started operating again under their own name they added the Van to Sweringen. It was a legitimate enough addition, since their earliest ancestor in America had been a Dutchman who called himself Van Sweringen. How much family tradition had to do with their decision is questionable; for what they planned to do the added syllable represented prestige as well as a slight shift from the name that was soiled in the courts.

The Vans now devoted themselves exclusively to higher priced residential property, and by virtue of long hours, persuasive salesmanship and fresh ideas, were beginning to do moderately well. For $3,000—$1,000 down, most of which they borrowed, the rest to be paid in installments—they purchased property at the south end of Cleveland Heights, running along Fairmount Boulevard, just east of the city's limits. It was desirable land, except that it was three miles beyond the end of the streetcar line of the Cleveland Railway Company. The brothers promptly visited the president of the company. By promising to pay a monthly addition to the fares collected they convinced him that he ought to extend his tracks. The Van Sweringens then had no difficulty selling their lots, but the profits they accrued could not have been as important as the significance of the winning of three miles of track. The two broth-

(69)

ers learned early that suburbs could not succeed without transportation; eventually, this sense of the commuter's need was to lead to positions of power in real estate and transportation. Their understanding of the commuter's problem was as instinctive as John Jacob Astor's understanding of the direction of Manhattan's growth.

Success on Fairmount Boulevard convinced the Vans that their talents were ideal for undeveloped areas suitable for high-priced housing. Accordingly, they looked a short distance south and were confronted with the Shaker property, all but deserted by its owners. The brothers went to Buffalo and convinced W. H. Gratwick, the head of the syndicate which held the land, that they could do something with it. Gratwick had nothing to lose, of course, and agreed to a thirty-day option on a small section. The Vans insisted on one proviso: if they took up the first option they would then be permitted a second one for twice as much land and for twice as long a period, and, if they took that up, a third, and so on. This did not seem an especially exorbitant demand to Gratwick, and he agreed. To the Vans it was to be the basis for expansion with a minimum use of their own funds. To reduce their risk even more, they formed a syndicate to develop their new land. Their skill as salesmen was undeniable. With only the slightest indication of their vision of Shaker Heights they convinced some of Cleveland's leading bankers and businessmen that the land was a good investment. Among their earliest subscribers was Newton D. Baker, then city solicitor, later mayor of Cleveland and Woodrow Wilson's Secretary of War. With substantial backing, the Van Sweringen ambitions grew. After picking up the first and then the second option, they decided it was a slow method for expansion, and bought the entire property.

With 1,400 acres on their hands (their holdings were

eventually to reach 4,000 acres) the Vans had room to express themselves. "There had been no instance in the history of an American real estate development," *Architectural Forum* commented thirty years after the Vans started their new venture, "where any man or set of men had set such a definite plan for the development of so large a piece of property along such rigidly controlled lines." The young men knew precisely what they wanted. In getting it, they established standards not only for the suburbia of their own day but for the present as well.

In the face of a tradition that called for gridiron blocks and identical lots divided by enough road for traffic, the Van Sweringens were radicals. From two main boulevards, 180 and 190 feet wide, they ran curving and semi-elliptical roads. The width of the main roads was "a liberality that was looked upon at the time as prodigal, if not downright foolish," a writer later noted, and the winding filigree of streets an ornamental waste. But the Vans had gauged their time and their potential buyers. Their basic idea was to provide for homes in several price categories without hurting the values of the most expensive ones. They divided their land into sections, each of which had its own rigid standards and prices, and separated the sections with the winding roads lined with trees and with parks and lakes. It is a testimony to their skill that Shaker Heights did not break up into a series of separate settlements but has remained a unified community with estates costing half a million dollars not far from homes built for under twenty thousand.

The restrictions established by the Vans were published in a plush booklet called "Shaker Village Standards." (The brothers always called their development Shaker Village to emphasize its rural nature, but Shaker Heights was the name Clevelanders always used.) The requirements

(71)

pertained not only to the use of the land and the architectural style of the homes to be built but even to interior decoration. Depending on the section, houses had to be set back from the front lot line from 50 to 200 feet. Favored architectural styles were conservative, of course, and in practice Colonial, French and English styles dominated. "Appropriate" color schemes were listed, as well as the proper "trim and sash, shutters, doors, chimneys, fly-screens, roof, mortar, balconies, stucco, shingles, stone work." And before building could start, architectural drawings had to be approved by the Van Sweringen management. Among other things, the Vans did not want identical houses in Shaker Heights. There were to be no multiple dwellings, and, naturally, no businesses, although in time the Vans built apartments and a shopping center at the western entrance of Shaker Heights, which is called Shaker Square. Neither of these has changed the nature of the community. In the words of one of the expensive promotional brochures the Van Sweringens favored, "no matter what changes time may bring around it, no matter what waves of commercialism may beat upon its borders, Shaker Village is secure, its homes and gardens are in peaceful surroundings, serene and protected for all time."

Although their concept was magnificent and their autocratic implementation amazingly inoffensive, the land they held might have remained untenanted if the Van Sweringens had not also remembered the lesson of Fairmount Boulevard—transportation. They had not anticipated an overnight profit, but rather a long-term return (they correctly predicted that 1923 to 1928 would be the peak years), but they were understandably eager to assure a good start, and this meant that a quick, safe and economical means to travel to and from Cleveland's business district was needed. The first buyers did not require this service; they were wealthy men who presumably owned a motor vehicle. The Vans built a home for themselves and their sisters, in an English style that was on their approved list, to help improve the sparse look of their property. Then they returned to the Cleveland Railway Company to seek an extension of the line that had been previously brought out to Fairmount Boulevard. This time they offered to build the line themselves and donate it to the company. But with no population in sight to service, the company could not foresee profits in operating that far. The president told the Vans that such extensions were "bleeders instead of feeders" and that until the Vans "first supply the people" there would be no line. Oris P. promptly responded, "If you will first supply the line, I will supply the people," which showed that he understood the situation better than the myopic president of the streetcar company, but he lost his case nevertheless.

This rejection was a turning point for Shaker Heights and, eventually, for the history of American railroading. The Vans continued to push for the extension, and finally by 1913 got a partial one, which did not entirely solve their problem. From the time of their first discussions with Cleveland Railway, and even more after the rather decrepit cars began to rattle their way between the city and the edge of the suburb, the Vans were determined to provide their own transportation for Shaker Heights. As they had since they first entered real estate, and were to do before nearly every major decision, they consulted the proper maps. "My favorite authors are Rand and McNally," Oris P. once explained to a friend. A government topographical map showed a ravine called Kingsbury Run through which tracks could be laid directly into Cleveland without a single grade crossing en route. The Vans created a company which they named the Cleveland and Youngstown Railroad, and started to buy parcels of land which would accommodate their future commuter line. In 1909 they bought four acres near Cleveland's Public Square where they planned to build a terminal, not only for their own line, but for several interurban lines into Cleveland. Seemingly they were on their way to getting the transportation they wanted for Shaker Heights—a high-speed electric railway system which, without the slowdowns caused by grade crossings, could bring cars from Shaker Heights to Public Square in less than thirty minutes.

Now came the most important snag in the lives of the Van Sweringens. Two-thirds of the way from Shaker Heights to Cleveland was a two-mile stretch of land owned by the Nickel Plate Railway, on which it planned to erect freight facilities. (The railroad, which was founded as the New York, Chicago & St. Louis, got its modern name from William Vanderbilt, who, seeking to extend his rail empire, paid an exorbitant price to bring it under the control of the New York Central. "It might as well have been nickel-plated," he said of his purchase.) It was no longer an important railroad, and had been referred to by Newton D. Baker as "a toy railroad that ran its trains just often enough to make it dangerous." Baker, as a supporter of the Van Sweringen interests, may have been prejudiced since the small piece of Nickel Plate land was an impassable obstacle.

Then, during the protracted negotiations between the Vans and the railroad, which were not leading to the desired results, an announcement from Washington turned a desperate situation into a hopeful one. The Interstate Commerce Commission ordered the New York Central to divest itself of the Nickel Plate because its lines paralleled those of the parent company. To the Van Sweringens this meant their problem was solved. Instead of buying the railroad's right of way they would buy the railroad.

Oris P. and Mantis J. Van Sweringen had managed by astute methods and sound vision to become wealthy and important businessmen without using much of their own money. They certainly could not have changed methods to purchase the Nickel Plate, the prices of railroads being what they are. The price established for the New York Central's controlling stock in the Nickel Plate was $8,500,000, a nice round figure in view of the fact that the market value was at least a million dollars less and that no dividends had been paid on its common stock in six years, and very few on its preferred or common since it was opened in 1882. But for what the Van Sweringens had in mind, the Nickel Plate had promise, not alone for Shaker Heights, but for Cleveland as well; there was also the possibility that if it were properly run it would show a return.

With these arguments the Vans were able to borrow $2,000,000 from three banks to meet the required down payment; the rest was to be paid in ten annual installments of $650,000. The loan was made, not to the Vans, but to the Nickel Plate Securities Corporation, a holding company they created for their new enterprise. The new corporation then issued $2,075,000 worth of preferred stock and $12,-500,000 of common. To purchasers of preferred stock the Vans gave an equal amount of common stock. In a comparatively short while they sold $1,575,000 of the preferred to outsiders and $500,000 worth to themselves. This was used to pay off the bank loan. The Vans retained the remaining $10,000,000 worth of common stock for their own account. It was well that they did, because they had to use this stock as security for the $500,000 they borrowed to buy the preferred shares. On July 6, 1916, the 523-mile Nickel Plate belonged to the Van Sweringen brothers.

The reluctance of the Vans to part with their own money in no way inhibited the boldness of their plans. They put the Nickel Plate under the direction of John J. Bernet, considered by railroading men one of the ablest operators in the country, and he turned the rundown road into a remarkably successful one; by 1920 its common stock earned more than 10 per cent, in 1921 more than 25 per cent. Although this kind of management was to lead the Van Sweringens into greater preoccupation with American railroads, they did not neglect the original purpose of buying the Nickel Plate. In 1920 the Shaker Heights Rapid Transit began operations, and Shaker Heights started the phenomenal growth which the Vans had always expected. From 1919 to 1929 nearly 300 new homes were built each year; in 1925 alone, 556 building permits were issued for homes to cost $9,128,530. The population in that decade leaped from 1,700 to 15,500. The price of hundred-foot lots went from $20 a foot to more than $200 a foot in some sections. The valuation of the property which the Buffalo syndicate found high at $240,000 had gone to $80,000,000. By 1923, the Vans felt it necessary to keep the public from being carried away by the staggering statistics. "The dollar sign does not appear on the Shaker Village coat of arms," they wrote.

Despite their other interests, the Van Sweringens actively presided over the growth of Shaker Heights, which always remained their first love. They added twenty-six miles of new streets, laid pavements, water mains, gas pipes, installed new street lighting, and supervised the construction of eight public and three private schools, three churches and four country clubs. During this period the first buildings in the projected shopping center at Shaker Square were also going up, and the Van Sweringens kept buying adjoining property until they held 4,000 acres reaching to the banks of the Chagrin River, ten miles east of Shaker Square. They planned to sell the more desirable parcels, above the river, for country estates. Nor would they lack buyers; Shaker Heights was an assured success.

Cleveland's growing population—1,000,000 by 1929 —and the prosperity which it shared with the rest of the nation, were no doubt factors in Shaker Heights' surge in the twenties. But the Van Sweringens did not depend on these circumstances alone to keep their lands productive. Having established real estate fortunes with a rapid-transit system, they soon after made plans to improve both the system and their fortune. What they now proposed would have only an indirect effect on Shaker Heights, but a drastic and direct one on the city of Cleveland.

Years before the first rapid-transit car made the run from Shaker Square to Cleveland's Public Square, it seemed to the Vans that the four acres they held there could be put to a useful purpose. Offhand, it would have been difficult to see how. At one time the area had been the center of Cleveland, the site for public hangings, and more recently its most important business area. But from World War I to 1920 it had begun to deteriorate. Shops and offices moved up Euclid Avenue as soon as their leases expired and Public Square, surrounded by slums, the dirty yards of the Nickel Plate, Erie, Baltimore and Ohio, and Wheeling and Lake Erie railroads was on its way to dismal oblivion. The Vans decided to change all this. For one thing, it detracted from Shaker Heights to have its residents discharged in such seedy surroundings, and in the open where they were exposed to all kinds of weather. For another, they may have felt the need to follow suburban victory with an urban triumph. They announced that they were going to build a Union Station for Cleveland on the site they owned near Public Square. Furthermore, they planned to top it with Cleveland's tallest office building, and surround it with shops, a hotel and a department store.

Now, under normal circumstances such public spiritedness usually wins the approval of progressive-minded citizens, officials and newspapers. Not in this case. It was as if the Vans had been profane at a woman's club. Nor was it that the city did not need a railroad station. The old station, less than a mile away on the lake front, handled New York Central and Pennsylvania traffic, but was physically even more unattractive than the yards at Public Square. Things were so bad, in fact, that the city had put up a sign where rail passengers approaching Cleveland could read it: DON'T JUDGE THIS TOWN BY THIS DEPOT. Money had been voted for a new lake-front station, but World War I had prevented its start. Nevertheless, the city's businessmen prepared to battle the Vans over the revival of Public Square. The real estate owners and merchants on upper Euclid Avenue complained that the Vans were tampering with the "natural" trend of the city, and that recently increased real estate values would drop. The Vans did not deny that possibility, although they pointed out that the new real estate values were too high and that Cleveland needed a modern center if it were ever to qualify as a major American city.

The controversy did not end until 1923. Public hearings were held, at which Cleveland citizens expressed themselves loudly. Negotiations had to be worked out with the seven railroads which would use the new station. Since railroads are under government regulation, the Interstate Commerce Commission was involved. When the issue was put to a public referendum early in 1919, Cleveland voters backed the Van Sweringen proposal by a three-to-two vote on condition that the railroads ratify the plan within a year. In November, New York Central gave its assent, but a few days later the Pennsylvania said no. This called for the writing of a new ordinance and, naturally, more time for opponents to gather strength. In August 1921, the I.C.C. dismissed the Cleveland plan because it was not specific enough. In December the Vans were back in Washington and won federal approval, with one commissioner dissenting strongly because of what he considered loose financing methods by the Vans.

For more than a year after passing their last hurdle, the two brothers were involved in hundreds of negotiations before construction could actually get started. New companies were formed, contracts written with the participating railroads, and land purchased around the square. The Vans supervised the razing of some 2,200 buildings— including many historic houses, hotels, restaurants and breweries the relocation of some 15,000 people, and the moving of the graves in three cemeteries. Much of this did not get done without lawsuits. Meanwhile, the architects and railroad experts were assembling their working plans. Finally, on September 29, 1923, the first shovelful of dirt was thrown and the complex to be known as the Union Terminal, dominated by the seven-hundred-foot Terminal Tower Building, was under way.

By June 1929, when the Van Sweringen brothers were carried by a fast-moving elevator to their paneled offices on the Tower's thirty-sixth floor, more than $200,000,000 had gone into the project: $88,000,000 for the station, $18,-000,000 for the Tower Building, $8,000,000 for a department store, and $4,000,000 for a hotel, among others. But as suburban real estate men first and railroad men second, the Vans may have been most pleased that for the first time commuters from Shaker Heights arrived in Cleveland under a roof and could continue to their destination by train, taxi or streetcar without going outdoors. Or as *Business Week* noted just before the official opening, a Clevelander would soon be able to "work, eat, sleep, play golf, go to theaters, ride taxicabs, watch the stock market, see his doctor, all without leaving the Van Sweringen domain." *World's Work* said that the changing of Public Square marked "the transition of the city from an overgrown country town to a real metropolis." The men who managed this came out of the long fight with more than accolades. The project was carried out by the Cleveland Union Terminal Company, which was controlled by the New York Central, with lesser holdings scattered among the other participating railroads, including, of course, the Nickel Plate. The Van Sweringens had conveyed their rights to the land they had purchased around Public Square to this company in return for the air rights above the terminal. Thus they ended up with the ownership of the whole complex except for the station and its terminals, and even had a say in those because of their position with Nickel Plate. In keeping with past practice, no Van Sweringen money was used throughout.

In the years between the end of World War I and the stock market crash, as Shaker Heights expanded and the Terminal Tower Building rose in Cleveland, the Van Sweringens found time for other activity. The success of the Nickel Plate indicated that their talents might be appreciated on the national scene. They were not well known outside Cleveland; New York bankers and businessmen were hardly aware of their local accomplishments. Their natural antipathy to publicity had a lot to do with this, of course. They lived quietly with their sisters at Daisy Hill, a sixty-five-acre estate near the Chagrin River. Even among the mansions the Vans had encouraged at Shaker Heights Daisy Hill was outstanding; one estimate was that the brothers had spent $500,000 on buildings, land and furnishings, among which were some fine antique pieces. When the furnishings were auctioned by the Parke-Bernet Galleries in 1938 it required a 220-page catalogue to describe the 1,250 articles; a four-day sale brought $90,000. Friends recalled that the Vans were entirely relaxed among their possessions, and with one or two exceptions—Oris loved automobiles and Mantis rode horses—enjoyed and did the same things together for pleasure that they did for business. They belonged to no clubs, rarely entertained—and then only business associates—wore conservative clothes, took no vacations, ate sparingly, and went to bed early, usually by nine. Both men were at their offices by nine each morning, ready to act on decisions they had reached at Daisy Hill the evening before. When they left the city for business they traveled together in one of three private Nickel Plate cars. After maps, their most important bases for action were figures. They assembled the numbers into a definitive pattern, had them thoroughly checked by staff experts and then reduced to graphs, charts or even more capsulized form. If this was an idiosyncrasy, their opposition in business deals failed to see its humor. By the time the Vans decided they were ready to conquer the American railroad world, this total preoccupation with the affair at hand gave them an advantage most adversaries could not match.

Having watched developments in railroading since they acquired the Nickel Plate, the Vans had reached a major conclusion: small railroads were uneconomical and should be made part of a large rail system. Other people had come to that conclusion too, but thought any such consolidation unlikely because of the conflict of interests and personal rivalries which had grown in the industry. Least of all was it believed that any line except one of the giants could absorb the small companies. The Vans thought otherwise: the single-track Nickel Plate running from Buffalo to Chicago was going to be the base for a coast-to-coast railroad empire encompassing nearly 30,000 miles of track. Early in 1922, after five months of quiet negotiations, the Vans picked up the Lake Erie and Western from the New York Central for $3,000,000, of which $500,000 was to be in cash, the rest in five annual installments. By their favorite expedient of forming a holding company—this one called the Western Company which in turn was under the control of one called the Vaness Company—the Van Sweringens managed to raise the required cash. While these negotiations were under way the Vans also obligated themselves for about $3,500,000 more to get the controlling stock of the Toledo, St. Louis and Western, which was known as the Clover Leaf.

Under state laws the two new lines were merged into the Nickel Plate System, making it a 1,700-mile operation with an authorized capital of $105,500,000. These mergers were not enough to catch the attention of anybody except railroaders, but before the year was out the Vans stirred public attention; they bought the 2,500-mile Chesapeake and Ohio and the Hocking Valley, a subsidiary. This was to bring them to New York, the banking house of J. P. Morgan and Company, and the kind of publicity they did not want. When, by 1924, they took control of the 2,400-mile Erie and the 2,200-mile Pere Marquette, their names were as well known to the public as those of movie stars. But their faces were rarely seen, they hardly spoke to the press, and they were known as men of mystery. One publication said, "Writers have called them the 'mysterious' Van Sweringens, these twin-minded brothers who buy a piece of single track largely on credit and make it a system 9,000 miles long.

They give no interviews, they make no speeches, their public statements are about as florid as military orders; and as for their history—it is written in the county recorder's office and in deposit agreements. . . . Unlike railway geniuses of the past, they came into transportation neither from the operating end nor the stock market, but from real estate, and suburban real estate at that . . ." One paper found a former schoolteacher who recalled that Oris had once said he wanted "to drive a horse car" when he grew up, which was naturally treasured as the first clue to the brothers' "transit instinct."

The Van Sweringens were still some distance away from their goal of a truly transcontinental line, with branches penetrating into lucrative side areas. In 1930 they bought the Missouri Pacific and were firmly established west of the Mississippi. When that year James W. Gerard, former United States Ambassador to Germany, made a list of sixty-four men who "ruled America"—a list and phrase which remained in the public mind during the depression years—the Van Sweringens were on it. They were two of the five railroad men among the financiers and industrialists whose positions, Gerard said, gave them "a permanent influence in American life," who were "too busy to hold political office, but determine who shall hold such office." But the real effect of the stock market crash was not yet felt in the country, and it was still too early for anyone, including the Vans, to know that the Missouri Pacific was the end of their lines.

By virtue of a pyramid of holding companies they had managed to control all their holdings with imperceptible investments of their own. Although they had borrowed heavily in order to buy each succeeding railroad, the debts were no major burden as long as the roads showed a profit. And there was no question that their roads were run as well as their real estate operations. At the height of their power, the assets of the companies they controlled were worth some four billion dollars. But in the face of the depression, even sound management was not enough. The Missouri Pacific was first to go into the red. To keep their empire going, the Vans had borrowed $48,000,000 from a syndicate formed by J. P. Morgan and Company. In 1935 the House of Morgan called in the loan, and the Vans could only respond with their collateral: their shares in all their companies. The collateral was bought by the Mid-America Corporation—a new holding company—at open auction for $3,000,000. How much control the Vans had in Mid-America is questionable; but they were retained to manage the new company because, as a Morgan partner later said, "they are the only ones who can handle this intricate situation." For the first time since they had clerked at the turn of the century, the Vans were on salary. Although they were paid $150,000 a year—just enough to meet their expenses, they estimated in a memorandum to the House of Morgan—the large personal fortune they had acquired was gone, and their stake in the real estate and railroads had gone with it.

On December 12, 1935, Mantis James Van Sweringen died at Lakeside Hospital in Cleveland, of intestinal influenza which was complicated by a weak heart. He was fifty-four. Less than a year later, on November 23, 1936, Oris Paxton, who was fifty-seven, suffered a heart attack when the train which carried his private car was struck by another in Scranton, Pennsylvania, while he was on his way to a Morgan conference. He died soon afterward in the Hoboken, New Jersey, yards of the Lackawanna Railroad. Under an agreement of long standing, the surviving brother was to inherit everything left by the other. When Mantis James died his personal estate was worth $3,000 in cash plus life insurance, although this is less dramatic than it sounds because the estate he jointly shared with Oris Paxton was then estimated at $200,000. Even so, this was quite a comedown from their peak personal fortune of nearly $130,000,000. Oris Paxton left more; having been the beneficiary of his brother's insurance, and having worked nearly twelve months longer, he left $700,000 worth of personal property and real estate, and insurance policies worth $500,000.

Once they were dead, reorganizations, court actions and property sales dispersed into hundreds of other hands the material things once held by the Van Sweringens. Their dream of a unified rail system has been unfulfilled; the major roads they once held are separately run. Their Rapid Transit was bought by Shaker Heights at its junk value to keep it from being abandoned. The Cleveland buildings are owned by a separate company. The Vans' town house went for back taxes and its land was cut into six parcels; Daisy Hill was bought by a family which carved the sixty-five acres into twenty parcels, most of them of a size large enough to accommodate the kind of country estate the Vans always wanted in that part of Shaker Heights. After thirteen years the liquidating agent for the Vans' creditors grossed a little more than $366,000. Had the brothers been alive, they would still have owed more than $60,000,000.

The unpaid debts, the sufferings of thousands of people when two of Cleveland's major banks perished in the wake of the Van Sweringen collapse, may have been, as John T. Flynn wrote in 1934, the result of "the kind of disloyalties and betrayals by which the resources of a great city were forged into weapons for inordinately acquisitive men." Twenty-one years later, with the bitter memories of the depression receding, a Cleveland writer could say of the same men that "whatever else, they were great—and their legacies are all about us in Cleveland today, in a tall tower, a handsome suburb, a smoothed countryside . . . better ways of doing things. Where would today's Cleveland be without their impact?"

In Shaker Heights itself, where fireworks marked the finale of a month-long fiftieth anniversary celebration in 1961, the community's Architectural Board—three architects, the mayor and a city councilman—meets every Monday morning to determine whether building plans accord with restrictions established by the Van Sweringen brothers. It is likely that these meetings, and their results as they are reflected in the well-kept lawns and homes of Shaker Heights, are the memorial the Vans themselves would have appreciated most.

"Just follow the crowd."

4

Flagler, Florida and Fantasy

The tenacity of historical legends being what it is, chances are that the story of Juan Ponce de Léon's search for the Fountain of Youth, like that of George Washington's cherry tree, will never get much competition from the truth. For one thing, the idea of an aging man's bootless chase of the unattainable has an enduring quality. For another, it has the all but official support of an entire state, a rare distinction for a make-believe story. Florida does not acknowledge that Ponce de Léon failed to find the restorative waters within its borders. Since the state's economic well-being has in large measure derived from the spending habits of people seeking physical well-being, keeping the legend alive in Florida has obvious merit. The truth, on the other hand, has no exploitation value at all. In 1513, when he discovered and named Florida, Ponce de Léon was fifty-three years old, a veteran of an expedition with Christopher Columbus and the Spanish conquest of Puerto Rico, and healthy enough without a liquid diet. He had to be in order to lead three ships across the Atlantic and along Florida's long coastline, and to make occasional hazardous marches inland. His real

(87)

goal, according to an official historian of the Spanish court, was identical to that of the other explorers of the period: to "gain honor and increase his estate." Since Florida was blessed with about as many gold mines as fountains of youth, Ponce de Léon had nothing to show for his troubles except possibly a gain in honor. Despite the failure during his own lifetime and a subsequent rank among historians as a minor explorer, Ponce de Léon has survived because he combines in legend and truth the only appropriate symbol for the state of Florida.

No one knows the name of Florida's first tourist after Ponce de Léon, when he made his appearance, or whether he came seeking pleasure or a favorable climate for ills of the body. By the Civil War, St. Augustine, founded in 1565 and the oldest city in the United States, was doing a brisk tourist trade and could even drop names like that of Ralph Waldo Emerson, who visited there in 1827 to try to rid himself of a "bronchial ailment." Long before that, and until Florida achieved statehood in 1845, the area attracted adventurers, pirates, smugglers and a scattering of planters, although its largest population consisted of Indians who had broken away from the Creeks in Georgia and were called Seminoles. Spain held Florida until 1763, first against French and then against British encroachments. But that year, when England defeated both Spain and France and thereby gained control of North America, Florida was one of the prizes. Before it could be considered the fourteenth American colony, however, the Revolution had broken out, and Floridians showed their loyalty to the Crown by hanging John Hancock and Samuel Adams in effigy. When the thirteen colonies won their independence, Florida was returned to Spain. But Americans were convinced the territory belonged to them, and after thirty-eight years of almost constant military and diplomatic bickering, Spain ceded its colony to the United States. From the time it became a territory in 1821, Florida began to lure permanent settlers and, properly enough, tourists.

Florida's main attraction, then as now, was its weather, which at its best in some areas comes close to the perpetual springtime which has been claimed for it. This is not by any means a unanimous claim; one early settler recoiled from marshes and swamps, and described Florida as "pestiferous," and others since then have had unhappy experiences during recurrent hurricanes. Floridians do not acknowledge the existence of any weather but sunshine, and since territorial days have been remarkably sensitive to criticism of their climate. In 1832, John James Audubon, the famous naturalist, called St. Augustine "the poorest hole in Creation" and the area south of it distastefully changeable. "The thermometer has made leaps from thirty to eighty-nine in twenty four hours," he wrote. "Cold, warm, sandy, muddy, watery, all of these varieties may be felt and seen in one day's traveling." He was promptly spanked by the *Florida Herald* for his myopic vision as well as for "the most ungrateful feelings towards . . . hospitable people." Implications that Florida's climate is less than perfect, even when made by as objective an authority as the United States Weather Bureau in the course of its official duty, tend to be dismissed or minimized in the state's promotional literature. Over the years, Florida has made its point and, except when there is palpable evidence of a hurricane or a cold spell, tourists have flocked there. In the 1880's a resident of St. Augustine said that the city lived "on sweet 'taters and sick Yankees."

Before 1890, the diet and the clientele were drastically changed. Henry Morrison Flagler, a healthy and wealthy Yankee, made St. Augustine fashionable and profitable, and thereby established once and for all a personality for Florida. It is not very remarkable that in doing this he invoked the name and legend of Juan Ponce de Léon.

Flagler was in his late forties in 1878 when he saw Florida for the first time. He accompanied his first wife there that winter on her doctor's suggestion that the climate would be beneficial to her failing health. It wasn't, but by the time she died in 1881, Flagler had seen enough on their annual visits to realize that Florida offered vast potential to an astute businessman.

Henry Morrison Flagler was an astute businessman. He was also, according to Matthew Josephson's *The Robber Barons,* "a bold and dashing fellow." Flagler employed his talents wisely from the time he quit school at the age of fourteen to earn his own living. He left Hopewell, New York, where he had been born in 1830, the son of a poor Presbyterian minister, and worked his way to Republic, Ohio. On a job in a country store that paid five dollars a month and board, he managed to save money. By 1850 he was a grain commission merchant and had an interest in a distillery in Bellevue, Ohio. He did well there on two major counts. In 1853 he married Mary Harkness, whose father was a wealthy whiskey distiller and salt manufacturer, and in the course of his business he sold grain through a produce firm run by a young man named John D. Rockefeller. Some years later the two men met again in Cleveland, where Flagler had moved his grain business and Rockefeller his produce business. In 1865, Rockefeller switched from produce to oil refining in a company called Rockefeller and Andrews. Two years later Flagler was invited into the partnership, and, with $70,000 of his father-in-law's money, accepted. The firm became Rockefeller, Andrews and Flagler, and on the basis of the fresh capital opened a second refinery, which made it the largest oil producer in Cleveland. In

1870 the name was changed to the Standard Oil Company of Ohio.

Next to Rockefeller himself, the most important man in the company was Flagler. "For years and years this early partner and I worked shoulder to shoulder," Rockefeller wrote in his *Random Reminiscences* in 1909. "Our desks were in the same room. We both lived on Euclid Avenue, a few rods apart. We met and walked to the office together, walked home to luncheon, back again after luncheon, and home again at night. On these walks, when we were away from the office interruptions, we did our thinking, talking and planning together." These conversations eventually led to the giant monopoly which ruled the expanding American oil business, and which made Rockefeller the richest man in America. Flagler, as vice-president and one of the largest stockholders in the company, did nearly as well. When he visited Florida again in 1883, this time on a honeymoon with his second wife, he decided to act on the possibilities he had envisioned on his initial visit. By then he not only had a high annual income from his Standard Oil stock, but had acquired over the years with Rockefeller a shrewdness in business dealings as keen as his partner's.

Flagler's choice of St. Augustine as the starting point for his Florida venture was a wise one. Although rail transportation from Jacksonville was a haphazard affair on a rundown narrow-gauge road, St. Augustine, only thirty-five miles to the south, but blessed with a better climate, had managed to remain Florida's main tourist city. This does not say a good deal for it; St. Augustine lacked the luxurious facilities that enticed wealthy tourists to northern and European resorts, a deficiency which Flagler set about to remedy. He announced that he was going to build the Ponce de Léon Hotel, a structure so elegant that St. Augustine would immediately become another Newport, and its shore another Riviera. Equating his project with American society's favorite and most impressive resorts was the first indication of the heights Flagler planned to reach, and the amount of money he was prepared to spend. As he started to assemble parcels of land, a wave of speculation hit St. Augustine. Prices rose fast, but Flagler did not gamble with real estate. "I have no desire to speculate in St. Augustine property," he wrote one man who offered him land at an inflated price. "I only want to buy certain property which will be needed for the new hotel." Property values did increase greatly as a result of what Flagler did in St. Augustine, but he remained single-minded about his goal.

Flagler chose John M. Carrère and Thomas Hastings to design his hotel. Although they are now better known as the architects of the New York Public Library, the interior of the Metropolitan Opera House and the Memorial Amphitheatre at the National Cemetery in Arlington, Virginia, the Ponce de Léon Hotel was a distinctive achievement in its own right. It was built of poured concrete, one of the first large buildings in America on which this technique was used, and was faced with coquina, a soft, whitish rock formed of marine shell and coral fragments. The rock had to be hauled from Anastasia Island across the Matanzas River. Permission to do this was required from the city of St. Augustine, the state of Florida and the federal government. Flagler found the service of the Jacksonville, St. Augustine and Halifax River Railroad thoroughly inadequate for his needs, and when its owners refused to improve the line, he simply bought it. He changed the narrow-gauge tracks to standard size, extended them into St. Augustine and brought his building materials almost to his hotel site. Some of the fine furnishings, though, were shipped by steamboat from New York. Flagler seems to have found in the construction of the hotel some of the excitement he may have lacked at his desk in Standard Oil. He came to St. Augustine as often as he could to watch the construction.

The official opening of the Ponce de Léon Hotel at an elegant dinner on January 10, 1888, was a prime social event. The guests entered through a main gate on whose grand arch mermaids supported a shield bearing the name of the explorer. Vine-covered verandas ran along the street on each side of the gate. The interior court had a multi-colored fountain in its center and was surrounded by more verandas. On the other side of the fountain was the twenty-foot-wide entrance to the hotel itself, which led to a rotunda inlaid with rich mosaic, its high dome supported by massive oak pillars. All figures and ornaments were in Spanish Renaissance style. Beyond the rotunda was a great dining room which was reached by two polished marble staircases. The dining room was oval-shaped, could seat seven hundred diners comfortably, and was decorated with stained-glass windows and columns of antique oak. Flagler had provided for 450 rooms and suites, each spacious and luxuriously furnished. He had also installed electric lights, which would have been enough cause for comment that year, and steam heat, thus revealing an un-Floridian attitude toward the climate, but a sensible solicitude for the clientele he hoped to reach. Throughout the building were comfortable rooms for reading, games, refreshments and private meetings. The grounds, building, furnishings and decorations cost Flagler $2,500,000.

Flagler had accurately gauged the needs of St. Augustine and the taste of high society. The Ponce de Léon flourished from the day it opened. Before then Flagler realized that in the wake of the very wealthy and socially prominent would come the less endowed. It may have been less from reasons of snobbery than from practicality that

Flagler built another hotel across the street with rates lower than those at the Ponce de Léon. This one, which he called the Alcázar, and which cost him $1,250,000, was built on Moorish lines, had seventy-five rooms, as well as shops and restaurants, and a large tropical garden in its court. Behind the hotel, Flagler built a casino, which in addition to gambling tables had sulphur and salt-water pools and game rooms. To compensate for the evils of gambling, which was a business opportunity he could not overlook although it went against his religious upbringing, Flagler also financed the construction of the Memorial Presbyterian Church. Historians of the period record hundred-per-cent occupancy of Flagler's hotels during the tourist season, and great activity at the casino, but have no figures on church attendance.

As the only hotel keeper of any consequence in St. Augustine—he bought a third hotel there in 1889—Flagler was the social arbiter during the winter season. In fact, the season did not officially open until the Ponce de Léon received its first guests in mid-January. The arrival of the first visitors at the railroad station was always a ceremony. They were met by a "great omnibus drawn by six white horses." As the vehicle approached the hotel, a cannon was fired, flags were raised, and the gates leading to the inner court lifted while an orchestra played "The Star Spangled Banner." Flagler himself traveled to St. Augustine in a private railroad car called the *Alicia* in honor of the second Mrs. Flagler. The Flaglers entertained in style both at the hotel and at their home. Mrs. Flagler's clothes and jewelry were carefully noted by guests and the press, and one event she sponsored was inevitably called the Pearl Ball as a tribute to the quality of the gems she wore. Public parties, especially for causes close to the hearts of high society, were delightful challenges to the ingenuity of the Ponce de Léon's

management. On one occasion, according to a guest, the
hotel "was a dream of beauty bathed in rainbow colors and
decked with butterfly wings and laden with gleaming gold
so absolute and complete as to allure every sense and bring
all to the verge of paradise." Beauty was also provided by a
menu which included "bass, grouse, quail, woodcock, turkey, *foie gras* and partridge, as well as meats, pastries,
wine and ices."

While Flagler had from the start anticipated the kind
of guest who would appreciate this lavishness, he may not
have foreseen all the consequences. A rather cynical student of his career has noted that along with the wealth and
the society there came "anglers, invalids, heiress chasers,
gamblers, confidence men, real-estate men and Methuse-
lahites. The city of St. Augustine became, after it had been
Flaglerized, the high-society and con-man capital of the
United States during the winter season."

Whether Flagler was distressed at some elements of
the new population or simply had, even at sixty-three,
a strong urge toward new conquests, he now looked south
of St. Augustine. His first stop was Ormond, a coastal town
a few miles north of Daytona Beach, where the Hotel Ormond, an enormous wooden building, had an embarrassing
surplus of empty rooms each winter. Flagler saw no reason
for this state of affairs. The hotel was situated between the
shore and the Halifax River, which gave it space, Flagler
immediately discerned, to install a golf course. He bought
the hotel, refurbished it, manicured the grounds, optimistically enlarged its capacity, and constructed an eighteen-
hole course parallel to the ocean. As at St. Augustine, tourists eagerly sought accommodations. To bring them to
Ormond properly, Flagler acquired another narrow-gauge
railroad, whose rails were described as "two streaks of
rust," and converted them to standard gauge as far as Day-

tona. Later, when the hard-packed beach sand was found ideal for automobile racing, enthusiasts of the newfangled sport fought for rooms at Flagler's hotel. Their competition included people who wanted not so much to see a Vanderbilt drive a Mercedes as to gape at John D. Rockefeller taking his swings on the golf course.

Once Ormond provided further proof of his genius, Flagler moved deeper south. This time he was preceded by his own railroad tracks. In 1892 the state of Florida awarded him a charter authorizing a line paralleling the Indian River as far as Miami. Flagler did not then see any possibilities in a city so far away; his immediate goal was Palm Beach, at that time a handful of houses between the ocean and Lake Worth, which separated it from the mainland. The largest single piece of property was owned by Robert R. McCormick, heir to a farm machinery fortune, who had a winter home by the lake. In 1893, Flagler bought the McCormick land and several adjoining lots for $75,000. He announced the imminent construction of a new hotel to be called the Royal Poinciana, which would make all previous Flagler hostelries as out of date as last season's hats.

Before Flagler got started, and before the railroad was extended to Palm Beach, real estate prices soared. Among the beneficiaries of this development were a number of homesteaders who had stayed on nearly worthless land because there was nowhere else to go. When prices went to $150 and, in some cases, $1,000 an acre, the homesteaders reaped the profits of the new demand. Disregarding such crass activity, Flagler established quarters for his construction workers on the west side of the lake, which meant they had to row to and from the job every day. The site, which is now West Palm Beach, became a shack and tent city. It is likely that this use of the land led to Flagler's decision to keep Palm Beach itself uncluttered by commercialism or the unwashed. When he later started construction at West Palm Beach he was quoted as saying, "That is the city I am building for my help." On March 22, 1894, Flagler's railroad reached West Palm Beach. By that time, the Royal Poinciana had been open a month.

When Flagler first purchased the McCormick estate he said, "I shall build upon this spot a magnificent playground for the people of the nation." Although it had cost less than the Ponce de Léon, presumably because it was made of wood, the Royal Poinciana exceeded its predecessor in all other respects. It had 800 rooms and 1,400 employes to look after the guests who filled them from December to April. In the dining room, which could seat 1,600 at a time, there was one waiter for every four diners. The service alone would have brought the clientele Flagler sought. As it was, the food was also highly admired, and there was always a brisk demand for rooms at $100 a day, which included meals, although less expensive quarters were also available. As before, Flagler mined gold in its most liquid state, the assets of wealthy Americans seeking release from northern winters. Escape from climate often meant an escape from restrictions usually associated with home. Palm Beach became the playground Flagler envisioned, if not for all "the people of the nation" then at least for those who could afford it.

Play was continuous. The daily rounds of golfing, sailing, swimming, fishing and bicycling were topped by the evening entertainments—dances, concerts, vaudeville performers—and annual fetes such as the George Washington Birthday Ball, which was the main social event of the season. "The gay nineties," one of his biographers noted, "were perhaps nowhere gayer than in Palm Beach." Flagler enjoyed the fun, as well as the profits. One day, Henry Bradley

Plant, who was then working to develop Florida's West Coast, made an attempt to belittle Flagler, who had not strayed from the East. "Friend Flagler," he asked, "where is that place you call Palm Beach?" Flagler hardly paused. "Friend Plant," he said, "just follow the crowd."

Operating on the proven principle that if one hotel encouraged a crowd, another one would increase it, Flagler in 1895 started construction of a hotel a quarter of a mile east of the Royal Poinciana. It was first called the Palm Beach Inn, but after a few seasons, when it was enlarged and redecorated, it was named The Breakers. It was opened in January, 1896, after which Flagler extended his railroad across Lake Worth so that his guests no longer had to be rowed from the railroad station to his hotels. He also built a footbridge which made the guests more accessible to the residents of West Palm Beach who, as fishing guides, sailors and employees at the Flagler hotels, recognized the visitors as the root of their winter prosperity. The natives referred to the Royal Poinciana as the Royal-pounce-on-em.

Flagler had no objection to sharing his wealth with the year-round residents, but in 1898 he found a way to divert most of the stream to where he no doubt felt it properly belonged. He opened a gambling casino, which he called the Beach Club. Unlike St. Augustine, where Flagler eased his conscience by building a church after games of chance were installed, Palm Beach had had the weekly services of a minister since 1895. Flagler had even built an annex to his hotel called the Royal Poinciana Chapel, where gambling and other forms of sin were regularly denounced. Thus fortified, he invited Colonel Edward R. Bradley, a professional gambler, not quite forty years old but with a wealth of experience in his field, to run the Beach Club. It was to become, as one historian wrote, "the most celebrated gambling hell in the New World." It was also to make Palm Beach the closest thing to the Riviera ever seen in the United States, and Bradley second only to Flagler as the most influential man in Palm Beach.

Bradley was forced to operate under some narrowly conceived restrictions; that he did so successfully is a tribute to his ingenuity. To start with, Florida had laws which made gambling a crime subject to heavy penalties. Bradley did not consider this an overwhelming obstacle. He simply ruled that no native or resident of Florida be permitted entrance to the Beach Club. Under the club's charter he received approval "to run such games of amusement as the management and members may from time to time agree upon." Since Bradley made it a firm policy never to keep a record of the club's finances, there was no way for the curious to determine the profits derived from amusing the members. To further guarantee the state legislature's keeping a proper distance, Bradley banned anyone who did not *look* twenty-four years old, who was obviously drunk, or who, according to sources he considered reliable, was not financially solvent. This was to reduce possible public complaints to a minimum. Aside from this, Bradley fixed a rule of his own: evening clothes were required. It was also the only rule to which Bradley attached an exception. Gamblers who planned to take the afternoon train north the next day could appear in business suits.

Despite his careful planning, or perhaps because of it, there was an initial lack of interest in Bradley's enterprise; he was disconcerted to find that he showed a loss during his first year. About then, however, a female guest of the Royal Poinciana sought entrance to the gaming rooms. Bradley and Flagler, gentlemen of a school which takes a dim view of women gamblers, objected to the intrusion. Bradley's brother, who was present, spoke up on her behalf. Things

(99)

were so bad, he pointed out, that the closing of the Beach Club was imminent, making it unlikely that the problem would ever come up again. Bradley and Flagler bowed before the logic. There is no record of the pioneer woman's name, or whether she won or lost, but as soon as the doors were opened to female guests, the Beach Club flourished.

Bradley became expansive in his prosperity. He hired Conrad Schmitt, a Swiss chef, to preside over an elegant kitchen. The food Schmitt prepared was the best in Florida, and among the best in the United States. Schmitt received $25,000 a year for his talents, which in time included the creation of green turtle soup, a delicacy for which Bradley charged a dollar a plate, and variations in the preparation of Florida lobster. To keep the standards of his service as high as those of his food, Bradley paid his employees as much as $35 a day. He selected his staff with great care, preferred single men, and laid down firm rules against mingling with the guests. This did not prevent them, however, from reporting unusual behavior by players which might have an effect on Bradley's activities.

The greatest risk Bradley ran was the possibility of a guest's claiming in public that he was cheated. If this was even intimated in the club house, Bradley immediately offered to return the player's losses before he left—on condition that he tear up his membership card at the same time. Male players who lost heavily were sometimes invited by Bradley to have one last throw of the dice on a double-or-nothing basis. Women were treated more gently, perhaps because Bradley was sentimental about the role they had had in his success; if he felt their losses might harm their relationship with their husbands he occasionally reduced their debts. By means of policies such as these, and despite reform movements and attacks from the pulpit, Bradley stayed free of trouble. His position was undoubtedly made secure by heavy contributions to both the Democrats and Republicans and to every church in Palm Beach, regardless of denomination. In time, as a result of loans and a purchase at a bankruptcy sale, Bradley also owned two Palm Beach newspapers and part of the third. The nearest thing to a problem for Bradley was his sponsor. Flagler had become increasingly distressed at the growth of gambling, which he had seen initially only as a small operation to amuse hotel guests while providing a moderate profit. He is said to have offered Bradley $350,000 to fire himself as manager of the Beach Club. Bradley turned him down. When Bradley's nightly take continued to rise, Flagler considered closing his hotels, the source of Bradley's clientele. Rumors of this reached Bradley, who immediately sent word that he would have Flagler indicted for promoting a lottery at a fair run by the Royal Poinciana Chapel. Lotteries, Bradley let Flagler know, were illegal under Florida state law.

Bradley's total profits will almost certainly never be known. Guesses have been made about some aspects of his affairs. They probably are not reliable. When *chemin de fer* was added to the club's repertoire in 1923, it was reported that some $3,000,000 changed hands during the year. Bets running to $50,000 on the turn of a card are also remembered. Bradley assured the safety of these sums by the clever disposition of guards armed with machine guns behind a white trellis which decorated the walls of the Beach Club, and by hiring eighteen Pinkerton detectives who, flawlessly attired in dinner jackets, mingled unobtrusively with the players. Thus protected both inside and outside his domain, Bradley prospered beyond Flagler's lifetime. Only a liberal policy on food cut into his winnings; he complained that he lost two dollars on every lunch and four dollars on every dinner he served. Eventually age halted Bradley's winning streak. In 1941, when he was eighty-two, Bradley closed the Beach Club. He died five years later, leaving a will which called for the club to be destroyed, its gambling paraphernalia taken out to sea and sunk, and the club site given to the city. It has since been made into a public park.

Whatever he felt about Bradley's achievements and the evils of gambling, Henry Morrison Flagler did not allow them to divert him from fulfilling his own ambitions. Still farther south on Florida's East Coast were cities to be transformed and hotels to be built. Even before Palm Beach was an assured success, Flagler's vision extended to Key West, the southernmost point in Florida and the United States. In 1893 the charter of his Jacksonville, St. Augustine and Indian River Railroad Company was amended to permit Flagler to lay tracks all the way to Key West. That year, too, a sympathetic state legislature encouraged Flagler's ambitions by granting him 8,000 acres of land for each mile of railroad he constructed south of Daytona. While the land Flagler eventually received—between 1,500,000 and 2,000,000 acres—did not come close to the grants the federal government had made to Jay Cooke, it was still a substantial property. After all, Flagler's railroad, which in 1895 was definitively named the Florida East Coast Railway Company, never had more than 765 miles of track. On the way to its ultimate depot at Key West, Flagler bought, built and developed. Collecting new cities and hotels was not quite an obsession with him. Rather, he was pushed, he told a friend, because he had found that "satisfaction and contentment are not synonymous."

Of all the cities with which Flagler was involved, he should have had both satisfaction and contentment from Miami, the major stop on his southward push. It was a swampy town when he found it; it was well started toward its present-day distinction when he left it. It probably should have been named for him—an idea which had sizable support at one time, although not from Flagler himself—but sentiment prevailed for the Indian name which had long identified the site. Flagler did not immediately recognize, as he had at St. Augustine and Palm Beach, the opportunities in Miami. The scales were lifted from his eyes by Mrs. Julia D. Tuttle, an early resident who owned 640 acres on the north bank of the Miami River. It took her three years to enlighten Flagler, but she was an enterprising and determined woman, the first Miami booster, as it were.

Mrs. Tuttle knew that a railroad was necessary if Miami and her property were ever to amount to much. In 1892, while Flagler was working on his plans for Palm Beach, she offered him half her acreage if he would bring his railroad that far south. Flagler firmly, but diplomatically, declined. "I am in no fit condition mentally or physically, to consider your proposition," he wrote. "I am tired out, and a mole seems a mountain." But he did not completely shut the door. "If my life and health are spared," he added, "it seems more probable that I will extend the road to Miami within a few years." Flagler's life was spared, and Mrs. Tuttle finally won her point with an assist from nature. In the winter of 1894-95, Florida as far south as Palm Beach went through a devastating spell of freezing weather. James E. Ingraham, one of Flagler's most trusted agents, traveled through miles of ruined citrus groves and vegetable farms to report on the damage. To his amazement, when he crossed New River on his way to Miami, he found no sign of the freeze. Mrs. Tuttle drove home the obvious point to Ingraham, who carried the news of the weather phenomenon to Flagler. Negotiations on the conditions of Mrs. Tuttle's original offer were started soon afterward.

At the outset Mrs. Tuttle generously offered Flagler 100 acres on which to build a railroad station, train yards and a hotel. In addition she proposed to share with him alternate strips of a 525-acre section, and she persuaded W. B. Brickell, another landowner, to do the same with 400 acres he had on the south side of the river. For this, Flagler was to build a hotel within eighteen months, bring his railroad to Biscayne Bay, lay out streets and erect a water works. He started at once to keep his end of the bargain. As at Palm Beach, tents and shanties sprang up to house the workers who arrived as soon as they heard the reports of Flagler's new activity. By September 1895, tracks were being put in place and intermediate stations were constructed, around which new towns were built. Seven months later the first train entered Miami, carrying serious settlers and the usual hangers-on. Some 3,000 people were more or less installed by the summer of 1896, most of them on the north bank of the river because, with a shortage of rowboats and lack of a bridge, the south side was inaccessible. In January 1897, Flagler opened his Royal Palm Hotel, a five-story building, not quite as imposing as any of his previous hotels but nevertheless impressive in the newborn city. By that time Miami had incorporated itself and had elected a mayor and other officers, all of them, not surprisingly, Flagler friends and supporters.

In the months to come Flagler was to need them. Almost immediately after his men took office, a formidable opposition to Flagler's grip on Miami developed among its citizens. His holdings—valuable land sites, the railroad, hotel, power plant and water works—were derided as "The Corporation." Many articulate Miamians felt that the city could not attain its full possibilities as long as both economic and political power were controlled by one man. Pro-Flagler partisans were loud in their defense of the Corporation, and arguments were often settled, according to a resident, "in fist fights with an occasional display of knives." Violence was part of the frontier spirit which pervaded Miami's early days. As maturity came, there was restraint in the discussion, but opposition to the Corporation did not diminish. It was blamed for power failures and for destroying the city's beauty. There was some merit in these charges; Flagler's electric generators could not be enlarged fast enough to meet the needs of the growing population, and they used pine wood and coal as fuel, which sent smoke, soot and smelly gases over the residential areas. "Probably no other town along the Flagler line of march kicked more strenuously against its benefactor," the authors of a history of Florida wrote a few years ago.

Flagler, although dismayed at the state of his popularity, did not let it interfere with his gathering the fruits of his labors. As Miami grew, so did the value of the land he was given to come there in the first place. Neither Brickell nor Mrs. Tuttle, his original sponsors, came out as well as he did. On the basis of her expectations for the city's future Mrs. Tuttle bought Miami land extensively, mostly on credit. As a long-term investment this made sense, but she could not turn purchases into immediate cash. When she asked Flagler for help his response was less sympathetic than she probably felt was proper. "I do not want you to suffer," he wrote her, "but I cannot accept the responsibility of your suffering. For months past, I have advised against you becoming so deeply involved in debt." Mrs. Tuttle died in 1898 without personal benefit from the city she helped bring into existence. The results of Brickell's partnership with Flagler are not as well documented as Mrs. Tuttle's, but he seems to have finished badly, too. His properties had little value until a bridge could be built across the Miami River. An old Miami story has it that he and Flagler argued over the location of the bridge and that when Flagler persisted in his view Brickell left Miami forever. It is likely that he sold his alternate strips before departing, if, indeed, he did go. Flagler, without the disillusionment of Mrs. Tuttle and Brickell, and in the face of Miami's opposition to his monopoly, could speak well of the city. "It is," he said, again invoking the legend, "the city of eternal youth."

By the time Flagler's railroad came to Miami he had acquired, from the state and by purchases and gifts, a vast accumulation of land on Florida's East Coast. In February 1896 he established the Model Land Company to manage, develop, publicize and sell some of his holdings. James E. Ingraham, who had been impressed by Miami's weather and Mrs. Tuttle's arguments, was put in charge of the company. He was an ideal choice. He had had a leading part in the construction of the rail lines, especially in the choice of town sites along its route. In the course of this he had attained a wide knowledge of the land's potential for fruit, vegetables and livestock. He was also a natural promoter and, with Flagler, quickly understood that the encouragement of settlers on Florida's East Coast meant not only a profit on land sales but future profits for the railroad. Flagler once estimated that new settlers were worth $300 each to him; everything they brought in to use and everything they produced had to be carried by his railroad. Although Flagler and the Florida East Coast Hotel Company, which managed his hotel properties, never neglected the profits represented by tourists, the emphasis in promotion was increasingly aimed toward permanent residents. Flagler himself owned large farms where he raised potatoes, pineapples and oranges, and he encouraged Ingraham's employment of farm experts to help new arrivals get properly started.

Ingraham sent a steady barrage of brochures, advertisements and even a magazine, *The Florida Farmer and Homeseeker,* throughout the northern states. Salesmen were placed in key cities to supplement the printed matter. It is not likely that they could have surpassed his words. "The gates of death are farther removed from Florida than from any other state," one of Ingraham's broadsides intoned. Florida's climate was, as always, invoked as the source of all good, whether for long life or productive land. Ingraham did not overlook any possible land buyer; he sold to individuals who sought farms or homesteads, to groups who wanted to establish cities, to real estate companies that wanted to resell. Prices varied from $1.50 to $5 an acre depending on location and quality of land, and installment payments were permitted for an additional charge of 8 per cent interest. As the population of the East Coast grew, and new towns were founded, the importance of Flagler's railroad increased, as he intended it should.

Despite the influx and the activity, the railroad itself was never profitable. It also brought Flagler into conflict with the area he had all but singlehandedly created. Until 1896, the railroad operated without any restrictions. That year, Florida passed a law establishing a Railroad Commission with power to regulate passenger fares, schedules, freight rates, services and the construction of depots. Flagler lost both his fight against the bill and, in the years that followed, his efforts to control the commission. Passenger fares were not reduced by the commission, presumably on the ground that tourists were by definition able to afford their passage, but freight rates were cut sharply. This pleased the growers, who up to then had no recourse but to go along with Flagler's monopoly. In 1901 they formed the Fruit and Vegetable Growers Association, to bring pressure of their own on the commission. They cited flaws in rail service; one city which gave the road $50,000 worth of business a year was without a station agent; freight was carelessly handled, and sent at the shipper's risk; claims for damages were ignored. Before the fight was over—and the commission prevailed—the state was also criticized for its land grants to Flagler, and many of them were revoked. In the wave of anti-Flagler feeling it was generally forgotten that during the big freeze of 1894–95 he had lent money and materials to farmers to restore their lands. Those who did remember cited his actions bitterly as a case of Flagler's self-interest; he needed the farmers to keep his railroad going.

The antipathy aroused by Flagler as a businessman was intensified by an incident in his personal life. In 1894 his second wife had a mental breakdown, and in 1899 she was declared legally insane by the New York Supreme Court. Flagler wanted to remarry, but in neither New York nor Florida was insanity grounds for divorce. In April 1901, two years after Flagler made Florida his legal residence, the state legislature passed a law establishing such grounds. At once the opposition to Flagler leaped on this as a moral issue. His enemies protested at the speed with which the law was passed; it had been introduced on April 9, passed by the Senate on April 17, by the House on April 19, and signed by the governor on April 25, possibly a record for such legislation. Newspapers hinted that it took $20,000, properly distributed, to guarantee such speed, and referred to the results as "The Flagler Divorce Law." Flagler himself said nothing publicly, but he instituted divorce proceedings in August, an act which the papers considered tantamount to an admission of all their charges. The courts were even faster than the legislature; Flagler was awarded a final decree in forty-eight hours. A week later he announced his engagement, and, three weeks after that, his marriage to Mary Lily Kenan. He was then seventy-one. Later, when Flagler donated $10,000 to the Florida Agricultural College and another $10,000 to the University of Florida, which succeeded it, the newspapers regarded the gifts as further evidence of guilt. They continued to be critical of the law until 1905, when another session of the legislature repealed it.

Flagler's wedding gift to his wife was a Palm Beach house, his most grandiose gesture since the Ponce de Léon. He recalled Carrère and Hastings, his first architects, and in effect said, "Build me the finest residence you can think of." They did, at a cost of $3,000,000. For that kind of money, Flagler had his house completed in eight months. In it were, among other things, sixteen guest suites, each decorated to represent a different period in world history, including "modern America," which was distinguished by a set of twin beds, said to be the first in Florida. Another first, a sunken bathtub, graced Mrs. Flagler's bathroom. The dining room could seat fifty with a different table service every night of the week, Mrs. Flagler once boasted—on chairs covered with Aubusson tapestries, all different. The ground floor, to take it chronologically, had a library in Renaissance style, a ballroom in the style of Louis XIV, a music room, with a tremendous pipe organ, in Louis XV, and a salon in Louis XVI. The billiard room was Chinese, period unknown. The largest room was not identified beyond its name, Marble Hall. It was so called because seven shades of marble were used to decorate its 110-foot length and forty-foot width. The speed on which Flagler insisted undoubtedly raised his costs. It is estimated that rugs which should have taken five years to weave were completed in five months, and that one of them cost some $35,000. At their new home, which they called Whitehall, the Flaglers entertained lavishly and often, and disregarded their critics.

(*109*)

Whitehall was neither the last, nor, for all its treasures, the most impressive of Flagler's creations. In 1905, shortly after his seventy-fifth birthday, Flagler undertook the extension of his railroad lines to their logical—to him, at any rate—terminus at Key West. The logic was not apparent to everyone. One of Flagler's closest friends told him, "A railroad in that God-forsaken section? You need a guardian." Engineers were just as skeptical, and only one contractor bothered to make a bid on the job. None of this skepticism bothered Flagler. Across ninety miles of the Florida Strait was Havana, main port of Cuba, now independent of Spain and presumably ready to ship its goods to American customers. Flagler also owned large shares of Cuban railroad stock, and thus had an added incentive to promote the island's industry. Key West already had a fine harbor and a population of 20,000. Patently, Flagler had good arguments for his Overseas Extension.

The job took seven years. The trackage from Miami to Key West amounted to only 156 miles, half of it over water which separated the long strand of islands, but it cost Flagler more than $20,000,000. It was, according to the *Scientific American*, "one of the most . . . difficult works of railroad construction ever attempted." Although Flagler took personal charge of the project, the actual direction was under a skilled engineer with experience on the Panama Canal. From 3,000 to 4,000 men were employed at a time. Since fresh water was not available on the Keys, flatcars brought it in daily, often from points a hundred miles away. Food and other supplies were sent three times a week from a town called Marathon. In many instances preconstruction planning had to be completely revised to meet changing conditions. Wind and waves did more damage to the viaducts than had been anticipated. Before they could be placed between the tiny islands the road had to be built over swamps and marshes. As if there were not enough problems, three hurricanes swept over the area during the road's construction. The first, in 1904, struck while Flagler's survey party was at work and did little harm. Another, two years later, caused considerable damage; equipment was lost, ships were destroyed or blown out to sea, and men injured. By the time the worst of the three came, in 1909, Flagler's engineers had anticipated its dangers and had, in fact, built so well that their viaducts and bridges have withstood every hurricane since.

The first cars to traverse the Overseas Extension arrived at Key West on January 22, 1912; they were met by the mayor and some 15,000 townspeople, many of whom had never seen a train in their lives. This was not a freight train for Cuban products, but an engine and five private cars carrying, besides Flagler and his associates, a representative of President Taft and a clutch of congressmen. Flagler was presented with a gold medal, 1,000 children strewed his path with American Beauty roses, the Cuban National Band, imported for the occasion, played as soldiers, sailors and Boy Scouts marched in review. Other trains followed later in the day, including one which labeled itself a through train from New York to Havana, whose passengers were forthwith put aboard a ferry for the Cuban port. For the next few days a Cuban circus, a Spanish opera, receptions, dinners and dances livened Key West. There is no question that Flagler enjoyed the show more than anyone else present. The *Miami Herald* expressed the hope that the celebrations at Key West "will in some degree convey to him the appreciation in which he is held by the people of the entire East Coast. . . . Every city and every hamlet on the line of the road . . . has been built and fostered by the development undertaken by him." These were pleasant words, especially when contrasted

(*111*)

with the kind of editorials the anti-Flagler press had published a few years earlier at the height of the freight rate battle.

Since losing that fight, Flagler had hoped to put his road in the black on the basis of the Overseas Extension, trade with Cuba, and the development of Key West into a great port and America's "Gibraltar." But on January 15, 1913, he slipped and fell while descending the white marble stairs at Whitehall, breaking his right hip. He was eighty-three, and already quite feeble, and he never recovered; he was bedridden until his death on May 20. His estate was valued at $100,000,000. At his own request, Flagler was buried at St. Augustine, the scene of his first triumph in Florida. The Flagler system did not survive its founder by many years. Its strength was dissipated as the various properties it encompassed passed to other owners. The last blow came, ironically enough, from a hurricane. In September 1935 the Keys were struck by one of the fiercest hurricanes in Florida's history. Winds and a tidal wave eighteen feet high brought death to nearly 500 people, injured hundreds more, destroyed a train racing to rescue survivors, washed long stretches of embankment into the sea, and twisted miles of tracks into distorted uselessness. Only the finely built trestles and bridges remained upright. After the storm few but die-hard Key Westers talked of rebuilding the Overseas Extension. The railroad itself had barely squeaked through the depression and could not meet repair costs. An Overseas Highway was built on the sturdy trestles laid out by Flagler. The road was completed in 1938 and, even if it is not quite what Flagler had in mind, it remains today the most impressive part of his legacy in Florida, although in a broader sense the legacy is the state's entire East Coast resort area from St. Augustine to Key West.

If at times the history of Florida since Flagler reads like a postscript to what he had written across the map of the state, it is simply because, like all pioneers, he had left much to be done. In the thirty years he devoted to Florida's development he had barely scratched its potential. Those who followed—serious developers and get-rich-quick speculators, visionaries and cynics, honest men and charlatans—operated, whether they knew it or not, on the same assumptions he made in 1883. The main difference was that Flagler had faith in Emerson's dictum and built his mousetrap first; many of his successors felt that they needed the world beating a path to their doors while their mousetraps were still on the drawing boards. Amazingly enough, they were successful for a while, and never more so than during the years between 1920 and 1926, which saw the frenetic climax and dismal bust of a boom which ranks among the most incredible in American history.

The road to the Florida madness of the 1920's was preceded by a bridge. It spanned Biscayne Bay from Miami to Miami Beach, a euphemism for a long stretch of mangrove swamp then inhabited by snakes, mosquitoes and rats. Collins Bridge, named for the man who conceived it but lacked the finances to complete it, was opened on June 12, 1913, less than a month after Flagler's death. John S. Collins, a horticulturalist, had planned to clean up the swamps and grow grapefruits and avocados. Carl G. Fisher, whose money made the bridge possible, and who bought large sections of Miami Beach, felt that the swamps had possibilities exceeding the virtuous, but risky, venture of farming. His was not a farmer's personality anyhow. He was a promoter, and a notably successful one. He had raced bicycles as a youngster, graduated to automobiles—in which he barnstormed with Barney Oldfield, America's first speed champion—and had earned a fortune on an invention which made automobile headlights possible. When the Collins bridge was completed, Fisher began to dispose of his fortune at the rate of $52,000 a day by filling in the mangrove swamp at Miami Beach. When he was done he had a sandy beach, and trees, shrubs and grass to keep it from blowing away. He also managed to build a one-mile narrow-gauge railroad to which he gave annual passes to the presidents of all the major railroads in the United States.

The passes were the first of a series of publicity stunts which Fisher sponsored, and which contributed much to the early personality of Miami Beach. In 1915, when Miami Beach was incorporated, it was still all but deserted, and Fisher had no takers when he offered free land with a sixty-foot ocean frontage to anyone who promised to build a $200,000 hotel. But Fisher had patience, and it was rewarded when World War I ended. By then the automobile was coming into its own, and good roads—among them the Dixie Highway to South Florida, which Fisher promoted—were being built all over the country. Prosperity and the postwar urge toward fun and frolic did the rest, with a boost from Fisher. He created the Miami Beach bathing beauty, without whom no photograph of the beach is ever quite official. Two elephants, which he had previously employed in removing stumps from the swamp, were the source of reams of free publicity; one of them was photographed caddying for President Warren G. Harding on a Miami Beach golf course. Big-name bands played at Fisher's hotels and big-name people stayed at Fisher's home. His success was complete—and the Florida boom well on its way—when Will Rogers, than a comedian with the Ziegfeld Follies, called Fisher "the midwife of Florida." Lots sold at rapidly rising prices, hotels were built, and business increased with the jokes. "Fisher rehearsed the mosquitoes so they wouldn't bite you until after you bought," Rogers said.

Publicity of the sort Fisher inspired now became standard, not only at Miami Beach but everywhere else along the coast where speculators felt there was a chance to sell an undeveloped lot. The outstanding entertainers of the period were brought to Florida; Helen Morgan, Ruby Keeler, Gilda Gray and Elsie Janis performed regularly at speakeasies. Texas Guinan, a famous night club hostess of the prohibition period, ran the Silver Slipper in Miami, where a glass of cracked ice sold for two dollars and fifty cents. The purchase entitled the customer to hear, among other things, Walter O'Keefe sing a song entitled "So Mister Engineer Open Up the Throttle, I'm Gonna Throw Away My Hot-Water Bottle, We'll All Be in Miami in the Morning." Songs were considered ideal promotional material and were swiftly commissioned by real estate dealers and hotel proprietors. From this period have come "On Miami Shores" and "When the Moon Shines on Coral Gables." Popular orchestras, among them those led by Jan Garber and Paul Whiteman, were hired to play the new compositions. For potential customers with higher musical tastes, Madame Alda and Boris Chaliapin, the opera singers, and Ignace Paderewski, the pianist, were on hand to perform. Sports lovers could see Gene Tunney train, and even buy real estate from him, or watch Red Grange on a football field. Spiritual uplift was provided by William Jennings Bryan, who conducted "the largest outdoor Bible class in the world" on Sundays and spoke of the glories of nearby Coral Gables real estate on weekdays, for which he received $50,000 a year in cash and $50,000 in land.

Bryan's enthusiasm was not limited to Coral Gables. He also had nice words to say for Miami. "It is the only city in the world," he once remarked, "where you can tell a lie at breakfast that will come true by evening." Not all the lies came true the same evening or, for that matter, any evening, but with entertainers and statesmen to beckon them, people rushed to Florida from all parts of the country. Aspects of the California Gold Rush of 1849 were there, but with the modern variations—automobiles instead of horses and mules, down payments instead of pickaxes, lots instead of lodes. Stories of overnight wealth were widespread, and widely believed. A popular one was of the New York taxi driver who took a load of passengers to Miami when they missed their train, and made a fortune with just his fare and tips as starting capital; history does not record how his passengers made out. Barbers who also did it on tips, bank clerks who made enough to marry the boss's daughter, itinerant actors who arrived broke and left rich, and schoolteachers who invested their savings were also part of the folklore. Little or no intelligence was required; as in previous gold rushes, the only requisite was to be where the money was.

As the new San Francisco of this race for riches, Miami generated its own kind of excitement. Ben Hecht, the writer, who visited there during the boom, recalled some of it later with a mixture of awe and horror. "The City of Miami had turned itself into a real-estate cornucopia," Hecht wrote. "A hundred thousand people were getting rich selling building lots to each other. They raced up and down the hot sidewalks in bathing suits, bathrobes and jiggling sweaters. A colored boy had sold his shoeshine stand for ten thousand. The news of great profitable sales spread like the arrival of a Messiah. Strawhatted salesmen waved 'new development' maps in the air and chanted the names Silver Heights, Coral Gables, Picture Bay, Montezuma Manors, Sea Cove Crest, Biscayne Bay, like the signal towers of a Promised Land. Symphony orchestras played in salesrooms. Buses full of bonanza-hunters roared through the streets and down the coral dusty roads. Tumbling out of their tallyhos, these Argonauts looked at rubbish heaps and reeking swamps and visioned the towers of new Babylons.

"Everybody was trying to get rich in a few days. Nobody went swimming. Nobody sat under the palm trees. Nobody played horseshoes. Seduction was at a standstill. Everybody was stubbing his toes on real-estate nuggets. People who had been worth only six hundred dollars a few weeks ago were now worth a hundred thousand dollars— not in money but in real estate.

"You could hardly move in the main streets. They were choked with fortune hunters. These were not gamblers or adventurers. They were chiefly people from nowhere who had come to Florida for a two-weeks' tan."

To divert the attention of these visitors from the benefits of sunshine to the benefits of land, the promoters soared well beyond earlier uses of language as a salesman's tool. Words were distorted to take on a peculiarly Floridian meaning. The late Alva Johnston, a journalist of wit and perception, collected a number of the key words in the course of writing the biographies of Addison and Wilson Mizner, who were prominent in the Florida boom at one stage of their lives. *Near*, Johnston discovered, meant far. It was most often used the way Charles Ponzi, a well-known swindler, described his tract of land; it was "near Jacksonville," meaning sixty-five miles away. *High* meant low. This usage derived from a certain sensitivity to the flatness of the Florida landscape which led to calling an area Okeechobee Highlands because it was twelve inches higher than anything around it. *Heights*, Johnston said, was usually reserved for an altitude of twenty-four inches, although a place called Baldwin Heights was found by the National Better Business Bureau to be under water. *By-the-sea* usually meant "far back in the hinterland." When J. W. Young, a California developer, called his Florida site Hollywood-by-the-Sea, it was barely in view of the ocean. In time, Young bought adjoining properties and did indeed reach the Atlantic, whereupon he dropped the hyphenated addition in favor of plain Hollywood. *Waterfront* and *oceanfront* were loosely used, too, although many promoters tried to maintain a certain honesty by digging canals around their properties to give them a waterfront.

Of all the words used during the Florida boom, three attained a special status. When all else failed, the word *proposed* came into use. Kenneth Roberts, the novelist, who covered the boom for the *Saturday Evening Post,* wrote of a group of promoters who proposed a major project and hired a painter to create a large sign reading, "A Million Dollar Hotel Will Be Erected Here." When the sign was delivered the gentlemen could not raise the eighteen dollars to pay for it, whereupon the painter sold it to another group. *Vision* was not just a word, but a gift, wrote Johnston, "that enabled an observer to mistake spots before the eyes for magnificent cities. . . . The greatest disgrace that could befall a man in Florida was to be suspected of not being a man of vision. . . . You qualified as a man of vision the moment you saw the Manhattan skyline rising out of an alligator swamp. The realtor's standard question for testing a man's vision was, 'Can you imagine a city *not* being here?' " One word alone was banned from the lexicon of the Florida promoters; they hated *boom.* Florida, they said, was not having a boom but a development.

Whatever the word and whatever the meaning, real estate dealers and their salesmen were in the ascendancy. In Miami in 1925, 7,500 real estate licenses were issued. Some of the sales were unbelievably swift. One day a 400-acre tract of sand-covered swampland was put up for sale at 8:30 A.M. By 11:00 A.M. the real estate office had to close its doors. A mob had formed, forcing checks and cash on

salesmen to a total of $33,734,350. The money was brought
to the bank in barrels. Another time, N. B. T. Roney (whose
initials were said during the boom to stand for No Back
Talk), a former governor of Florida, formed a company
to buy some oceanfront land for $3,000,000. In a sale
lasting six and a half hours, it was sold for $7,645,000. The
most impressive single profit has been attributed to Carl
Fisher. He bought a tract at the northern end of Miami
Beach for $8,000,000, for which he paid $3,000,000 down.
Within two weeks he had sold it for $11,000,000, of which
he received $4,000,000 down. The quick turnover at such
levels would have been enough to set this transaction apart,
but Floridians were soon enjoying a final twist. Fisher, they
said, had his customer committed before he entered the
deal, but did not have the $3,000,000 to support the check
he wrote. He saw to it that his bank did not clear his check
until the resale was complete. Sales like these contributed
to the enormous figures which were linked to Florida at the
height of the boom. Because of the universal exaggeration
there is no way of getting at the truth, but students of the
period are convinced that real estate turnover in Florida
in the twenties amounted to several billion dollars.

The money which made up this total did not come
solely from large transactions. Most sales, in the tradition
of earlier booms, were made on the basis of deposits, or, as
they were most often called, binders. A binder of 5 per cent
was usually enough to close a deal; by law, the next payment, which could be as much as 25 per cent of the total
price, was not required until title to the property had been
legally cleared. With so many sales going on, such clearance
often took four to six weeks. During this period, the
"binder boy"—the holder of the binder—started operating.
Since he had no intention of keeping the land on which he
made his deposit, his job was to find someone who would

buy his binder at, naturally, a higher price than he had paid. The next buyer, having a similar goal, looked for a new buyer, and so on. Thus as binder prices moved upward, the property changed hands a half-dozen times or more before an actual transfer of property took place. Binder boys increased their take by hiring youngsters who were known as "bird dogs." The function of a bird dog was simply to find customers for the binder boys, not an especially difficult task in view of the thousands who came to Florida for the express purpose of making a quick profit. Bird dogs received a commission for their efforts and, presumably, graduated to the ranks of binder boys. The beauty of the system was that it took so little money to get started, and, of course, any number could play.

Through all this, warnings were broadcast by northern bankers and businessmen, many of whom were aghast at the amount of money being withdrawn for land gambles in Florida. The secretary of the National Credit Association called attention to the dangers in Florida, and was immediately criticized by the Florida Credit Association, which asked that he be dismissed. When the New York Better Business Bureau pointed out some of the shortcomings in certain Florida projects, Florida real estate men called the findings malicious. When W. O. McGeehan, the sports editor of the *New York Herald Tribune*, made jokes about the boom a St. Petersburg newspaper responded with an editorial entitled "Shut Your Damn Mouth." Occasionally Florida itself took some action, but only, apparently, against the most flagrant violations. Charles Ponzi, whose Charpon Land Syndicate guaranteed a dividend of 200 per cent within three months on "certificates of indebtedness" which sold for $310, was indicted and convicted for breach of Florida's trust laws. Other outright frauds were uncovered by the Better Business Bureau and the Post Office Department. Eventually there were hundreds of arrests and law-suits, but fraud and illegality were less prevalent than might be expected in such an excitable atmosphere. Most developers, a recent study of Florida concluded, "were determined to carry out what they had planned and were convinced that it could be done." In their enthusiasm for their own private "vision" and their eagerness to succeed, most developers simply got carried away by their own promotion.

Of all the mirages created on Florida's East Coast during the boom, none stirred as much attention at the time, or has been so well documented since its disastrous failure, as Boca Raton, twenty-six miles south of Palm Beach. Boca Raton was the invention of Addison Mizner, a successful architect who specialized in homes for wealthy clients. He was the subject several years ago of a lengthy study by Alva Johnston, who thereby provided posterity with a look at post-Flagler Florida as well as a case history of the rise and fall of a development during Florida's boom years.

Addison Mizner picked up architecture in the course of a short apprenticeship in San Francisco when he was quite young. He had, wrote Johnston, "uncommon powers and odd weaknesses. He knew his profession at the top and at the bottom but not in the middle. At the high level, he had an imagination that teemed with beautiful façades and interiors, with striking vistas and splendid theatrical effects. At the low level, he was a master artisan, skilled in nearly all the building trades, from carpentry and cabinetmaking to ironwork and plastering. About the middle, or technical, part of his profession, he was strangely defective; he knew little about plans and specifications, stresses and strains. His mind was almost a blank on the sciences to which the architectural student of today is required to devote four or five years." Regardless of shortcomings Mizner became, after several years of wandering around the world, a social and commercial success in New York in 1904. By 1916, however, due to a penchant for travel and social resorts which kept him out of the city much of the time, the demand for his services had fallen off. He not only had no money, but had also become seriously ill. Friends suggested that Palm Beach was a pleasant place to die. Unlike others who chose the same route, Mizner found something akin to Ponce de León's fountain of youth in Florida; he lived seventeen more years, and his talents flourished.

The turn for Mizner came when he met Paris Singer, the youngest of twenty-four children of Isaac Merrit Singer, who made a fortune in sewing machines. Paris Singer had come to Palm Beach to recover from a broken romance with Isadora Duncan, the famous dancer. His consolation came in remaking Palm Beach with Addison Mizner's help, a monumental job to which both men brought enormous energy and imagination. Palm Beach, they saw at once, had not changed much physically since Flagler had shaped it, but its high society, Singer decided, had deteriorated. Thereupon, he commissioned Mizner to design the Everglades Club, which became the social center of the city. Singer ran the club ruthlessly; a membership card was granted for one season at a time, and whether it was renewed the following season depended on Singer. His standards were capricious. A woman was dropped for laughing too loudly; Colonel Bradley had to be content with his own coterie at the Beach Club because Singer would not let a professional gambler join the Everglades Club.

High society, or those members of it who came to Palm Beach, enjoyed Singer's domination, but what he accomplished at the social level was surpassed by Mizner at the architectural level. Mrs. E. T. Stotesbury, who had been the leading hostess at Palm Beach since the turn of the century, liked Mizner's design of the Everglades Club, and commissioned him to do a house for her. By the time he finished El Mirasol, which Mrs. Stotesbury liked very much, a house designed by Mizner was as much a requisite of Palm Beach society as a dinner jacket.

Between Mizner and Singer, Palm Beach became a city Flagler would not have recognized. The construction of luxurious homes led to a longer season; people arrived in the late fall, instead of January, and remained until late spring. When they were not entertaining at home they were at Singer's Everglades Club or shopping in the business district which Mizner had carved out of something called Joe's Alligator Farm, which he bought with Singer's backing. In time, they also spread—or at least, the males among them spread—a fashion which Mizner inadvertently started. At a time when the winter colony still dressed conservatively, Mizner dashed around Palm Beach with his shirt tail fluttering behind him. Because Addison was such a pace-setter in nearly everything, Johnston wrote, even this quirk was copied. Palm Beachers began to take off their jackets, then their ties, and then to leave their collars open. Soon a haberdashery stylist finished the job by cutting off part of the shirt tails and putting a neat hem at the bottom; he called it a sport shirt.

Setting the style in clothes was not Mizner's métier. His conscious efforts were devoted to architecture and interiors. "As an antiquarian," wrote Johnston, "he had a sure touch in adapting the architecture and decoration of past ages to the Mizner Palm Beach period. As a landscape expert, he had a feeling for the melodramatic botany of Florida and knew how to mount his colors with bold and dramatic effects. As a veteran wit, courtier and social comedian, he possessed the best qualities of showmanship and salesmanship for recruiting a billion-dollar clientele.

(123)

. . . His more or less misspent life turned out to be the perfect preparation for his Florida career." He did so well that competition was inevitably imported. Joseph Urban, an outstanding architect in his own right, was brought to Palm Beach by a wealthy resident. By that time, Wilson Mizner was in the city helping his brother spend his new-found fortune. Wilson "blasted Urban out of the picture with one wisecrack—'Harry Thaw shot the wrong architect.'"

Mizner's architecture at Palm Beach, and later at Boca Raton, is usually called Spanish, although a former American Ambassador to Spain said, "It's more Spanish than anything I ever saw in Spain." Johnston pointed out that it has been called by many names, "adding up to the Bastard-Spanish - Moorish - Romanesque - Gothic - Renaissance - Bull - Market-Damn-the-Expense Style." Mizner turned Palm Beach into a medieval city of enormous houses, which were usually referred to by their owners as cottages. Among his innovations were battlements, parapets, towers and turrets. Mizner explained that in his imagination Palm Beach was a stronghold on the Christian-Mohammedan frontier and he could not leave his clients defenseless. In one of his citadels he also, for no apparent reason, put a large woodburning fireplace in the bathroom. Often, as he made changes during construction, he would be warned by the contractor about the added costs. "Listen," Mizner said, "these people can't stand the sight of anything that doesn't cost a lot of money." In pleasing his clients' tastes he kept away from anything "that looked like a mathematical formula with a roof on it. He wanted his structures to give the impression that they had evolved from century to century, not that they had sprung ready-made from a blueprint." This may be the reason that once, after a house was built, he discovered that he had forgotten to put a staircase between the first and second floors. Mizner was annoyed at himself for the oversight, but rather than spoil the beauty of the rooms he had designed he had a staircase built on the outside of the house, which presented no problems except on rainy days.

Mizner's experience at Palm Beach was possibly the best he could have had to move properly into the Florida land boom. He had learned early, says Johnston, that "business getting was the chief of the seven branches of architecture, and he regarded salesmanship as a form of poetry. He was the first to hear of it when a socially ambitious matron with a silo of money arrived in Palm Beach. The most accidental of meetings, some lyrical conversation on the glories of Old Spain, a personally conducted tour of Mizner-land, and Addison would soon be heaving and hacking at a new bank roll. . . . Addison was adept at egging on feuding social leaders to fight it out with Mizner architecture, and he stirred up terrific duels in which great ladies delivered tremendous blows with new Moorish patios and frescoed porticoes, only to receive savage counterthrusts in the shape of neo-Byzantine loggias, baroque staircases, and colonnaded orangeries." Salesmanship, especially if it were poetic, was precisely the skill required to rise above the binder boys, bird dogs and the other scurrying real estate agents in Florida. Mizner had it, and thus was able to launch the most superb "vision" of the Florida boom.

Mizner called his creation Boca Raton, which is Spanish for Rat's Jaw, but which was never, if it could be helped, translated. This was in keeping with boom practice. Spanish names were popular—Los Gatos (The Cats) was one—along with such Romanesque borrowings as Naples, Venice and Riviera, and romantic inventions like Coral Gables. Established cities, which could not be renamed, had to be satisfied with subtitles: Miami, the Magic City; Orlando, the City Beautiful; Fort Lauderdale, the Tropical Wonderland; and St. Petersburg, the Sunshine City, for example. Mizner did not have this problem when he convinced some of the most prominent men in American business that Boca Raton under the direction of the Mizner Development Corporation had possibilities forever denied to all other Florida developments. He drew to his board T. Coleman DuPont, a former United States Senator; Jesse L. Livermore, a prominent capitalist; George S. Graham, a congressman from Pennsylvania, and several others of comparable stature. Addison Mizner reserved the presidency of the corporation for himself and the portfolio of secretary-treasurer for his brother Wilson. Thus fortified, the new corporation claimed in its first advertisement: "World leaders in finance, society and arts establish an international resort on the Florida East Coast."

Whether it was the quality of the sponsors, the flavor of Mizner's prose, the vision he conjured or the ability of his salesmen, Boca Raton was an immediate success. Before a single building was erected lots were offered for sale. On the first day $11,000,000 worth were sold. Cash—"immediate filth" as an old friend of Wilson Mizner's called it—flowed into the Mizner offices at Palm Beach and in Washington, D. C., where the firm had the ground floor of the Munsey Building, a short walk from the Treasury Building. During the next six months sales averaged $4,000,-000 a month while Addison projected a Ritz-Carlton hotel, a golf course, airport, polo grounds, yacht harbor and lagoons and canals for which he planned to bring gondolas and gondoliers from Venice. In that period completed structures amounted to a small hotel and two hundred houses, which by Florida development standards was quite an achievement; most developers were happy with one imposing structure around which their city of the future would revolve. The non-stop flow of money prompted another advertisement which reported that "the public has demonstrated its faith in the men and women back of Boca Raton." Competitors watched jealously, and called the Mizner project "Beaucoup Rotten."

To assure the continued faith of the public, the Mizners employed a public relations man, Harry Reichenbach, whom Johnston identifies as "the most gifted mob psychologist since P. T. Barnum." Reichenbach had a simple theory: "Get the big snobs and the little snobs will follow." He saw that the problem with many of the other Florida development promotions was that they appealed to the middle classes. No one, Reichenbach felt, wanted to belong to the middle classes, and he promoted Boca Raton by hinting that it was impossible for any member of the middle classes to get near the city. Nobody, his ads, brochures and press releases repeated, could buy at Boca Raton except certified celebrities and YOU. To lend credence to his campaign, he and the Mizners enlisted a number of bona fide American celebrities. They already had an imposing board of directors, but they managed to add Elizabeth Arden, Irving Berlin, Marie Dressler and Herbert Bayard Swope to their list of supporters. Reichenbach seemed to be happy with Boca Raton's roster of celebrities until a rival development, Floranda, announced that Prince Paul of Greece and the exiled King George of Greece were planning winter residences there. This aroused his competitive spirit, and he sought loose royalty for Boca Raton, even going so far, Johnston says, as to try to kidnap the King of Greece from the opposition.

Reichenbach's finest adjectives were saved for the gaudiest production in Boca Raton—El Camino Real, the King's Highway, which led from the Dixie Highway to Lake Boca Raton. El Camino Real was 219 feet wide, enough for twenty lanes of traffic. There was no question that it was the widest road in the world, but Reichenbach found seven or eight other superlatives to establish its rank. It was not only landscaped, but waterscaped. Down its center ran a duplicate of Venice's Grand Canal, with Rialtos, ornamental buildings and electrically driven gondolas, which were actually made in Venice. Wilson Mizner contributed to the road's nocturnal beauty by using concealed lights in the curbs instead of open lights in lamp posts. El Camino Real had several defects, however. Addison Mizner, Johnston reports, had his heart set on beautiful blue water in the canal, but it stayed muddy. He kept scores of workmen cleaning out mud and silt, but the harder they worked the muddier the canal got. Another flaw in the road was its length—slightly less than half a mile—making it, unfortunately, the shortest road in the world. On Mizner's maps and blueprints it was projected past Boca Raton and other nonexistent cities. In actuality, it died among the brambles and swamps. But if it had little value for water or land traffic, it was heaven-sent for real estate salesmen. To lot buyers looking for evidence of a city with a future, El Camino Real suggested unlimited possibilities. Corner lots in Boca Raton rose in price from a few hundred dollars to a hundred thousand dollars. Wilson Mizner, sensing the profits in quick turnover, once offered a prominent society man $50,-000 for his lot and was turned down. Selling accelerated, and foundations were actually laid for the $6,000,000 Ritz-Carlton.

That was about as far as Boca Raton was to prosper under the Mizner management. By the fall of 1925, the boom had begun to dwindle. Conservative New York bankers who had never been enchanted with it were convinced that the peak had been reached, and although Floridians did not agree, land buying did start to slow down. A fire at Palm Beach destroyed the Breakers and Palm Beach hotels, which helped kill a good deal of the enthusiasm in that area. And in November the Finance Committee of the Mizner Development Corporation resigned. A few months later the company declared its insolvency. By then, the man who rejected Wilson Mizner's $50,000 was having difficulty finding buyers for his lot at $200. Harry Reichenbach, in Europe and unaware of the collapse, was trying to drum up an exiled king, queen or prince for Boca Raton.

On July 7, 1926, the *Nation* printed an article entitled "Florida Cashes in Her Chips." The author, a Florida resident, reported the increasing scarcity of buyers, starting in November, until, "like a giant balloon that had been punctured, the gas began noiselessly and gradually but surely to escape. . . . By early March it had to be admitted by all, even the most frantic Florida boosters, that the end had come and that nothing but the shriveled skin of that enormous thing was left." The admission of defeat was actually much longer in coming. Newspapers were still saying that "business is good" and that the collapse was "merely a readjustment that had to come." But then, in mid-September 1926, Miami was hit by a vicious hurricane. More than a hundred people were killed in Dade County and nearly a thousand more hospitalized. The property damage was highest in Miami—more than 2,000 homes and other buildings destroyed and 3,000 damaged—but few coastal cities escaped unhurt. Much as Florida real estate men might have liked to keep it a secret, a storm of that size had to produce large headlines. The news was followed by quotes from developers that the damage was exaggerated and that a new boom was in the making. The major effect of these statements was to make it difficult for the National Red Cross to collect funds for Floridians who really needed help. Before Florida recovered from the 1926 hurricane, another one hit the coast in 1928. A year later, the stock market crashed and not even the most optimistic promoter could talk that away.

The victims of the bust could be counted in the thousands, of course. Among them, even in death, was Henry Morrison Flagler. His East Coast Railway could not survive the hurricanes, the collapse of the boom, and competition from the Seaboard Airline Railroad, and in 1931 it went into receivership. Carl Fisher, who owned property said to be worth $100,000,000 on the boom market, left an estate of $53,000. Addison Mizner used up all his funds by taking personal responsibility for the debts incurred in the Boca Raton development; he lived on loans from wealthy friends and was insolvent at the time of his death in February 1933.

Perhaps the most poignant note was written by W. O. McGeehan, the sports writer who, having been told to keep his damn mouth shut because of his skepticism, may have taken special delight in reporting the collapse as he witnessed it during baseball's spring training season in Florida in 1926. Real estate men, he wrote in the *New York Herald Tribune,* had been caught representing themselves as rookies on the New York Giants so they could get free meals by signing checks at a restaurant that catered to the baseball players.

"We'll never get the job done."

5

Abraham Kazan vs. the Slums of New York

Amalgamated Housing, the residence of 1,435 families in fourteen apartment buildings spread over a six-block area in the New York borough of the Bronx, is a monument to the deliberate violation of several basic rules in the real estate canon. For one thing, the Amalgamated Clothing Workers of America, the trade union which sponsored Amalgamated Housing, has never sought to make a dime. It has succeeded completely in this, and in keeping its buildings solvent. Refusing to profit from the housing shortages following World War II and the Korean War was tantamount to ignoring the law of supply and demand which, when government controls do not apply, determine real estate prices more precisely and more swiftly than those of any other commodity except, perhaps, stocks and bonds. In 1927, when the first units were ready for occupancy in the Bronx, and a waiting list had already formed, tenants paid an average of $11 a room per month; in 1957, when the demand for housing was high and costs had soared throughout the

(*131*)

country, the tenants of Amalgamated Housing paid an average of $13 a room per month. To cap its disrespect for the usual guidelines to real estate success, the Amalgamated put its building plan in the charge of the man whose inspiration it had been, but whose only experience in housing was based on several years of residency in the slums of Manhattan's Lower East Side. This may have given Abraham E. Kazan—then thirty-eight, a brisk, energetic, slightly built man with the gentle bearing and soft-spokenness of a Talmudic scholar—some ideas of what housing should *not* be like; it certainly was not what real estate men would consider the ideal preparation for dealing with architects, carpenters, masons, electricians, lawyers, bankers, and city and state officials. Kazan did have an unbounded faith in his project, though, and applied himself to it with zeal and enthusiasm. This would have made him right at home with the outstanding figures in real estate, who despite their abiding dependence on cost accounting, have usually succeeded as a result of such intangibles as faith; Astor's belief in the future of Manhattan and the Van Sweringens' in Shaker Heights are examples. Kazan's faith moved some good-sized mountains, and his pioneer project in the Bronx has become the prototype for nonprofit housing, which in recent years has had growing support as an attractive solution for the housing problems of middle-income city dwellers. As for Amalgamated Housing itself, it is considered an unqualified success, even by real estate men who found it hard to believe that most of their rules could be broken.

Amalgamated Housing is a cooperative; its tenants are actually its owners rather than renters—in a sense their own landlords. When Amalgamated Housing was organized, tenants paid $500 a room, which gave them a vote in the management, and which was returnable if they moved out. The monthly payments are not rent as such but the cost of building maintenance, mortgage interest and amortization. Co-op apartments ordinarily are associated with wealthy occupants who may pay upwards of $10,000 per room and correspondingly high monthly charges. The cooperative aspect of these buildings, as *Architectural Forum* pointed out in its issue of July 1959, "is scarcely more than a financing gimmick of the builder—a device that enables him to take his capital and his profits out of the venture as soon as it is completed, so that he will not have to remain locked in for many years as an 'investor-owner,' with a sizable equity tied up behind a . . . mortgage." This kind of housing makes peculiar sense for rich tenants. The higher their tax bracket, the more mortgage interest and real estate taxes they are allowed to deduct from taxable income.

In attempting to create a true cooperative, the Amalgamated Clothing Workers and Kazan were far removed from the problems of the rich. Their inspiration derived from a group of weavers in Rochdale, England, who in 1844 established a set of principles for mutual aid which led to the growth of the consumer-cooperative movement in many countries. In the United States, until Kazan enlarged the concept, cooperatives had been mainly concerned with providing consumer goods and services to their members on a nonprofit basis. Kazan, an advocate of cooperatives since 1910, when he first heard about them, sought to extend to housing the same principle which reduced the cost of a quart of milk to an individual if he bought it in concert with a number of other individuals. In fact, Kazan, who was employed by the Amalgamated Credit Union, itself an application of the cooperative idea, had early in 1925 conceived the idea of buying ice and coal at wholesale for credit union members. The ice purchasing proved unfeasible, but Kazan delivered coal at a saving of seventy-five cents a ton. Kazan was aware that cooperating to construct apartments is more complicated than joining to buy a fixed amount of coal, but he felt so strongly about the possibilities of cooperatives that he did not consider the problems overwhelming. Late in 1925, the A.C.W. Corporation, which had been formed to handle the purchase of coal, became a housing company. Its purpose, Kazan said, was to find a way "to build housing . . . without the risk of having the rent increased beyond the ability of the tenants to pay, and without the risk of being evicted." It was also decided that the new housing had to be "near the open spaces, parks and trees where families could enjoy plenty of light and fresh air, and be generally convenient to places of employment."

These goals were a sort of Utopian dream, but understandable enough considering the housing conditions which most workers in New York had known for generations. The slums they lived in were overcrowded and unsanitary, and rent was taking a disproportionate part of their wages. Rents after World War I had risen sharply, and slum tenements had deteriorated; rent strikes, evictions and court actions became as common as the illnesses and deaths caused by the poor housing. However dreamlike the goals of Kazan and his associates, they were not only worthy, but urgent, even if they could be attained for only a handful of the hundreds of thousands of New Yorkers who lived in substandard tenements. Kazan's quest, which was to become his life-work, eventually led to even more than had been outlined in 1925. He may very well have made the most important single contribution to the seemingly endless battle to clear New York of its slums, and to replace them with decent housing at a reasonable price.

With the possible exception of brothels, no aspect of housing in America has been viewed with so much alarm as city slums. Of these none have been damned more often

than the tenements of New York. For well over a hundred
years now, men and women, alone or in committees—often
with burdensome titles: Association for Improving the Condition of the Poor and Committee on the Expediency of Providing Better Tenements for the Poor, for example—have
been trying to ameliorate the dismal living conditions in
slums. Newspapers have run campaigns against slums and
their owners. Ministers, sometimes those whose churches
are supported by rent from the worst housing in the city,
have delivered sermons on the evil of slums. In 1897, during a period of particularly strong agitation, the ministers of
the city set aside February 23 as Tenement House Sunday,
and nearly every sermon in New York that day was devoted
to the denunciation of slums. In recent years, one New York
minister attained a degree of renown and success by following his spiritual appeals with direct action; he took a good-
sized ax to the doors and walls of some of the uglier buildings in his parish. Government officials at the city, state and
federal level have studied the slum problem, have confirmed
what was common knowledge, have promised, and on occasion delivered, remedies of sorts. Yet slums, like the poor
who inhabit them, have always been with us, and the surprise and consternation with which they have been discovered by each new generation has not led to their elimination.

If ridding the cities of slums seems at times as distant of
achievement now as it did to some of the early American
figures in housing reform, it is not for lack of some great
creative efforts over the years. We have come a long way
since 1909, when a trustee of Trinity Church in New York
responded to a magazine article on the church's vast holdings of slum properties with the suggestion that "the public
should mind its own business if it has any." The statement
was in the tradition of W. H. Vanderbilt's "the public be

damned" some thirty years earlier, and J. Pierpont Morgan's "I owe the public nothing" in 1901. But the tradition was already dying. Charles Edward Russell, who had written the article for *Everybody's Magazine*, simply replied that breeding places for tuberculosis—which he had shown the Trinity-owned slums to be—were very much the business of the public. They could not be permitted to exist, he said, any more than "an institution for the dissemination of small pox." The Russell view has prevailed, and it is now taken for granted that government has a right to establish certain standards for decent housing which private builders and property owners must maintain. And Trinity, wrote Ray Stannard Baker in the *American Magazine*, was, as far as its real estate was concerned, "a big business corporation: calling it a church does not change its character."

The attack on Trinity Church was the culmination of nearly seventy years of off-and-on preoccupation with slums by concerned citizens. The shock of the Trinity articles resulted not so much from the housing conditions that were revealed, but from the fact that they were sponsored by a respected church which reaped inordinate profits on the misery of others. Citing specific names of slum owners had not been part of the method of the early critics. It seemed to them enough to show the abuses and to trust what Dr. John H. Griscome, an early advocate of housing reform, called "the humane and philanthropic capitalists." Griscome, however, established the pattern for criticism of the slums. It was, before photographs and motion pictures, simply to illustrate in words the actual conditions that prevailed. Describing the damp and filthy cellars in which people lived, Griscome told a New York audience in 1844, "You must descend to them; you must feel the blast of foul air as it meets your face on opening the door; you must grope in the dark . . . ; you must inhale the suffocating vapor of

the sitting and sleeping rooms; and in the dark, damp re-
cess, endeavor to find the inmates by the sound of their
voices, or chance to see their figures moving between you
and the flickering blaze of a shaving burning on the hearth,
or the misty light of a window coated with dirt and fes-
tooned with cobwebs—or if in search of an invalid, take
care that you do not fall full length upon the bed with her,
by stumbling against the bundle of rags and straw, digni-
fied by that name, lying on the floor. . . . All this, and
much more, beyond the reach of my pen, must be felt and
seen, ere you can appreciate in its full force the mournful
and disgusting condition in which many thousands of the
subjects of our government pass their lives . . ."

Griscome suggested that these conditions could be alle-
viated by a city law regulating cleanliness and by the construction of better housing by private industry. But, as a
special committee appointed by the New York State legislature in 1856 pointed out, "astute owners or agents of property [perceived] that a greater percentage of profit would
be realized by the conversion of houses and blocks into barracks, and dividing their space into the smallest proportions capable of containing human life within four walls."
These profits, the committee said, were "twice or thrice the
amount which a legitimate lease of the building . . .
would bring." The crowding of more people into less space
continued at such a rapid rate in New York that by 1864 the
Council of Hygiene and Public Health of the Citizens Association found that the "tenant-house population is actually packed upon the house-lots and streets at the rate of
240,000 to the square mile. . . . Such concentration and
packing of a population has probably never been equalled in
any city . . ." Long before the end of the nineteenth century it was apparent to every objective investigator of housing that, Griscome to the contrary, owners were not going to

improve the situation voluntarily. As the studies continued, each new one confirming or enlarging on the evils discovered by an earlier one, an impact was made on public opinion; slum dwellers, once considered immoral criminals, were now seen to be poor workingmen and women. Sympathy for their lot rose and, as a student of slum housing wrote, "it became something of a commonplace to remark that [the tenants] were obliged to pay high rents for accommodations that compared unfavorably with the stables of beasts." A writer for *Scribner's Magazine* said that "you are liable to arrest if you allow your stable to become filthy and a nuisance. The landlord may do pretty much what he pleases with his tenements."

With public support growing, advocates of housing reform campaigned for legislation to curb the most flagrant abuses—lack of sanitary facilities, ventilation and fireproofing, among others—and to suggest what model tenements ought to look like. The first laws were not much more stringent than those Griscome had suggested to regulate cleanliness, but gradually they were made tougher, to the point where cities were granted the right of seizure and demolition of dangerous tenements. Even so, most violations went unpunished; there were not enough inspectors to enforce the laws. Nor did the enthusiasm for model tenements hide the fact that most of them were not much better than the buildings they were designed to replace. The "Big Flat," built in 1855 by the New York Association for Improving the Condition of the Poor, was the first of the model buildings, and very nearly the last. It simply perpetuated the dark, windowless interiors, allowing light only to the rooms in the front and rear of the elongated railroad-type flats. A competition in 1879 produced three winning sets of plans, none of which showed windows for interior rooms. The reason for this, aside from the fact that no architect sat on the board of judges, was fairly obvious: property owners invariably used the entire width of their twenty-five-by-hundred-foot lots, which meant the buildings had no space between them. The problem could have been solved, as Richard M. Hunt, one of the city's leading architects, pointed out, if New York adopted the standards of Paris, which allowed only two-thirds of a lot to be used for a building.

In 1886, New York's slum landlords were slightly intimidated, but only temporarily. Henry George, the advocate of the single tax and the author of *Progress and Poverty*, became a candidate for mayor. His denunciation of landlords attracted huge crowds, and worried the politicians. The Republicans reacted by putting up young Theodore Roosevelt, who had served in the state legislature and whose record for reform was a good one. Tammany Hall selected Abram S. Hewitt, an advocate of labor unions. The three men left conservatives with as difficult a decision as they have ever faced in New York City. All three were for improvement in tenement housing, and their speeches brought the living conditions in the slums to the attention of the entire city. It was a close election: Hewitt received 90,000 votes, George 67,000 and Roosevelt 60,000. But with Tammany in control, Hewitt could not carry out his promises, and the slums remained filthy and overcrowded. In 1888 Hewitt ran as an independent, but could not win without Tammany, and retired from politics.

The campaign of 1886 had its effect, however. Non-slum dwellers were made acutely conscious of the lives of their fellow citizens, and they were in a receptive mood in 1890, when a book appeared which all but brought them the stench of the tenements. Jacob A. Riis, a Danish immigrant who had been a police reporter on the *New York Sun*, published *How the Other Half Lives*, which described the slums accurately and with compassion. Coming after the years of academic discussion and the passions of the election four years earlier, Riis's book and its plea for reform had a deep sense of urgency. Its effect may have been strengthened by contrast to another popular book published that year, *Society as I Have Found It,* by Ward McAllister, New York society's social arbiter and inventor of the phrase Four Hundred to designate the elite of the city. Riis gave New Yorkers the strongest word pictures of New York slums since Charles Dickens had described them some fifty years earlier. And Riis could not be labeled a Socialist, which was the inevitable response of landlords to all other housing reformers. Riis did not talk about the ills of society, nor was he particularly sympathetic to workers as such. He did make the point that people lived in the slums, not because they were too lazy or immoral to do anything else, but because they had nowhere else to go; overall, his was a simple warning to the society Ward McAllister represented that, unless it acted, the crime and disease which were nurtured in the slums would spread to the whole city, including fashionable Fifth Avenue.

The warning was not entirely unheeded, but at the start of the twentieth century slums were still being discovered, investigated and deplored—and were getting worse. In 1901, though, an important breakthrough occurred. Three years earlier, the Charity Organization Society of New York had established a tenement house committee, among whose members was Jacob Riis. In the spring of 1900 the group sponsored an exhibition of slum conditions which was so effective that it finally brought results, starting with the appointment of a New York State Tenement House Commission by Theodore Roosevelt, who was now governor. Although much of the information in the exhibit was not new, it was presented so graphically that it had an effect unlike any previous marshaling of facts. Detailed maps, more than a thousand photographs, and scale models of tenement buildings showing the most glaring shortcomings of slum housing were displayed, and reams of statistics were produced on disease, crime and death. One of the most startling points of the exhibit was that new buildings worse than those already in existence were being built by the thousands in the city's newer districts. The conclusion was inescapable: poor New Yorkers were living under worse conditions and paying more rent than those in any other civilized city in the world.

The exhibit, much of whose material was incorporated in the two-volume report issued by Governor Roosevelt's commission, led to the Tenement House Law in 1901, which established minimum standards of sanitation and safety in buildings. It was, all students of American housing agree, the most substantial step forward taken up to that time against the slums. Yet it was still not enough to cope with the problem. As immigration continued and the need for housing increased, the slums grew. The law remained in effect until 1929, when it was replaced by the Multiple Dwelling Law, which raised the standards. In those twenty-eight years some 7,000 tenements were built in Manhattan alone. They housed more than 850,000 people, more than 120 to a narrow five-story building. Meanwhile the older tenements still stood—82,000 of them, gradually diminishing to slightly under 68,000 in 1929. The landlords of the "old law" buildings bitterly fought the new codes which would have forced them to spend money for the installation of minimum safety features. Some converted their buildings to lodging houses to avoid the Tenement House Law altogether. Some fought in the courts, and occasionally won. And as always, enforcement was a problem; there were never enough inspectors, and those who did take inspectors' jobs often did so for the sake of the bribes which came their way.

Not many years after the passage of the Tenement House Law, the slums were discovered once more, and again as if for the first time. These investigations and exposés were undertaken by a new breed of journalist, the muckrakers, who, unlike earlier critics of the slums, identified landlords, and optimistically predicted dire consequences for them. Someday, Charles Edward Russell warned in 1907, there would be "an accounting for every rotten tenement, every foul alley, every reeking court, every life without light." And among those to be held accountable, he and the other muckrakers made clear, were Trinity Church, the Astor Estate and some of New York's foremost families, who profited from the worst of the slums. Trinity, more sensitive to public opinion than other slum owners, hired the secretary of the tenement house committee of the New York Charity Organization Society to supervise its houses. But "landlord missionaries," as these agents were soon called, were not effective either. The problem had reached overwhelming proportions. The area south of Fourteenth Street on Manhattan's East Side, which was one of the most crowded in the city in 1855, when it contained 417,476 people, held 750,000 by 1907. In some places, investigators found eighteen men, women and children sleeping in three tiny rooms. Reformers who thought that exposure alone should have been enough to bring action were disappointed. They did not quit investigating, however, even after Edith Abbott of the University of Chicago, one of the most experienced of their number, decided that investigations had become "only further demonstrations of the futility of investigations."

Before World War I, when it was apparent that legislation could not force decent housing and private landlords

were not eager to change profitable habits, the reformers
started to suggest public housing. The idea of governments
actually building and operating apartment houses was not a
novel one. European cities had taken such action; pictures
of municipally owned workers' homes had been shown in
the 1900 tenement house exhibition. William Dean
Howells, the noted editor, critic and novelist, wrote that the
United States could settle for nothing less than "public control in some form or another," else "the very poorest must
always be housed as they are now." In 1913 an official
commission reported to the Massachusetts legislature that
"in nearly every country of standing among the civilized
nations the government has actively aided and encouraged
the creation of a larger supply of good homes." In 1914 the
convention of the American Federation of Labor adopted a
resolution calling on the federal government to finance
"sanitary homes" by loans.

These were premature expressions. Government subsidy
of housing was not to make any significant contribution to
the solution of the problem until the New Deal administration of Franklin Roosevelt undertook large-scale slum-
clearance projects. Since then, federal assistance in one
form or another has made it possible to provide decent, low-
cost housing not only in New York, but throughout the
country as well. Public housing has not been the definitive
answer to slums that its advocates had foreseen, but as one
of a number of approaches it has been undeniably significant.

The fight against slums is far from over, of course.
Substandard housing still exists in the cities. While immigration from Europe has all but ended, a constant flow of
southern Negroes and Puerto Ricans has combined with an
accelerated population growth to keep northern cities as
crowded as ever. Under these conditions slum landlords—

or slumlords, as many newspapers have taken to calling them—still find it profitable to squeeze a maximum of rent out of a minimum of space. Despite this there are signs of progress. The small victories of the housing reform movement over the years are not likely to be snatched away. Laws establishing basic standards of comfort and safety are being strengthened where enforcement is lax and penalties so trivial that it is often cheaper for a landlord to pay fine after fine than to install proper sanitary facilities or supply a coat of paint. Encouragement of slum clearance by the federal government has, even with abuses and scandals, brought low-cost housing to many cities under the auspices of private builders. Cities and states have helped, too, by providing tax abatements to encourage building. Today it is almost possible to foresee, as Jacob Riis and the muckrakers at their most optimistic could not, cities entirely free of slums.

The efforts of Abraham Kazan to speed that day were so modest at the outset that it is unlikely he, his associates, or anyone even moderately knowledgeable about housing, could have anticipated their eventual impact. Kazan's plan for cooperative housing was not conceived to solve the entire slum problem but, as with many successful ventures, simply to meet an immediate need. However sympathetic he may have been with all slum dwellers, his primary concern was with those of them who happened to be members of the Amalgamated Clothing Workers of America. As it turned out, there was space in his project for others as well, including a number of professional men and women. It is not surprising that a fresh approach to the housing problem should have been sponsored by the Amalgamated. Traditionally, it has been more concerned than most unions with the well-being of its members outside their working hours.

In the beginning, so many of them were foreign-born that the union frequently had to function as a settlement house; it sponsored English-language lessons, group theatricals, lectures and recreational facilities, and founded banks and credit unions to keep members from paying exorbitant interest rates elsewhere. In addition to having union sympathy for his project, Kazan was fortunate in his timing. By the mid-1920's the garment workers' pay scale had gone up and their work day had been shortened as a result of unionization of the industry. The garment shops had moved uptown, and were no longer within walking distance of the Lower East Side. For the first time in their lives many workers could contemplate living outside the slums—until they faced the rents of better apartments. Kazan's goal was to make apartments available at prices garment workers could afford.

Kazan came to his task from long experience with the problems of garment workers. He had emigrated from Russia with his family before he was twelve. After a few years on a New Jersey farm, the Kazans moved to the Lower East Side. As a result of life on a farm he may have reacted more strongly to the dismal slum conditions than other teenagers. His first job, when he was fifteen, was as an errand boy for the International Ladies Garment Workers Union. In his twenties he was made secretary of one of the union's locals and performed so well that the Amalgamated hired him as director of its Records Department. In a few years he was made secretary-treasurer of the New York Joint Board, but also found time to act as secretary of the Amalgamated's credit union, which operates on much the same cooperative principles he had found appealing. Forming the A.C.W. Corporation was the first step toward a goal he once articulated on the Lower East Side. A union member who had been on the same ship from Europe and had seen Kazan from time to time in New York recalled that once Kazan looked around a small, unventilated room in a slum building and said, "Some day, people like us will have a decent place to live."

Translating that youthful expression into reality required the solutions to dozens of problems which neither Kazan nor his fellow workers had ever faced before. The first decision confronting Kazan's A.C.W. Corporation was the choice of a site. Union members wanted open spaces, light and fresh air, so the search was almost immediately removed from Manhattan. The spot which Kazan and his committee found in the Bronx adjoined Van Cortlandt Park, the largest public park in the city, and Jerome Park Reservoir, a peaceful expanse of water; in addition, it had access to the subway. A $5,000 deposit was required to hold the property, which was priced at $315,000; this was merely the first expense in what Kazan estimated would be a $2,000,000 project. The members of the A.C.W. Corporation managed to raise the $5,000, which has to be considered an act of faith rare in the history of real estate; they did not have the slightest notion as to where the other $1,995,000 was coming from. At the time the Amalgamated was not officially involved, and the group in the corporation was acting on its own. Their plans called for 303 apartments with a total of 1,185 rooms, but they could not assume that they could raise money from prospective tenants before they had something more tangible to offer than a dreamhouse. "Undertaking the construction of a development of this size," Kazan later recalled in undramatic understatement, "was not a simple matter." Kazan believed a start could be made if members of the cooperative could put up $200 per room, the rest of the estimated cost of $1,500 per room to be raised by mortgage. But, he said, this still left some pertinent questions—such as "who was going to lend a group such as this a million dollars or more on a venture that had not been tried; what would happen if construction was started and there were not enough funds to finish the project; what if the costs were eventually much higher than anticipated; and what if the carrying charges turned out to be too high for the members to pay? The pioneers of this group spent sleepless nights going over these problems. A way had to be found to give this new organization financial standing in the community."

In finding that way, Kazan got the education in real estate he lacked at the outset. He quickly learned to cope with the ordinary matters—title search, legal restrictions, and architect's drawings. But since everything depended on raising nearly $2,000,000, Kazan devoted most of his time to that. It was not easy, and when hope of success was especially low, some of the original supporters withdrew their money and sought housing elsewhere. By the end of 1925, the A.C.W. Corporation had collected only $10,-000, and prospects for more were not especially bright.

That was Kazan's worst period, however. In 1926, Governor Alfred E. Smith had prodded the New York State legislature into passing a bill to encourage low-cost housing. Tax abatements for companies willing to accept limited dividends on their investment were the most important lure. Kazan attended the hearings which preceded passage of the governor's bill, and saw clearly for the first time the solution to his problems. He returned to New York City and convinced the Amalgamated officers that the union itself should sponsor the housing project which until then it had sympathetically, but unofficially, encouraged. It was precisely the kind of thing which the Amalgamated's president, Sidney Hillman, believed was the proper province of the union. Its completion, under Amalgamated auspices, at a time when private enterprise was not filling the need for low-cost housing or, worse, was indulging in speculative excesses in Florida, would do more toward strengthening trade unions than the most intensive organizational drive. Hillman gave his approval, and the Amalgamated Housing Corporation was formed. It became the first limited dividend company organized under the State Housing Act of 1926. Kazan was named president. He also remained president of the A.C.W. Corporation, which was reorganized as the construction company for the project.

Despite the law, and the union's active support, the problem remained essentially the same: raising money. The manner in which this was done is remarkable testimony to how much Kazan had learned in so short a time. For one thing, he had to raise more from prospective tenants, or as Kazan always referred to them, "cooperators," because under the law mortgages could not exceed two-thirds of the cost of the project. Thus, members had to invest $500 a room, instead of the $200 they had originally been asked to put up. On the three- and four-room apartments, which were to be the most numerous, this meant $900 to $1,200 more per family, a formidable sum in most cases. Kazan and the Amalgamated, through its bank, solved this one quickly. They called on the officers of the Forward Association, publishers of the *Jewish Daily Forward*, a Yiddish-language newspaper with great sympathy for trade unions, and especially those in the needle trades, many of whose members were subscribers. The Forward Association pledged $150,000 as a credit fund, which permitted the union's bank to extend credit to members who sought to join the cooperative.

The initial requirement that one-third of the project's cost be supplied by its sponsors thus met, Kazan and the union now had to find a financial institution willing to take them on as a mortgage risk for the other two-thirds. Kazan had by this time reduced his estimated cost figure to $1,800,000, and was therefore seeking a mortgage of $1,200,000. This was a sum which under ordinary circumstances does not necessarily terrify insurance companies and savings banks seeking profitable investments. Whether it was the union sponsorship and a hard-headed appraisal of Kazan's plans, or the fact that 5 per cent interest was the maximum allowed under the new law, the mortgage was not immediately forthcoming. Finally, after several spirited and persuasive sessions with Sidney Hillman, the Metropolitan Life Insurance Company granted the mortgage. For loans on housing not under the law, the Metropolitan could have received 5½ per cent interest. Foregoing close to $100,000 over a twenty-year period is a gesture not normally associated with hard-headed investors; what the Metropolitan did can only be construed as a monumental act of good will. The company also topped its generosity by going along with the city and state in waiving all recording fees, revenue stamps and other fringe costs which accumulate in the course of transferring such large sums.

Kazan now had all the money he expected to need for his apartment buildings; actually, he was to fall short by $125,000, but that final crisis was overcome by a short-term loan from the helpful *Jewish Daily Forward*. On Thanksgiving Day, 1926, ground was broken on the plot in the Bronx. Kazan hovered over every feature of construction. His estimate allowed little margin for error, and he had a deep sense of his responsibility in the expenditure of other people's money. He became an expert bargainer in the year it took for the first group of houses to be completed. By insisting on paying cash, he cut down on the usual carrying charges added by contractors. As a result of that, and the size of the job, bids for the work were not hard to get.

The cost of excavation and building the foundation came to $180,000; masonry, $279,000; plastering, $167,000; plumbing, $134,000. Further savings were made by omitting elevators, no great sacrifice for the prospective owners since none of the buildings was to run more than five stories high, and slum buildings were that high or higher.

However much satisfaction he derived from raising the money and watching it being transformed into bricks, cement, pipes and wiring, Kazan was infinitely more pleased with the design of the development and what it was to mean to its future tenants. To former slum dwellers, the plans of architects George W. Springsteen and Albert Goldhammer must have appeared impossible of accomplishment; most of the union members who had invested in the project spent hours of their free time watching the buildings go up. By the standards of all but luxury apartments in New York, the rooms at Amalgamated Housing were large; living rooms were twelve by seventeen feet; bedrooms, eleven by fifteen; kitchens, eight by twelve. Every apartment had cross ventilation, and was equipped with a gas stove and heated by a central oil furnace. The buildings themselves covered less than 50 per cent of the land and were built around the perimeter of the plot. This left room for a garden enclosure, 550 feet long and varying from 50 to 100 feet in width, broken by walks leading to the separate building entrances. The ultimate effect, whether viewed from the inner court or from a distance, was that of an Ivy League campus.

The seasoned look was still some time away, though, when Kazan led a handful of impatient tenants into the first apartments on November 1, 1927. The stairs leading to the entrance of the buildings were not finished, electricity had not yet been connected, and a heavy autumn rain had turned the future garden court into clammy mud. Although the formal opening, with proper ceremonies, was scheduled for December 25, Kazan has recalled the November day as the true inauguration. The general elation in the Amalgamated, and especially among those who were to live in the new buildings, was gratifying to Kazan, of course, but he also knew that his most important test had still to be faced. He had set out to prove that cooperative housing was possible, but so far had provided only the framework for his experiment. While others praised him and the union, sometimes in terms as extravagant as those used by Congressman Fiorello La Guardia, who called the project "the greatest step forward in housing improvements ever made in this city," Kazan was pushing fresh plans for the apartments. He was moved by the evaluation of the *New York Times* that he had brought about "the finest and largest development of low-rent housing in the entire city," but he had also to make sure that cooperative purchasing of ice, milk and eggs by the tenants would work.

He need not have been concerned. The buildings themselves were the best salesman Kazan could have had. Representing as they did the palpable evidence of cooperative effort, the establishment of the A.C.W. Service Corporation to run food markets was considered by tenants to be a logical step. The nearest public school was about a mile away from the housing project, so members of the cooperative agreed to an assessment of $15 per family to buy a school bus. From the start, the members supported Kazan's contention that "families who own their own homes take pride in them." Aaron Rabinowitz, an experienced real estate man who had been selected by the state as its representative on Amalgamated Housing Corporation's board of directors, recalled a number of years later some of the effects the cooperative had on the new tenants. "When they came to view the new buildings," he said, "their sense of pride would not permit them to move up with the things they had in the old tenements. It is difficult to explain where the money came from to enable them to move in with new furniture and new fixings. Their whole lives changed. Overnight these people took on new standards. After a while, 303 families, formerly unknown to each other, lived in peace and tranquility and with a sense of consideration for each other that was beautiful. The change was amazing."

Kazan had the Amalgamated's support in promoting a thoroughgoing cooperative community. In the issue of the *Advance*, the union's official newspaper, which commemorated the official opening of the building by devoting its entire contents to the project, Sidney Hillman pointed out the benefits of cooperative purchasing as well as of cooperative management of playgrounds, a social center and a library. To get these benefits efficiently, the Amalgamated Housing Corporation established several ground rules for the cooperative which have been adhered to ever since. Individual cooperators were made aware that they did not own the apartment they lived in, but that they were one of 303 owners of the entire cooperative, each with one vote in the affairs of the corporation. The union itself emphasized that its role was simply that of sponsor, not owner, and that its main interest was in the solvency of the cooperative. Speculation was prohibited on the sale of a member's equity stock. When a family moved from the cooperative it had to sell its share back to the corporation for the same $500 per room at which it had been purchased. To keep the board of directors from meeting too often on minor matters, a house committee was organized, its membership elected from within the cooperative. Its function was to settle grievances between members or against management. The directors, however, reserved for management the right to increase or decrease maintenance charges, to declare rebates and to name a project manager.

Kazan, who became the first manager, was also the only member of the board of directors who lived in the cooperative. In his new role he had the opportunity to create the kind of cooperative community he had foreseen. Early frictions, as noted by the *Amalgamated Co-Operator*, the housing project's newspaper which was published in both Yiddish and English, seem to have been no more than normal growing pains. In November, 1929, its editor was disturbed by the growth of the non-cooperative practice of tipping employees of the buildings. "In all cases where co-operators find that anything has to be done in their apartment requiring the services of building employees," he wrote, "they should notify the office without delay. In cases where . . . the work to be done is not part of the regular duties of the employees, arrangements for such work as well as for the amount of extra compensation will be made by the office." Concern for its employees led management to make another plea a few weeks later. "The task of our ice delivery men, which is not an easy one at best," the paper said, "is made far more difficult by the large number of tenant-cooperators who insist that their ice be delivered 'the first thing in the morning.' With more than three hundred apartments . . . it is clearly impossible for the ice men to make deliveries during the first hour to more than a very small percentage of the tenants." In December it was announced that an iceman was fired for accepting tips from tenants. This appears to have been an isolated case, and there was never any danger that Kazan's vision of a true cooperative would be destroyed by a carryover of such non-cooperative habits.

Kazan made it apparent that the rewards for coopera-

tion were real. Besides reduced costs for the material things
—inexpensive dental and medical clinics were added after
a few years—cultural activities at little or no cost were soon
available. Music, photography and art classes for children
were started, orchestras and dramatic societies formed,
theater parties organized and political discussions sponsored. Except in politics, differences of opinion were no
threat to the cooperative or its activities. And Kazan, by
adhering to democratic methods and a tolerant respect for
conflicting points of view, even managed to keep political
conflicts to a minimum. The most vexing during Amalgamated Housing's formative years was the battle between
Communist and Socialist residents. "We came out in favor
of political freedom," Kazan said, "[and decided that] a
group can carry on its own interests in our community but
this place cannot become a headquarters for a battleground;
no group can propagandize in the name of the House."
Meeting space was allowed any group as long as its activities did not interfere with the general cultural program and
the proper administration of the cooperative, but political
campaigning and the formation of political youth groups
were barred. "It wasn't all love and kisses," a long-time resident recalled years afterward. "But we learned how to get
along. Every kind of decent person can live here, and does.
Except fascists—I don't think we have any of them." The
art of getting along, at least politically, survived a test on
the evening of March 21, 1930, when members of the cooperative were invited "to learn the true and authentic
interpretations of these two aspects of social salvation—
Socialism and Communism." Norman Thomas and Scott
Nearing, identified as "the two greatest exponents of these
philosophies," were to meet in debate in the cooperative's
auditorium, an event which the *Co-Operator* described as "a
miracle, fellow cooperators, a miracle!" The miracle was,

in retrospect, more than a single debate peacefully conducted. In a period of intense political feelings, the Amalgamated cooperative survived intact.

In a report to the union in 1957, thirty years after the first houses in the Bronx were occupied, Kazan made a special point of the fact that "there has never been a single case of juvenile delinquency." He attributed this to the stability of the community—some 70 per cent of the original tenants were still in residence—and to the program of activities which directed the children to "worthwhile pursuits." There was occasional mischief—scratched doors, chalk-marked hallways—which required adult attention, and in which Kazan's theory of pride of ownership appeared to have been effective. The *Co-Operator* in 1930 ran an editorial entitled "A Word With You, Young Lads!" which, as much as anything else, indicates the atmosphere which dominated the cooperative. "Don't you realize what you are doing?" the paper asked. "Don't you take pride in your own property? Don't you wish your homes and entrances and courts to look neat and new? Of course you do. We know that in your hearts you don't wish to destroy. But you don't even think what you are doing. Remember, lads and lassies, these are your homes—your very own. Cherish them! Protect them!" No further incidents were reported.

The success of Amalgamated Housing as a low-cost residence, ably managed and meeting its financial commitments regularly, made expansion inevitable and relatively trouble-free. A list of applicants for apartments had been growing in Kazan's office, but few tenants moved out. In January 1929 ground was broken on land adjacent to the original site, and construction was started for 192 more apartments. No mortgage problems came up this time; the Metropolitan Life Insurance Company agreed to make the loan under the same conditions as for the first one. When a short loan was needed to get construction under way, the New York Trust Company provided $200,000. As before, potential tenants who did not have the required $500 per room could borrow up to half their down payment from the Amalgamated Bank at low terms to be paid back over ten years.

Later in 1929, Kazan and the Amalgamated achieved their finest triumph. They brought cooperative housing to the Lower East Side itself, for decades the center of the city's worst slums. The triumph was not theirs alone, but was achieved in partnership with enlightened capitalism. In a private venture, Herbert Lehman, then the lieutenant governor of the state, and Aaron Rabinowitz, a member of the State Housing Board and its representative on Amalgamated Housing Corporation's board, had purchased an entire block on Grand Street, one of the most congested of all the East Side's overcrowded blocks. They had intended to sponsor a low-cost housing development of their own, but were so impressed by Kazan's accomplishments in the Bronx that they decided to permit the Amalgamated to handle the project. The two men not only supplied the land, but agreed to finance construction until all the apartments were bought. Furthermore, they set up a fund to help prospective tenants borrow part of their equities. In all, Lehman and Rabinowitz made a commitment of $800,000. With this backing, the remaining financing presented no problem, and under the direction of a new limited dividend company, Amalgamated Dwellings, Inc., 236 new apartments were created in the midst of Manhattan's slums. In April 1931, the New York Chapter of the American Institute of Architects awarded Amalgamated Dwellings a medal for the best example of a six-story apartment house erected the previous year. The award committee was particularly pleased that "every room has desirable exposure" and that "the es-

sential elements of design have been used to achieve
esthetic results with the complete elimination of meaning-
less ornament."

By the end of 1931, Kazan and the Amalgamated
Clothing Workers of America had accounted for 856 low-
cost cooperative apartments in New York. (Taking advantage of falling costs, Kazan had managed to build a 115-
apartment unit in the Bronx while the Lower East Side
construction was in progress.) In the five years since actual
work had begun on the first Bronx apartments, he had not
only made his point about the advantages of cooperative
housing, but of cooperative living as well. He had proven,
not alone to himself, but to the most skeptical, that idealism
could be made practical. He had no illusions that he was
about to revolutionize the real estate industry by causing it
to dispense with profits, or that he alone would eradicate all
the city's slums. He did feel that he had shown one way to
do it, and could only hope that others would follow. In a
series of articles in 1930 and 1931 he repeatedly pressed
the arguments for cooperative housing, and with full occupancy in his Bronx and Manhattan buildings, he was
finding receptive audiences.

By all the rules for American success, Kazan should
have surged ahead, with one building following another.
But starting in 1932, as the depression deepened in the
United States, the rules were being broken not only for
the successful men on Wall Street but for those on the
Lower East Side and the Bronx. From 1932 to 1936, Kazan's
cooperatives went through their severest crisis. By the summer of 1932, the incomes of tenants in the Amalgamated
buildings had dropped sharply as unemployment spread in
the needle trades. Tenants fell behind in their monthly
maintenance payments, and those in particularly bad straits
resold their apartments to the management in order to raise

cash. And now there was no long list of applicants for the vacancies. With money short, few people were willing to put $1,500 to $2,000 into an apartment, however low the rent; the slums began to recapture former residents. For Kazan, the personal pain caused by the problems of friends and neighbors was intensified by his knowledge of the financial commitment the Amalgamated buildings represented. Mortgages were being foreclosed all over the city, and the properties sold by lenders as quickly as possible. He had to maintain not only the faith of his tenants in the cooperative, but that of the Metropolitan Life Insurance Company as well.

Because the years leading up to the depression had been ones of steady growth and full tenancy, neither Amalgamated Housing nor Amalgamated Dwellings had felt it necessary to lay aside a reserve for the repurchase of tenants' equities. This had been no problem when new tenants were immediately available; it was an enormous one when there were none. Kazan realized that the reputation of the cooperatives were threatened if he could not buy back a tenant's share, and that his whole concept of cooperative living could be quickly destroyed. The problem was readily solved at Amalgamated Dwellings, where Lehman and Rabinowitz authorized a loan up to the par value of the stock. At Amalgamated Housing, Kazan had to be more resourceful. He used the funds of the cooperative shops and services—which were now called A.H. Consumers Society —to meet the crisis. Even so, he was not able to pay all tenants in full at the time they left, although all commitments were eventually met. At one point during the depression years, the A.H. Consumers Society had $275,000 worth of Amalgamated Housing stock. Rather than hold apartments empty for reluctant buyers, Kazan authorized a system of temporary purchase. For $100 a room, families were permitted to sign a two-and-a-half-year lease with a fixed rent from five to ten dollars higher than the going rate. At the end of that period the tenant could withdraw and receive his $100 a room equity. If he decided to purchase at the full price, the excess monthly charges were credited against his investment.

Meeting cash commitments to cooperators who pulled out and to the Metropolitan Life Insurance Company was made harder by the financial difficulties of those who elected to stay. Many of them simply did not have money for their monthly maintenance charge. By the end of 1936, Amalgamated Housing recorded unpaid charges amounting to $156,000, and the grocery showed $15,000 in accounts receivable. Kazan's approach to this problem was direct and simple; and it prevailed: as long as he and the board of directors were convinced that honest efforts were being made to pay, no action was taken; members who deliberately avoided paying when, in the opinion of the management, they could do so faced eviction. It is a reflection of Kazan's skill as a landlord that eviction proceedings were taken against only two members during the depression, and that every dollar of back charges was ultimately paid.

Perhaps Kazan's most outstanding application of the cooperative principle was the establishment of a relief fund. He called on all members of the cooperative to contribute a minimum of a dollar a month, which would be returned at the end of the crisis, but without interest. Needy members could borrow from the fund up to a maximum of $400, without interest, but with a flat fee of 2 per cent of the loan to cover handling costs. "This plan . . . will demonstrate with what ease cooperatively a group of people can accomplish great results," Kazan wrote in the *Co-Operator*. In the early days of the depression, members who still had jobs contributed generously, and the fund helped many of the unemployed get through some difficult times. As the depression grew worse, however, fewer members could afford to contribute and the fund had to be discontinued. The practical results were not as great as Kazan had predicted, but it was one more way, along with the other methods he devised to keep the cooperatives solvent and their members housed, in which he kept the cooperative idea from dying.

"That was the worst storm," *Survey Graphic* reported in a review of the first twenty years of Amalgamated Housing. "It left the organization, at the end of its first ten years, physically exhausted but spiritually strengthened. Before the depression the cooperators had begun to take low rent and other advantages for granted . . . no protective measures for financial soundness seemed necessary. Now . . . they gradually accumulated substantial reserves for the repurchase of equity stock of owners who decided to sell, putting earnings from other cooperative activities into it." By 1940, Kazan could once again contemplate expansion, and that year he started, modestly enough, three two-story buildings designed for older residents. When World War II ended all construction, Kazan's plans had to be postponed, but he could rest for a while with the satisfaction that all his houses were in order.

In the immediate postwar years, and in the face of increased costs, Kazan brought the total number of Amalgamated cooperative units in the Bronx to 1,435 and those on the Lower East Side to 1,043. Carrying charges ran higher now, but at $16 a room per month, the Hillman Houses on the Lower East Side, named for the union's president, who had died in 1946, were still a great bargain. What is more, to make room for the three twelve-story buildings, gardens and playgrounds, sixty-five slum tenements packed on a four-block area were destroyed. It was the kind of frontal attack on bad housing which Kazan, who had once lived in that neighborhood, must have mounted with more than his normal zest for a new project.

The Hillman Houses and the new buildings in the Bronx were the last cooperative apartments Kazan built under the auspices of Amalgamated. In 1950, several cooperatives in New York City, including the three Amalgamated groups, labor unions, neighborhood associations and fraternal organizations, formed United Housing Foundation as a nonprofit organization to promote cooperative housing on a wide basis. Logically enough, they named Kazan president.

The years of trial and error had strengthened Kazan's convictions about cooperative housing. He was as skeptical of public housing as he was of private, profit-seeking housing. Public housing did not have the self-help principles which he felt were basic to the dignity of the residents. Further, because most public housing projects establish income limits for families to be eligible, they often lead to a sense of impermanence or, worse, put a damper on ambition. As for profitable housing, Kazan's views on that had not changed, except that they were expressed more strongly. He was, as he had been from the beginning, a missionary for cooperation. "The cooperative movement to me," he said in 1961, "is an attempt to reconstruct society, to bring about a better life for all the people. It is an attempt to help provide a greater share of comforts and happiness for the average man—the cooperator. To me, the movement is not a political instrument, nor is it a religious sect. Every cooperative should be an organization set up on the principles of self-help and mutual aid. Housing is but one of the basic needs of the average man, and cooperation is not confined to this particular activity. . . . The housing de-

velopments are . . . schools where the member-coopera-
tors have an opportunity to learn to work together for the
common good."

Behind the idealism there was, as the United Housing
Foundation embarked on its crusade under Kazan's leadership, a wealth of practicality. Within ten years, UHF had
initiated or sponsored cooperatives which would house
15,000 families. One of them, under construction in 1962 on
the site of the old Jamaica Race Track in the borough of
Queens, would be the largest housing cooperative in the
United States, with rooms for 5,480 families, to be built at
a cost of $86,450,000. With plans for twenty-five acres of
public park, two elementary schools, a junior high school,
cooperative supermarkets and parking facilities for 3,900
cars, the project is more in the nature of a city than a housing development. Appropriately enough it has been named
Rochdale Village, for the English pioneers of cooperation.

Rochdale Village, though a long step from the first
Amalgamated Housing buildings in the Bronx, may not necessarily be Kazan's final achievement. In 1962, at the age of
seventy-three, he was still actively guiding Rochdale, as
well as a 2,500-unit project in Brooklyn, and a 2,800-unit
one in Manhattan, while contemplating sites and plans for
others. By then, the housing problem in New York, as in
most American cities, was to find suitable quarters for the
so-called middle income family—and Kazan felt that cooperatives were the only answer. "You can live in a public
housing project if you're poor enough, or on Park Avenue if
you're rich enough," Kazan said. "There's not enough profit
in middle-income housing to interest private builders. That
leaves only the co-ops to do the job, because they're not in-
terested in profits."

His bulldozers were tearing into ground which once
held filthy tenements and racing stables, and he had been

eulogized in the press in terms usually reserved for obituaries. "He figuratively, as well as literally, changed the look of the land in this city," the *New York Post* wrote in 1961. "He changed, too, the way that thousands upon thousands of families lived." *Architectural Forum* said that "without UHF, and Kazan's energetic leadership, many co-op projects would not have materialized."

In 1962, his achievements received the highest public recognition when President Kennedy attended ceremonies marking the opening of Penn Station South, a Kazan project that replaced a slum on the city's West Side. Kazan himself has few illusions about what has been done and none at all about how much is left to do. "We've made a start, but that's about all," he said a few years ago. "Co-ops open three supermarkets while the chains open fifty; we build a handful of cooperative apartments and the need is ten times greater. At the rate we're going, we'll never get the job done." This may be an accurate appraisal, of course, since Kazan's judgment on housing had by then been proven sound for nearly thirty-five years. What he overlooked was that without his contribution the job might never have been started.

6

The White-Collar Cities of
Fred F. French

Fred F. French, creator of Tudor City, a five-acre potpourri of apartments, hotels, gardens and garages on mid-Manhattan's East Side which was the city's first self-contained, giant economy-size (by Manhattan standards) residential enclave, never tired of attributing his success to salesmanship. The success, which came to him at the age of forty after years of failure and poverty, was largely of his own making, a matter which he felt should serve as inspiration to the less fortunate. French used to write accounts of his early, penniless years for the *Voice*, a publication he issued for the employes of the several companies he formed to run his real estate holdings, and he addressed his salesmen every business morning on the techniques of selling. These were not complicated, as far as French could see, and he believed that anyone could master them, even though it was his opinion that Jesus Christ was "the best salesman of all time." At one of his morning inspirationals, French explained the significance of "Knock, and it shall be opened unto you" (Matt. VII:7; Luke XI:9). "What He meant was," French said, "Keep knocking until the door is opened, and if it isn't opened pretty soon, kick down the door." And, French concluded, "That's my philosophy, too." French's knocking and kicking brought him considerable esteem, material reward and the control of twenty-seven office buildings, apartment houses and hotels worth some $100,000,-000. The satisfactions he derived from these must have been considerable in his lifetime, for, as *Fortune* once said, he "made a profession of his success." Since his death on August 30, 1936, however, most New Yorkers would be hard put to identify him, except possibly in terms of the office building at 551 Fifth Avenue which still bears his name. That is too bad, because the Fred F. French Building has no more to be said for it than hundreds of other undistinguished commercial warrens in the city, and, given the current trend to replace old mediocrities with new ones, it may not last many more decades. Tudor City, on the other hand, although an architectural anachronism (it was designed in the sixteenth-century English style from which its name derives), has a charm and character missing from New York's newest residential buildings, gives the feeling of belonging to its neighborhood, and is likely to remain the home of some 10,000 people for a long time to come. Tudor City is also a landmark in New York's physical history; it spurred one of the most dramatic shifts in the direction of the city's growth.

When French announced the Tudor City project on December 17, 1925, New York newspapers recognized its significance and ran the story on page one. In the *Times* it ranked with the opening of the Senate debate on American membership in the World Court and the charges of Mayor-elect James J. Walker that New York had become a "wide open" town under Mayor Hylan. The reasons for giving

French's plan such prominence were journalistically sound. The site of Tudor City, then called Prospect Hill, was a high ledge at the end of Forty-second Street, seventy feet above First Avenue; it was one of the city's most run-down sections and overlooked slaughter- and packing houses, lumber and coal yards and an electric power plant. Furthermore, except for Sutton Place and Beekman Hill, where some improvements had been made, New York's East Side was a badly neglected, ugly strip of tenements, crumbling old brownstones and commercial buildings. If French's plans materialized, they could conceivably be the impetus to transform the area east of the Third Avenue El, from Thirty-fourth Street to the Nineties. He saw the possibilities of a residential area as luxurious as Park Avenue, or Riverside Drive on the West Side, then ranked as the finest in the city.

French was forty-two when he started to acquire the acreage around Prospect Hill, and just beginning to get used to having his announcements treated with respect. The struggling years were not far behind him. He had been the oldest of four children in a poor Manhattan family. His father's income as a cigar salesman was negligible, and French had to work, as he later recalled it, before he was in long trousers. His jobs were in the tradition of late-nineteenth-century child labor—peddling newspapers, running errands, washing windows, mowing lawns. Despite the need for his income, French's mother, a graduate of the University of Michigan, insisted that he be educated. He attended New York's Horace Mann School on a scholarship, and won admission to Princeton, but remained there less than a year. He decided to work his way around the country, and became a ditch digger, a railroad worker, a ranch hand and a miner before returning to New York and an engineering course at Columbia. In 1907 he had finished a stint as superintendent of a construction job, and was beginning to have his first visions of the possibilities in real estate. But he was, as he had been so often before, completely penniless. By then, however, he had impressed many people with his seriousness and reliability. With no more than those assets to go on, he managed to borrow $500, on which he was able to start a modest real estate office in a Bronx cellar.

French's limited funds caused him to seek a partner. The one he found had been a missionary in Alaska, which spoke for his honesty if not his experience in New York land and buildings. Nevertheless, not long after the firm had increased its capital, French's partner pocketed it, and headed back to Alaska. French borrowed again, and started again, this time without a partner. He managed to survive the real estate doldrums of World War I, and although still far from financial strength in the early postwar years, was soon on his way to becoming a major figure in the great building boom of the 1920's.

The difference between struggling anonymity and prosperous respectability was a financing method of French's devising which came to be known, properly enough, as the French plan. Although it was rooted in the real estate tradition of operating with other people's money, the plan was really a closer relative of the financial techniques used in other fields of business. Simply stated, the French plan, invoking the salesmanship for which its author had such a high regard, was based on the sales of long-term security issues directly to the public to cover the cost of a contemplated building above a mortgage of 50 per cent or less. In this way, according to a study of real estate financing in the *Architectural Forum* for July 1929, "the French Company obtains a never-ending stream of millions of dollars of new capital . . . at a much lower cost than it would if it used the ordinary methods of either mortgage bond issues or long-term first and short-term junior mortgages." As French knew, the "ordinary methods" were not only extremely expensive but were difficult to use unless big and immediate profits could be shown. Slower profits, if accompanied by a growing equity value, had appeal for the general public, and the French plan promised this once an essentially small mortgage became amortized. For French this method of financing had even more to be said for it. For each share of preferred stock he sold, he gave the buyer one share of common, and kept one for the company as its profit. The preferred stock was to be bought back at the end of ten years, after which French and the public were partners on a fifty-fifty basis on the presumably profitable building. In addition, by virtue of the Fred F. French Management Company, which French later established, he received fees for management of the properties in addition to those for architecture, contracting, and underwriting the stock issue. All in all, the plan was workable and popular, and brought French the success which had until then eluded him.

French's reputation as a builder and real estate operator had grown steadily but undramatically during the early twenties. "Beyond his buildings, his business, and Bruce Bartonesque beliefs," *Fortune* said of him, "Mr. French's topography is rather flat." He considered the theater a waste of time, and refused to own an automobile. He was proud that, like Thomas Edison, he could work late, sleep little, and show up early in the office each day. He neither drank nor played cards, but permitted himself an occasional cigar "to have one sociable habit." Oddly enough, his hero was Theodore Roosevelt, one of the most gregarious men in American public life. In French's office hung photographs of Roosevelt as a big-game hunter; scattered among them were photographs of French in similar costumes and similar poses. With the announcement of his plans for Tudor City, however, French became a public figure whose views were sought by the press, who addressed audiences larger than his own sales force, and who, at last, acquired a press agent.

The premises on which French proceeded with Tudor City were, with one important distinction, the same as those which prompted John Jacob Astor to buy where the city was sure to grow. Whereas Astor held on and waited, French all but forced a steady growth around his land, which immediately increased its value. The property French accumulated had once been among the city's most desirable. It was named Prospect Hill by Bayard Winthrop, who built a comfortable home there during the Revolution. Until a few years before the Civil War the area was made up of large estates owned by prominent New York families. As waves of Irish immigrants moved north and east in Manhattan, the Prospect Hill area was deserted by its owners and was soon covered by small farms, and many huts and shacks. Paddy Corcoran ran a group of thieves called the "Rag Gang" which ruled the area as if it were an independent domain. Much of the strength and leadership of the New York draft rioters in the Civil War came from Corcoran's Roost. After the Civil War, many Irish residents sought better housing, and as they left Prospect Hill the city's new rich began to construct genteel brownstones there. For a brief period the area was marked by Victorian respectability. By the turn of the century this had vanished with the arrival of factories and slaughterhouses, and a long decline set in which was not arrested until French bought Prospect Hill.

French's confidence in the potential of Tudor City, despite its discouraging surroundings, flowed from a theory he had about New York. It seemed obvious to him, as it must have to innumerable others, that New York was being stifled by its own traffic. The city's growth as an industrial center was being threatened by the inability of workers to get from one place to another with any degree of speed or comfort. Most observers of this increasing inconvenience to New Yorkers saw its solution in terms of new transportation systems, more efficient subways, additional elevated lines. Not French. His was the frontal attack of his hero, Theodore Roosevelt. "The surest way to solve the traffic problem," French said, "is to eliminate it. That is, establish living quarters near one's place of business." Tudor City, he added, "goes a long way" toward doing just that, "by pointing the way for similar developments in other sections of the city." A single building in a business section did not make sense, he suggested, because residents could not be made comfortable in the noise, dirt and congestion. Tudor City, on the other hand, was "entirely isolated from either crosstown or north and south traffic and yet [was] within a stone's throw of all the important lines of traffic."

Once he decided his reasoning was sound, French proceeded to buy Prospect Hill lots at a dizzying pace. Speed and secrecy were essential to keep prices down. Few things raise land values swifter than the knowledge that a buyer with big plans and ready cash is in the neighborhood. In 1946, Leonard S. Gans, who directed the buying campaign for the Joseph Milner Company, which French had selected as his agent, recalled the buying spree. "Purchases started in November 1925," he said, "with the acquisition of a few tenements at the easterly end of Prospect Hill —a mere 35,000 square feet. But Mr. French's imagination and the scope of his project grew day by day, and the result was an exciting campaign of land assemblage. In only thirty-five days I and half a dozen associates had purchased an area nearly 200,000 square feet. Only the refusal of the meat packers to sell their slaughterhouse properties prevented Tudor City from spreading out even further along the river." Gans and his associates worked late into each evening, and averaged three contracts a day. This took some doing, because many of the properties had been under the same ownership for years, and there was occasional reluctance to overcome. Thanks to Gans, French acquired what he wanted, and although "many sellers received prices beyond anything they had previously hoped for," French put the total cost at less than half what he had paid for some sites on lower Park Avenue a short time earlier.

The low purchase cost, and construction savings he anticipated because of the bulk purchases involved in the size of his project, led French to announce that he would rent apartments at the average rate of $500 a room per year, as compared to the $1,000 he was charging on Park Avenue apartments. Nor did he intend to stint in the quality of the work. If anything, his concept of Tudor City promised more in the way of luxury than New Yorkers were accustomed to. Besides an inner garden court in the English style—in this case, a two-acre park with vine-covered arbors, shaded walks and flowers on the green grass—French promised a swimming pool, tennis courts, a children's playground, club rooms, and shops to make the marketing easier. He anticipated the hotel's height at twenty stories, and that of the ten apartment buildings at from ten to fifteen stories. In an editorial following French's announcement, the *New York Times* was slightly skeptical of the effect these heights would have on Tudor design. "New York is promised—or threatened with, as the event may prove—a vast community settlement," the *Times* said. "In itself, the building plan is not abhorrent. In order to make the proposed Tudor ar-

chitecture—which used to be low-lying and rangy—altogether appropriate, it might have to be stood on end; but we
live in an age of innovation." The *Times* suggested that
the approval of the city's architectural board be sought first,
since the location of Tudor City "makes it impossible that
this city should ever be hid."

This mild criticism was the worst French had to face.
Most of the response was enthusiastic. J. H. Burton of the
Save New York Committee said, "I consider this the most
important development for the midtown section of Manhattan since the Pennsylvania Railroad Company built its station at Thirty-third Street and Seventh Avenue. It means
that the social center of New York, which has been steadily
moving, will now move south and east." He foresaw the rebuilding of the whole area east of Park Avenue between
Thirty-fourth and Forty-second streets, the ultimate solution of the city's traffic problem, and the growth of New
York in "an orderly satisfactory way." French's move
brought out the prophet in many, but except for a gentleman who predicted the eventual razing of the Third Avenue
Elevated tracks, few of them came anywhere near an accurate forecast. The poorest prophet of all was French, at
least regarding his predictions on the effect of Tudor City
on Manhattan's traffic.

If French's crystal ball was clouded on traffic conditions, it was clarity itself on apartment living, and the influence of Tudor City on Manhattan's East Side. Long before
September 30, 1927, when the first two buildings in the
development were officially opened, every apartment had
been rented. Leases had been signed as early as the previous February, and by midsummer inquiries had been coming into the French Company offices at the rate of 250 a
week. The growing interest coincided with a spate of press
releases on the Tudor City Park, as the garden area was

now being called. As French well knew, it was one of his
best sales devices, and there were not only words about its
peaceful charm in the bustling city, but about its unique
status in New York: it was to be the first private park in
Manhattan since Samuel B. Ruggles had nurtured Gra-
mercy Park a little less than a hundred years earlier. Not
only that, but, falling in with a national fad, French
started construction of an eighteen-hole miniature golf
course—illuminated for nighttime play—on the south side
of the park. This, French's press agents breathlessly announced, was "believed to be the first outdoor golf course on
Manhattan Island, and certainly the first to be made a part
of a real estate development in this borough." The course
lasted only as long as the national taste for miniature golf,
but it helped rent apartments, which was precisely what a
salesman like French expected it to do.

The assured success of Tudor City was a tremendous
boon for French personally as well as for the companies he
headed. A month after its opening he announced that in
seventeen years in the real estate business the Fred F.
French companies had under construction or had already
constructed buildings with an approximate value of $44,-
000,000. This was a conservative figure, since $4,000,000
represented acreage at Tudor City on which work had not
yet been started. A year later, French was getting ready to
embark on an even more ambitious project. In October
1928 he announced the formation of Fred F. French Operators, Inc., with an authorized capital of $50,000,000. In
addition to buying land on which to build, the new organization would specialize in buying and selling real estate for
quick turnover or for holding against a long-term increase
in value.

The new company, he said, being ten times larger than

the Fred F. French Investing Company, which was building Tudor City, could therefore build ten Tudor Cities. "You
can't overbuild New York," French said. He predicted that
within a few decades there would be between 25,000,000
and 30,000,000 people in the city's metropolitan area. He
was optimistic; in 1961 the population was estimated at 11,-
000,000. This was the first time that French had publicly indicated any plans for real estate development beyond the city proper, since, in a sense, Tudor City was to
have been an alternative to the suburbs. Whether or not he
was hedging his city bet, French talked of the possibility of
buying several thousand acres in Westchester County. Perhaps moved by the example of the Van Sweringens, he suggested that he would install his own transportation system,
and thus bring suburbs close to New York. These suburban
cities, when built by the French Company, he said, would
embody features so advanced as to change the whole com-
plexion of suburban life.

How much of this was wishful thinking will never be
known. Not long after he projected his vision of a new suburbia, French addressed himself to Manhattan again, and
never embarked on any important project beyond the city
limits. In 1929 he bought the old Hippodrome, between
Forty-third and Forty-fourth streets on Sixth Avenue, for
$7,500,000. He planned to tear down the building, which
was then a major showplace for vaudeville, and build a skyscraper. New York, he told the press a few weeks later, was
in for a complete transformation. It would be made up of
residential communities like Tudor City—"to be constructed
by the score"—and office buildings like the Empire State,
which had just been announced, and the one he planned on
the Hippodrome site. To bring this about, the skyscrapers
"must straddle the very avenues to obtain the wind-bracing
for their towers of thousands of feet and hundreds of

stories," he said. "Tunnels would be bored under streets and perhaps through the great towers themselves for general traffic purposes. Perhaps the sidewalks in congested areas will be raised a story above the present curb levels, and present sidewalks be given over to automobile traffic. If Manhattan real estate is to serve its function and continue its upward trend, these gigantic projects are indispensable."

To show his own stake in the city of the future, French had earlier reported that he had turned down quick profits for two parcels of land he had bought on Fifth Avenue, one for an apartment house and the other for the office building which was later to carry his name. The total profit would have been $700,000, with no great expenditure of effort, but French said he had bought the properties to improve them, and that was what he intended to do. Along with his reiterated faith in the city to be, French had a conviction that only large companies could handle the large prospects. "No longer is it possible for the individual or small syndicate to keep pace with the tide of inflowing people and capital reaching into millions of dollars," he said. "Manhattan Island has after 300 years of real estate growth outgrown the control of individual owners."

Having expressed himself so forthrightly so often, French was ready by the end of 1931 to make public his own new contribution to giantism in New York City. He released a secret he had been keeping for four years—another "white collar city" for 10,000 residents of Manhattan, this one on the Lower East Side in a slum district lying between the Brooklyn and Manhattan bridges. The new one, to be called Knickerbocker Village, because the area had historical associations with the early Dutch settlers of Manhattan, was based on the same premise that inspired Tudor City. It would enable workers in the financial area around

(175)

Wall Street to walk to work. "Traffic in New York," French said, "is becoming not less congested but more so every year. . . . Manhattan Island must be reconstructed so that groups of residential buildings will be adjacent to groups of business buildings in the same way that Tudor City adjoins the Grand Central business zone." If those words had a familiar ring to newspaper readers, French this time had terrifying facts and figures to support his thesis. It was almost as if he were carrying on a campaign against any form of locomotion except a person's two feet. "Anyone who has traveled in the subways," he said, "understands the crowding, the waiting for trains in which a foothold may be obtained, indignities to women, foul air and danger to life from fumes in case of accident. Most people, however, have not realized that the two hours per day or more spent traveling back and forth to work means twelve hours per week, fifty hours per month, six hundred hours per year, thirteen and six-tenths weeks of eight-hour days. In other words, a person living downtown and walking to his work would be able to take three months of vacation every year and still devote the same amount of time to his work, and during the time that he did work save the wear and tear and unhealthful conditions of subway travel."

No one questioned the validity of French's statistics, and certainly no one would have quarreled with his picture of subway conditions, especially as it pertained to rush hours. French may have put himself through the test to come up with these conclusions, although he rarely rode the subway himself. He was an inveterate walker, and the idea for Knickerbocker Village came to him on a hike in Manhattan. Soon after the successful opening of Tudor City he had gone off to hunt grizzly bears in Alaska, and on his return started thinking about another undertaking of the magnitude of the one so obviously headed for success. He pondered best while walking, and as he "reeled off mile after mile," he told a reporter for the *New York Herald Tribune*, "the idea of reclaiming the old East Side and building there large apartment houses for bankers, brokers and office workers became more fascinating." To find the facts for himself he went down to the slum area and walked through one section after another to City Hall and Wall Street; he confirmed that some of New York's worst slums were within walking distance of the city's money center.

The area French chose for the new project had, even among the slums, one of the worst reputations for filth, disease and death. It contained what was known as the "lung block," the area bounded by Market, Hamilton, Cherry and Catherine streets. The name was coined by Governor Alfred E. Smith, a former resident of the area, because of an incredibly high death rate from tuberculosis. A social worker reported that "we care for 800 children in this section. Most of them have had pneumonia three times before they are six. That is the first step to T.B. They have pneumonia year after year because the walls of those flats run water. They are damp the year around. . . . There are no bathrooms. The toilets for a whole floor are at the end of the hall. The fire escapes are vertical and the staircases are wooden—a bad fire would end the lives of every person and child in the block. I wouldn't be sorry to see the block demolished."

The area's decline into slums was typical of the history of others like it in the city. During the Dutch and English colonial periods it consisted of large landed estates. Most of the street names on the Lower East Side reflect its history. The Rutgers, De Lancey and Bayard families were prominent citizens during and after the Revolution. Catherine Street, which was for a time the site of Lord and Taylor, Brooks Brothers and some of the leading yacht uniform houses, was named for Catherine Rutgers. Henry

Street was named for Henry Rutgers. Oak Street once had magnificent oaks, Orchard Street had apples, and Cherry Street cherries. As the established families moved north, the Irish, Scotch and German immigrants spread over the former farms. Small houses replaced the mansions. Shipyards went up at the waterfront, and soon the neighborhood became the city's Barbary Coast. Hamilton Street was one of the Manhattan's most famous hiding places for criminals. Pickpockets, confidence men, pimps, river pirates, and professional panhandlers inhabited the "Gap," as it came to be known. The street was only a block long, but one end could not be seen from the other because of a sharp turn at its mid-point. This came to be known as the "bloody angle" because of the number of men who died violently there.

Two houses on the west side of the street, just south of Market, were known in those days as "the Ships." The name came from their interior architecture, which was similar to that of a ship between decks. Heavy beams ran across the ceiling and rested on brackets which were connected with uprights similar to a ship's ribs. The generally accepted story was that a ship had been blown ashore many years earlier and had become embedded in the sand. When wind and tide packed it tighter into the shore pirates took possession and built brick walls around it. Whatever its origin, "the Ships" made a great hangout for criminals, and police did not enter except in large numbers. Trap doors and hidden exits abounded. Even on the Gap itself, the Ships were held in terror. At night, men who had entered earlier in perfect health came out on crutches, arms distorted, heads bent at odd angles. These were the panhandlers heading uptown. About the same time a number of handsome men in gentlemen's evening dress moved briskly north. They were confidence men looking for victims among the city's best hotels. Following the Civil War, a fresh increase in population filled the Gap and its neighboring streets with immigrants. The Ships was abandoned and the criminal population diminished as the Irish, the Italians and the Jews took over the neighborhood and moved into the over-crowded tenements which were erected for them.

French's motive was profits, not housing reform; he contemplated rentals of $20 a room per month, far more than slum dwellers could afford. But he was now familiar enough with public relations to know that the picture of a man replacing slums with decent housing was bound to be a favorable one. His original plan was by far the most ambitious he had ever made, perhaps the largest in urban housing up to that time. In the flush days before the stock market crash, he anticipated a development for 30,000 residents at a cost of $150,000,000. He started buying with this in mind, and imposed standards of secrecy worthy of a major military operation. Four dummy corporations were formed. The Allied Metal Yards, Inc., was to purchase in the southwest, the Tenement Renovations Contracting Company in the northeast, the Southern Markets in the southeast, and the Druiss Company in the northwest. A total of forty-two men and women were enlisted as purchasing agents, and made to sign a pledge drawn by French. They promised not to tell anyone, including "wife, friends, business associates and officers, directors and employes of the French companies" what they were doing. To show the seriousness of the pledge, French himself was "held just as strictly as anyone else in the compact and specifically agrees that if he deems it necessary to mention it he will bring the subject before the undersigned for approval."

As French's agents deployed themselves to buy, rumors spread through the district. But, amazingly enough, the secret was kept for more than three years, even though more than 500 separate negotiations had to be carried out. Once it was reported that a railroad terminal was to be built there. The story that John D. Rockefeller was buying up the entire Lower East Side for a model city was popular for a while. Perhaps the most outlandish rumor was that drillers had struck an enormous lake of oil under the streets and that an unknown syndicate was gathering the lots before turning them into a field of gushers. French himself did not dare enter the district during the buying period. He was too well known, as a result of Tudor City, and he felt his presence would reveal the secret. Although no one guessed who was behind it, the buying activity was so great that prices began to rise. When they doubled, and then tripled, French called a halt to the buying to permit the prices to collapse. By the end of 1930, when he had gathered some 250 parcels covering 14½ acres, he had spent more than $5,000,-000. By that time, too, the depression had taken a strong hold, money was getting tighter, and French stopped all buying, although he had acquired only one-third of what he had originally wanted.

Throughout most of 1931, French sought financial backing to build houses on the land he now owned. He interviewed businessmen, bankers, politicians and labor leaders, among them Henry Ford, Owen Young, Gerard Swope, John D. Rockefeller, Jr., Governor Roosevelt and William Green. His arguments went beyond the value of the housing itself. "We outlined to these various parties," French said, "that an immediate building operation in the neighborhood would be instrumental in avoiding the dole. We showed that we could employ 25,000 men for a period of two years, each being employed on an average of 20 per cent of his working time. We showed that we would not be throwing more unrented space on the market, but would be causing the shift of population between the lower east side

John Jacob Astor was a handsome
young man when he started on the
career which was to make him the
richest man in America—"a self-
invented money making machine."
Astor made his first real estate
purchases in an almost pastoral
New York, shown above as it appeared in 1794 (the road in the

center is Division Street, on the city's Lower East Side). Anticipating the city's growth,
he bought seemingly useless farms and lots in the path of expansion. By the time he
died in 1848, a few years before artist-lithographer John Bachman made the bird's-eye
view of Manhattan and Brooklyn (below), Astor had amassed $25,000,000.

Land speculation in the United States in the nineteenth century victimized thousands, including Charles Dickens, who got some sort of revenge by writing *Martin Chuzzlewit,* a novel in which he lampooned America. These sketches by Phiz, Dickens' illustrator, reflect the bitter text.

Jay Cooke, "the financier of the Civil War," had nothing in common with dishonest land jobbers of the period except a tendency to exaggerate the quality of the 47,-000,000 acres he had at his disposal.

This circular, dated 1873, is typical of the promotion used by the railroads to entice easterners to buy land in the West.

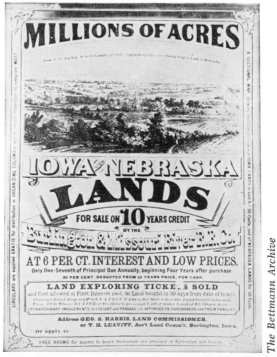

PEACEFUL SHAKER VILLAGE

People may not live longer in Shaker Village
—but they live better

M. J. Van Sweringen (left) and O. P. Van Sweringen, bachelor brothers from Cleveland, Ohio, created Shaker Heights, the first great American suburb. Ownership of the rapid-transit system from Cleveland to their new development started them in the railroad business, and led to control of more track and rolling stock than any other men in history.

The Vans encouraged the wealthy class to buy in Shaker Heights with richly printed brochures containing incentives like those shown here.

THEY play more, because there are facilities for play —golf, tennis, riding, boating, walking—all around them in their own community.

They enjoy their gardens because, with roomy homesites, every home has its garden and there is incentive to make it as colorful and picturesque as those around it.

They relax and are neighborly, for careful selection of purchasers assures people around them that they enjoy as neighbors.

They live in sunshine and clean fresh air, for Shaker Village is six hundred feet above the lake—far above the smoke and soot of the city.

Playing, gardening, relaxing in clean fresh air—Shaker Villagers certainly do live better, and the chances are all for their living longer, too.

Henry Morrison Flagler, a partner of John D. Rockefeller, had a love affair with Florida which lasted until his death.

Flagler single-handedly developed the state's resort cities, among them St. Augustine, where he built the fabulous Hotel Ponce de León

But the Florida boom during Flagler's lifetime was nothing compared to the real estate frenzy which gripped the state in the twenties. Flagler Street, Miami, shown here as it looked in 1922, was the address of most of the city's licensed real estate men—7,500 at the height of the boom.

The Jacob A. Riis Collection, Museum of the City of New York

Jacob Riis, a New York newspaperman, used tough words and a tough camera (he took this picture on the Lower East Side) to show New Yorkers *How the Other Half Lives.* His crusade led to the first important tenement house legislation in the state.

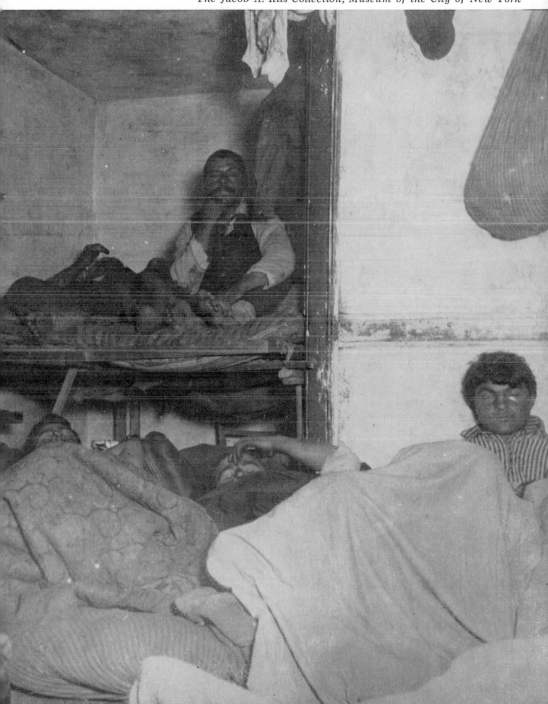

Wurts Brothers

In the Riis tradition, Abraham Kazan, who once lived in the slums, with no real estate experience developed low-cost, nonprofit cooperative apartments. His first, in 1927, in the New York borough of the Bronx, was started by pooling the savings of slum-dwelling garment workers.

Culver Pictures, Inc.

The first true skyscraper—a building in which the metal skeleton, not the walls, supports the structure—was the Home Insurance Company Building, Chicago, 1885.

Harry St. Francis Black inspired New York's skyscraper race with the twenty-one-story Flatiron Building at Madison Square, built on a site which was "a stingy piece of pie." Many people considered it unsafe to walk near it for fear it would fall; some said they saw it sway in the wind.

United Press International Photo

The skyscraper race was won, perhaps for all time, by the Empire State Building, here seen under construction in a photograph taken from the roof of its spiritual ancestor, the Flatiron Building.

Fred F. French was a good salesman who built Tudor City, an apartment development on Manhattan's East Side, because he felt the city's traffic problem would be solved if people could live within walking distance of their work. He was wrong, but Tudor City has never lacked tenants from the day it opened.

Bill Levitt (above, right), president of the company which started the postwar housing revolution, helps veterans and their wives choose a house from the Long Island site plans. Since then he has built Levittown, Pa., and Levittown, N. J. The severe housing shortage which followed World War II was met by adapting industrial mass production methods to home building. Levittown, Long Island (left), was the first of the packaged suburbs.

William Zeckendorf special-
izes in the big real estate
deal. He is seen here in 1953
at the conclusion of complicated negotiations whereby
he took control of the Chrysler Building, the Chrysler
Building East and the Graybar Building in New York's
Grand Central Station area.

United Press International Photo

Zeckendorf's lively imagination is dramatized in this artist's rendering
of X City, a plan to replace the run-down slaughterhouse district Zeckendorf had bought on New York's East Side. Before he could get started on
this project, however, he sold part of his land to the Rockefeller family
so that they could give it to the United Nations for its present site.

Drix Duryea, New York

and the outlying districts. We showed that . . . New York would greatly benefit by the increase in taxable property, that the worst slums in New York would be thus destroyed. . . . But to no avail."

The best French received from these men was sympathy and moral support, the strongest coming from Al Smith, the ex-governor, who was moved by the vision of modern apartments replacing the rookeries he knew as a boy. But French needed more than moral support as his own financial problems increased. Taxes alone on his new property were running $246,000 a year, and its income was not only negligible but decreasing. Collecting rents from poor—and often unemployed—residents was more difficult than it had been for previous landlords. French solved this by issuing circulars in the languages of the area in which he offered rent discounts for payments received before the tenth of each month. This helped some, but did not bring money in the quantities French needed; it barely covered his interest and taxes. French found it necessary, for the first time since the French plan had been inaugurated, to default on dividend payments on preferred stock in some of his projects, and holders of the stock were beginning to raise questions. On September 1, 1931, French and his board of directors decided that "they would proceed," as French put it, "to go it alone." Their bold decision was based on their experience with Tudor City, on which the French companies had spent some $10,000,000 in cash before they found money for a first mortgage.

On December 18, one of French's assistants asked the city's Board of Taxes and Assessments for a reduction on the taxes of the buildings on French's properties, and that day French called in the press to announce plans for his new "white collar city." It was, of course, page one news. Few builders were announcing major projects those days, certainly none of this magnitude or with the appeal of being a slum-clearance effort. For a short while French gloried in favorable press notices. It is possible that he paid more attention to them than to the realities. In addition to the stream of releases from his office, promising rehabilitation of slums, large parks and playgrounds, twelve-story fireproof buildings, "upper Manhattan"-size living rooms, and "the first completely 'electric kitchens' in New York," French was quoted as saying that since the banks were timid about loans he intended to erect the first units of Knickerbocker Village "free and clear of mortgages if necessary." During February 1932 he reorganized his sales staff, and presumably gave them fresh advice on the art of salesmanship. He had not entirely lost his touch; $100,000 worth of stock in the first apartment building was sold before March 1, and French ordered demolition to start on some of the old slum buildings. To help push sales, French personally sold Al Smith the first share of stock and chose as the site for the transaction, so that the press could not miss its significance, the razed block bounded by Henry, Market, Oliver and Madison streets, where Smith had played as a child. But not even French's brand of salesmanship and Al Smith's popularity could overcome the effects of the depression; he could not raise the money to start construction.

French now found that new doors were not only impervious to knocking and kicking, but that some of the old ones he had opened were being slammed shut. Holders of preferred stock in various French buildings were bringing suit because of the absence of dividends on some $14,000,-000 worth of shares. French's public image had been tarnished by the revelation in the Seabury investigation of New York City government that he had once made a payment of $25,000 to the law firm of a former Tammany

Hall leader to insure a favorable decision by the Board of Standards and Appeals. It may be that cynical New Yorkers would have forgiven him that dereliction, except that the incident showed another side of Mr. French's character. French, it turned out, had given his own lawyer $35,000 to make the necessary arrangements. French's lawyer closed the deal for $25,000 and, under the circumstances, felt justified in keeping the remaining $10,000 as his own fee for such sensitive work. French differed, and, the investigation showed, made his lawyer return $5,000. Furthermore, French had insisted that the $25,000 was payable only if he received the decision he sought, otherwise nothing was to be paid. French was a difficult witness, and merely repeated that he always insisted on such arrangements, and saw nothing wrong with them.

Perhaps more distressing to French than stockholders' suits and evidence of bribery was the end of a cherished project. In August 1932 he announced the abandonment of his plans to erect an eighty-three-story office building on the site of the old Hippodrome. The property reverted to the Farmers Loan and Trust Company, which had given French a $2,500,000 mortgage to finance the skyscraper. In 1932 giant commercial towers were as hard to attain as giant residential developments.

Dismal as French's prospects seemed in 1932, they were not altogether hopeless. That summer Congress authorized the Reconstruction Finance Corporation to lend up to $1,500,000,000 for self-liquidating public improvements, including limited-dividend housing. This permitted the same kind of operation for builders that the New York State law had permitted Kazan and the Amalgamated for their Bronx cooperative, with the added advantage that mortgage money was ready from the R.F.C. and did not

(*183*)

have to be sought from banks and insurance companies. French saw in the new law the possibility not merely of retaining at least half the loaf that was about to be snatched from him, but perhaps of baking a few more. He formed Knickerbocker Village, Inc., as a limited-dividend housing corporation which would undertake the demolition of forty-five acres of slums and replace them with housing for 40,-000 people. He estimated that the cost of such a project would run to $93,000,000, of which he felt that a loan of $75,000,000 from the R.F.C. should see him nicely through the worst part of his problems. With these figures, and the active support of his friend Al Smith, he appeared before the State Housing Board to present his case.

Four months and seven formal applications later, French won the State Board's approval—but not precisely for what he had sought. "The size of the original project had gradually shrunk," French said, "from a $93,000,000 to a $10,-000,000 project; from a possibility of giving out over 100,-000 jobs to 10,000 jobs; from accommodating 40,000 [tenants] to 4,000; from a project which would have served notice to the entire world that this country had embarked seriously upon the destruction of slums to a five-acre project which amounts, at best, to a mere experiment." In the course of winning even this much, French produced enough figures, he said, "to settle the war debts." He had to compromise on nearly every point where his judgment as to what constituted proper real estate practice was in conflict with that of the board. For instance, French wanted the land valued at the $18 a square foot he said he had paid for it; the board thought $10 was enough, and a settlement was reached at $14. Not long after French had the board's approval, New York State's Emergency Public Works Commission, under the chairmanship of Robert

Moses, compiled a list of projects which it considered eligible for R.F.C. aid under the new law. Knickerbocker Village was the only housing project on the list, and when Smith, Moses, and other members of the commission went to Washington, Fred F. French was with them.

In the course of venturing into the area of government sponsorship, French offended his colleagues in the real estate business. Anton L. Trunk, president of the Real Estate Board of New York, wrote strong letters of protest to Moses and to the R.F.C., asking that no funds be authorized to French until New York real estate men had been consulted. His main objection was that putting so many new apartments on the market at that time would merely add to the hundreds of vacancies already in existence, and compound the difficulties of owners. The provision for tax exemptions for limited-dividend companies was also irritating to other real estate men. One cited a report showing 200,000 vacancies in the city in buildings on which taxes were paid, and said that Knickerbocker Village would represent unfair competition. Another flatly called French's project dishonest in that it could not sustain itself at the monthly rental of $12.50 per room which was the maximum that could be charged. The Federal Grand Jury Association for the Southern District of New York filed a brief with the R.F.C. attacking Knickerbocker Village as a "misuse of taxpayers' money." The association also questioned whether the project could be self-liquidating at the $12.50 rental, wondered where the tenants would come from, considering that average rentals in the Lower East Side were then $7 a month, and opposed tax exemption. It also felt that a third of the cost projected by French called for payment for the land—to the French company which owned it—"at inflated prices." It was just this sort of thing, the association concluded, that brought on the country's economic troubles: "lenders advancing more on the mortgages and debentures than the actual cost."

The opposition was ineffective. On March 30, 1933, the R.F.C. authorized a loan of $8,075,000 at the rate of 5 per cent interest, for the construction of Knickerbocker Village, the first such loan in the country for housing. In May the city's Board of Estimate granted its first tax exemption, making it applicable to all buildings erected before January 1, 1937. Although the actual contract for the government money would not be signed until October 10, French had long before that regained some of the enthusiasm he once had for Knickerbocker Village. The press releases poured out again—with the intelligence that the plaster to be used in the project would cover an area twelve and a half times the size of Washington Square, that the bricks would reach from New York to Key West, and that all the partitions to be used in the project would make a wall ten feet high around Manhattan Island. French told the *Herald Tribune* that now that he had "broken the ice," similar loans would be made for housing projects elsewhere in the country. "It was the President and the Secretary of the Treasury who finally put this over," he said. "President Roosevelt is very enthusiastic about it." French also had kind words for Mayor La Guardia, Mrs. Roosevelt, and Frances Perkins, the Secretary of Labor.

On October 11, with appropriate ceremony, and to the cheers of thousands of slum dwellers, former Governor Alfred E. Smith swung a golden sledge hammer against a golden wedge to mark the demolition of the "lung block." Before the blow was delivered, Smith made a little speech in which he invoked "the dawn of a better day" and expressed the hope that "my old neighborhood will be brought up to date, and made to look as good as Park Avenue; there was a time when it looked better." Now, he concluded, "having given my song and dance, I'll proceed to bring down the house," and drove the hammer with great zest.

The ceremony not only made Knickerbocker Village official, it brought fresh attention to French as a public benefactor who, far from seeking profits, was concerned only with leveling slums, providing employment, and promoting the general welfare. This was not a universal reaction, however. An article in the *Nation* pointed out that despite the limited-dividend provision under which French had to operate, he stood to make money on the sale of the land by the Fred F. French Operators to Knickerbocker Village, Inc.; on construction, which would be handled by the Fred F. French Construction Company; and on the management of the buildings, which, when completed, would be handled by the Fred F. French Management Corporation. Although the readership of the magazine was small, French authorized his press agent to reply to the article with a proper display of humility and good will on French's behalf. French himself, thoughts of giantism momentarily behind him, gave his new code in a speech in January 1934. He recalled his own "shoestring" beginnings, deplored the "speculative builders" of the 1920's, and recited the lesson he felt the depression had for him. It was, he said, "the new deal in character that I believe most worth while. Be satisfied with fewer things owned outright, smaller businesses safely controlled and fewer ideas thoroughly digested. If all of us, in the future, will conduct our businesses on the pay-as-you-go basis, such financial troubles as the world is witnessing today, will . . . be greatly minimized."

On October 1, 1934, the first section of Knickerbocker Village was formally opened, although 140 families had moved in a week earlier. The French company reported occupancy by a total of 700 families, and that 93 per cent of the building's apartments had been leased. This is one of the more pleasant statistics in a statistic-conscious business, but unfortunately for the French managers, they had not measured the nature of the people who made up their figures. On October 23, the tenants announced that they were on a rent strike; they were not going to pay their rents until management carried out promises it had made in its prospectus. Several hundred gathered at a protest meeting in the auditorium of the neighborhood public school and prepared a bill of complaints to be submitted to French. Specifically, they found the floors unfinished, the walls unpainted, the refrigerators unconnected, the bathrooms unequipped or not functioning properly, no laundry dryers in the basement, the self-service elevators inoperative, playgrounds nonexistent, surrounding sidewalks still torn up, and the promised rerouting of a bus line unfulfilled. The playgroundless children were finding their fun in the elevators, and dog owners walked their pets on the roof rather than face rough sidewalks. Many tied their dogs there, and the howling made it difficult for radios to be heard—that is, the tenants said, when the radios were not buzzing anyhow because of the interference of the elevator motors. As a last blow, the building was mysteriously invaded by a swarm of fleas. To all demands for an exterminator, management responded with an ineffectual, "We'll see about it." This kind of response bothered some tenants even more than the building's shortcomings. They felt that because of the government's role in financing the buildings and the resulting low rentals, they were being treated as charity cases. "I have friends in other Fred F. French buildings," one woman said, "and they do not receive such treatment as we do. I am really losing my self-respect. I sort of feel that I am an object of charity."

French was in Europe when the tenant protests were made, and his subordinates did what they could. They said they would meet with the tenants' committee to iron out their grievances, but beyond that appeared inconsistent. According to the *Post*, officials of the Fred F. French Management Corporation blamed strikes for the tardy completion of the building, and "a small minority of agitators" for the complaints. According to the *Sun*, the officials conceded they had themselves fallen down in some respects, and had "no criticism to make of the tenants." "All we ask," one of them said, "is that [they] show patience while we do this final work. We are not children in managing buildings, and we know that a satisfied tenant is the best advertising we can have."

That kind of advertising was not immediately forthcoming. In mid-November, fifty tenants representing 600 who had formed the Knickerbocker Village Tenants' Association marched into the Fifth Avenue offices of the Fred F. French Investing Company and demanded the remission of October rent for the unreasonable discomforts they had suffered. Irving Broun, president of the company, gave them an audience for an hour and a half. He refused to make a blanket remission, but announced that differences would be settled on an individual basis. This was apparently satisfactory to the committee, although they announced they would hold off paying their November rent until satisfactory agreements were reached. On December 2, two months after the apartment building had opened, the rent strike was settled, with some 250 tenants receiving rebates varying from half a month to a month and a half of rent.

While French—or his lieutenants—was able to settle his differences with the tenants, there was not a great deal he could do about criticism at a different level. In January 1935, *Architecture,* a magazine which devoted itself to matters on a higher plane than landlord-tenant relationships, published "A Critique of Knickerbocker Village." Albert Mayer, the author of the article, conceded that the basic theories behind the project were sound: it was within walking distance of Manhattan business areas and its rents were within reach of medium-income tenants. "But having said this in praise," Mayer wrote, "you have said nearly all. . . . The specific result . . . is disappointing and fundamentally depressing." Among other complaints, Mayer found that only one-sixth of the apartments—two out of twelve on each corridor—had through ventilation. Most of the others had only one exposure. The corridor width, he found, was so "pinched," with a four-foot width and an average length of 120 feet, that "the effect is dreary." The extra cost of adding a couple of feet to the width, he said, "would have been negligible. But when you acquire the habit of pinching and cramming, you instinctively pinch and cram even when there is little or nothing to be gained." He said the exteriors resembled "relentless barracks of brickwork" and that the scale of the inner courts was all wrong. "On the whole, then," Mayer concluded, "Knickerbocker Village does a disservice to the theory of large-scale housing."

Despite such carping and the widely publicized conflict with its tenants, Knickerbocker Village did not lack occupants. In August 1936, the French Company announced that it had maintained 99 to 100 per cent occupancy of the 1,592 units soon after both buildings had been opened, and that there was a waiting list of 600 families. Some of these were able to move in when the French Company refused to renew the leases of eleven original tenants, who, it turned out, were active in forming the Knickerbocker Village Association. This brought another flurry of criticism, which Broun met head on. "It is the landlord's prerogative under the law to decline to renew or not to renew, just as it is the tenant's privilege to get another place when his lease is up," Broun announced. That prerogative, he said, would be exercised "if for any reason we feel that [tenants] are too much out of sympathy with the management's policies, or with the rest of the tenants, or are a disturbing influence. . . . After all, this is a private company, not a housing project."

Although Knickerbocker Village was, properly speaking, a private company, it would not have existed without public assistance, and it was operating with a tax exemption which in 1935 was equal to a gift of $137,505. It was profitable from the start, even with the limited-dividend provision of the law, and it may have been the surprising turnabout from what was almost a total loss to regular profits which gave French renewed optimism about New York real estate. In April 1936, French formed a new company known as Properties and Construction Co., Inc., as a subsidiary of the Investing Company. Its purpose was to buy properties and put up new apartments. The company was started, French told reporters, "to take advantage of the present low prices in real estate." He found, he said, that the lack of building during the depression had created a housing shortage. He predicted increased rentals, with a consequent increase in returns to investors in real property, and he expected the French companies to take the leadership in the coming building boom.

It was French's last prediction, and his last public statement. He died in his sleep on August 30, 1936, at the age of fifty-three. When his will was filed for probate a week later his estate was valued at "less than $10,000 in personal property and no real estate." This anomaly was explained by the *New York Times*, which pointed out that "all of his enterprises, from Tudor City to Knickerbocker Village, were listed in the name of corporations." The *Times* also paid cautious respect to a man who may have had a low batting average as a seer, but who also hit enough home runs to warrant respect. "The major building enterprises" French was contemplating just before his death, the *Times* said, "might have brought future changes in the Manhattan skyline."

New York's traffic problem is worse now than when French thought he knew how to eliminate it. His theory was essentially sound, however. Getting about on foot is still the only practical means of movement in Manhattan; it is certainly the cheapest, and, with experience, not necessarily hazardous. The observation of a German visitor to the city in 1913 that, contrary to an earlier impression, "one who wishes to cross the street need not make his last will and testament" is by and large still true, although the number of pedestrians killed and injured each year is shockingly high. Despite the risk, walking beats everything else New York has to offer in the way of transportation. Subways are crowded and uncomfortable, to say the least, and they do not travel any great distance crosstown except at Fourteenth Street. Buses move no faster than a healthy Boy Scout, and their jolting stops and starts are disconcerting to all but the iron-nerved. Taxis are expensive, invariably get blocked by double-parked trucks, and, like policemen, are never around when you need one. Private cars are out of the question.

If French did not make a lasting contribution to the alleviation of street congestion, which seems beyond any solution, he left his mark on Manhattan in another way. Tudor City did, as he said it would, open the way for the development of the entire Upper East Side along the river; today that area is one of the most desirable residential sections in the city. French's influence lasted long after his death, and while it had its effect on the entire real estate industry in the city, it was only natural and fitting that it found its strongest expression in his own company. A month after French's death, Broun was named president of the Fred F. French Company, the parent organization of all the companies, and two months after that, he announced that buying and building would be resumed on a broad scale. The voice was Broun's, but the words and the plans were those of Fred F. French. The firm's own capital would be used at the start, Broun said, but the French plan would be used for major financing. The new construction would be concentrated on the Upper East Side, and, Broun added with an optimism that traced directly to his predecessor, "A sustained rise in realty values is inevitable."

7

Harry Black, the Man Who Built Skyscrapers

Frank Lloyd Wright, the talented and outspoken architect, attributed the first skyscraper to Michelangelo, "when he hurled the Pantheon on top of the Parthenon." Whereupon, Wright said, "the Pope named it St. Peter's and the world called it a day, celebrating the great act ever since in the sincerest form of human flattery possible." Wright was no admirer of the imitative domes which have proliferated around the world since the sixteenth century, but he did like skyscrapers, or at least the *idea* of skyscrapers as created in the 1880's by Louis Sullivan, the man he always called "The Master." The skyscraper began in America, Wright once wrote, "when Louis Sullivan came through the door that connected my little cubicle with his room . . . pushed a drawing-board with a stretch of manila paper upon it over onto my drafting table, and, without a word, went back again into his own room and closed the door behind him. There it was, in delicately pencilled elevation. I stared at it and sensed what had happened . . . there was the very first human expression of a tall steel office building as Architecture. It was tall and consistently so—a unit, where all before had been one cornice building on top of another cornice building. This was a greater achievement than the Papal Dome, I believe, because here was utility become beauty by sheer triumph of imaginative vision." From this and his other achievements in skyscraper architecture, Sullivan created the philosophic base for building tall. "Form must express function," he said. "There shall be no form for which there is not a function." Wright believed this, too, and was hurt and disappointed when, in his view, later skyscraper builders forgot the Sullivan dictum and "the light that shone . . . as a promise, flickered feebly." Most existing skyscrapers, he said in 1931, have "no life of their own, no life to give, receiving none from the nature of construction . . . they have no relation to their surroundings. Utterly barbaric, they rise regardless of special consideration for environment or for each other, except to win the race or get the tenant."

Winning the race and getting the tenant have been the prerequisites of skyscraper building almost from the time they were created in the United States. The race, for height, at least, ended with the completion of the Empire State Building in 1931. But getting the tenant, the *sine qua non* of any office building, is as much the goal today as it was when Sullivan and his talented contemporaries first discovered the possibilities of cast iron, wrought iron and rolled steel as construction materials. This event took place in Chicago, and although most experts in the field agree with Wright that Sullivan was the spiritual father of what *Life* has called "the most American architectural form," the first true skyscraper was actually designed by William Le Baron Jenney. This was the Home Insurance Building, which was built in 1885 at the corner of La Salle and Adams streets,

(*195*)

also in Chicago and razed in 1931. It was only ten stories high, and not the tallest building in Chicago, but it was the first to use the principle of a metal skeleton instead of massive walls to support the structure, which has been the basis for skyscraper construction ever since. Jenney said he got the idea from the bamboo huts built by Philippine natives. But it took more than the skeleton idea to make skyscrapers feasible; rapid elevators and inexpensive structural steel were needed as well. When both became available in the late 1880's, the skyscraper race was on.

Buildings using the new technique rose twelve, fourteen and more stories in Chicago. In 1892, the Masonic Temple soared a breathtaking twenty-one stories, and the word skyscraper, until then used almost exclusively by sports writers and baseball fans to describe exceptionally high flies, came into popular usage as the synonym for a tall building. By that time, New York had started building skyscrapers as well, and was just a few years away from taking the height record away from Chicago. The Tower Building at 50 Broadway, the city's first, was thirteen stories high, its framework resembling a "steel bridge stood on end." Bradford Lee Gilbert, the building's architect, had more faith in the new technique than John Noble Stearns, a silk merchant who owned the land on which it was to be built, and the city's building department, which refused to issue a construction permit. Gilbert convinced Stearns by offering to rent the top floor himself, and the city authorities by two months of stubborn argument. Not everyone succumbed as readily, however. When the steel girders began to rise, the tenant of the nearest building moved away for his own safety. The big test came on a Sunday morning in 1889 when, with the building nearly finished, a storm with eighty-mile-an-hour winds struck the city. Gilbert had been waiting for just such a test, and so, too, apparently, had most of New York. Crowds gathered downtown at what they hoped was a safe distance from which to watch the building crumble. Gilbert carefully made his way to the top, carrying a plumb line. When he dropped the weighted string it showed only a slight vibration. He had made his point; skyscrapers were safe.

For the next ten years New York matched Chicago in the number and height of buildings, as a loud and articulate opposition to skyscrapers started being heard. The safety of high buildings was still questioned, and architects were concerned about their effect on the city's beauty and on the health of city dwellers. Some felt that by keeping the air from circulating properly at ground level, the buildings would turn the streets into a "hotbed of malaria." George B. Post, a New York architect who predicted this dire consequence, organized the Architectural League of New York in 1894, consisting of like-minded members of his profession, and drew up a bill which would outlaw skyscrapers. He had the support of New York newspapers, the Brooklyn and Buffalo chapters of the American Institute of Architects, the City Club of New York and many art societies. Post felt he had the backing of the state Senate and Assembly as well as the governor, but on the last day of the legislative session his bill was left in the speaker's basket. Post attributed his failure to a strong lobby of the state's real estate men.

The criticism did not abate, even when a writer in the November 1896 issue of the influential *North American Review* assured readers that although "buildings of fifty or sixty stories are evidently feasible . . . such enormous heights will . . . probably never be realized." He reasoned that "sooner or later, there will be found a limit in the height of buildings depending upon many and varied conditions for each locality, beyond which they will no longer be profitable investments." Nobody questioned this view, even as records were broken. Early in 1899 the St. Paul Building was completed in New York. It was taller than Chicago's Masonic Temple, and thus, briefly, the tallest building in the world, a title that was to remain in New York from that date. Before the year was out the Park Row Building—392 feet high with its tower—was completed, and surpassed the St. Paul. In the face of this, Post continued his campaign, now warning building owners that the bottom floors of the tall buildings would be unrentable when hedged in by other skyscrapers. He pointed out the danger of fire, and was one of the first to warn of the traffic problems which would ensue when buildings held large numbers of people. Thomas Hastings, who preferred the low-lying buildings of the kind he designed for Flagler in Florida, said "there is no excuse for the erection of skyscrapers." He also doubted the longevity of the steel skeletons, and predicted that inspection and repairs would be difficult. A Brooklyn alderman condemned skyscrapers as a public menace, and another man was sure that their interiors were breeding places for consumption.

In 1902 the skyscraper fight centered on a single structure, formally named the Fuller Building, but never known as anything but the Flatiron Building, because of its triangular shape. The Flatiron was not an entry in the race for height (the Park Row was twenty-nine feet taller). It became the most controversial building in skyscraper history because its location at Madison Square, the intersection of Broadway and Fifth Avenue at Twenty-third Street, was, as a guidebook called it, "the central point of the life and splendor of upper New York." The building's shape was symbolic, too, perhaps frighteningly so to the anti-skyscraper contingent which may have sensed the truth in an essayist's words in *Munsey's Magazine:* "Its front is lifted to

(198)

the future. On the past its back is turned." When the Flat-iron Building was completed, few could doubt that sky-scrapers were here to stay and to grow, and that with few notable exceptions, their future was to the north of the strange-looking building at Madison Square.

Harry St. Francis Black, president of the George A. Fuller Construction Company, which financed, constructed and gave a name, however transitory, to the Flatiron Building was in 1902 the country's most experienced sky-scraper builder, and well on his way to becoming one of the most influential men in American real estate. Although he reached this eminence by virtue of intelligence, ambi-tion and drive, his was not the rags-to-riches rise that has typified so many of the real estate giants. He was born in Coburg, Ontario, on August 25, 1863, the son of Major Thomas Black, a paymaster in the British Army. He was educated in the schools of Coburg until he took a job in a local general store. While still in his teens, Black joined a surveying party which explored the Northwest and the Pa-cific Coast. In 1882 he became a sales representative on the Pacific Coast for a Chicago wholesale woolen house. This was apparently no great challenge to Black's talents, although he remained with the company for ten years. Immediately after he left, he founded and ran two banks in the state of Washington, then he opened a store in Tekoa, Washington, and another in Menominee, Michigan. In 1895, while in Chicago, he met George A. Fuller, head of the construction company which had built the twelve-story Rookery and the fourteen-story Tacoma, two of the city's pioneer skyscrap-ers. Perhaps more to the point, Black also met Fuller's only daughter, Allon Mae, then seventeen, and, after a rapid courtship, married her. Black joined the Fuller company, and quickly became a vice-president. When Fuller died in

1900, Black, who had done much to expand the business, was his logical successor.

The construction company that Fuller founded in 1882 after he had left a lucrative partnership in a leading architectural office had made its reputation in Chicago. Black carried the firm's reputation to the most important cities in the East. About the time Fuller died Black established the company's headquarters in New York, and was constructing buildings in Baltimore and Washington. He himself knew little about construction, but he knew how to find and keep men who did; most of all, he had learned how to sell in his ten years of carrying woolen samples. He had an ingratiating personality which, in an area where the client-contractor relationship often determines sales and rejections, was an important sales tool. Paul Starrett, later to head his own construction firm, worked with Black for twenty-five years "with no serious disagreement," and said "he had a smile that would charm the birds off the tree. . . . He had a contagious sense of humor and told anecdotes . . . effectively. He was big-hearted and selfish and, according to my standards, rather unscrupulous." Starrett summed up Black as "a business genius, a gambler, a financial juggler." These were also useful qualities in Black's new position, although they were not so apparent when he sought building contracts as they were to be when he became a real estate mogul.

Black was as impressed with the future of the steel skeleton building as his father-in-law had been, and, with a fine supervisory crew headed by Starrett, soon made the George A. Fuller Company the country's foremost building contractors. He did not make a profit on all his buildings, but even where there were losses he benefited. Due to rising costs after he made his estimate, he lost $8,000 on the *Washington Star* building in Washington, D. C., but this led to his getting the contract for the new Willard Hotel, on which he made a substantial profit. In later years his company was to build the Lincoln Memorial and the National Cathedral, but at the start of the twentieth century a builder's goal was New York. There, it was clear, the towering buildings of the future would be erected. "Geographic and human forces," Paul Starrett wrote, "were creating on Manhattan Island the greatest concentration of business and wealth and the highest land values per square foot in the world. Higher land values justified, indeed demanded, higher buildings. The concentration of business produced by higher buildings, in turn, increased land values and justified still higher buildings. It was an interacting process." Harry Black, who was already beginning to feel that he could control this interacting process, set about to conquer New York—and thus assure his own future—with the most dramatic skyscraper the world had yet seen. As Starrett said, "Bigger and bigger" were his watchwords.

The site of the Flatiron Building, "one of the half-dozen most salient building sites" in Manhattan, according to Starrett, was once described as a "stingy piece of pie." It had belonged to Amos R. Eno, who was known in his day as a shrewd real estate trader; he paid $32,000 for the corner in 1857, and in the forty years in which it remained in his estate it produced millions in rentals. Given such profits, Eno and his heirs could find amusement in the various names the public gave to his property, "cowcatcher" being considered especially humorous by the wits of the day. In 1899 the Eno estate compounded the joke by selling the corner for $690,000 to Samuel Newhouse, identified in the press as a "copper king." It was actually a disappointing price for the sellers, because before the sale a bill appropriating $3,000,000 for the city to buy the site as an extension of Madison Square had passed the Assembly with no discussion. The almost too smooth handling of such a large sum aroused the curiosity of the *New York World*, which soon discovered, and published, that the sale was to be made by the firm of Peter F. Meyer and Company. The Company, the *World* pointed out, was Richard Croker of Tammany Hall, which were dirty words to its readers. "I thought it was a motion to remove a lamppost from Madison Square," one alderman explained. The *World's* crusade prodded public opinion, and the purchase by the city was dropped, whereupon the Eno estate found a less lavish buyer. Newhouse held the property for two years, and sold it to the Fuller Company for $890,000.

When Black bought the triangle, it was strategically located in New York's fashionable shopping district, which then extended from Fourteenth Street to Twenty-third. To give it the eye-catching architecture the site demanded, Black called in D. H. Burnham, who had designed many of Chicago's skyscrapers, and was one of the nation's outstanding proponents of the skeleton construction method. Before Black could get started on what the *New Yorker* was later to call "that noble, if bizarre-looking, old pile of steel and stone," he ran into a stubborn tenant, the first of many men who disapproved of what he planned for that corner. This gentleman, Colonel Winfield Scott Proskey, a member of the staff of the governor of Florida, resided in the Cumberland Apartments, which occupied the south end of the block. Whereas all other tenants left before the wrecking crew got started, Proskey, whose lease had five months to run, remained "as a matter of principle." After the gas pipes and stairway to his apartment were cut he obtained an injunction against the Fuller Company, which finally got him out by paying him more than it considered reasonable.

Criticism of the Flatiron Building started while construction was under way. It came from architects and that part of the public which was still unconvinced about the safety of skyscrapers. Real estate men were uncritical but jealous; during construction Black turned down an offer for the Flatiron site which would have given him a million dollars profit. The *Architectural Record,* however, called the new building "quite the most notorious thing in New York," attracting "more attention than all the other buildings now going up put together," and concluded with its own negative critique: "a vast theatrical 'wing,' which conceivably rests upon Titanic casters and is meant to be pushed about, instead of being rooted to the spot." The magazine also saw potential problems for tenants in the offices in the northern wedge of the building, each of which, at best, would be "a mere bird-cage" allowing "perhaps . . . wall space within for one roll-top desk . . . But suppose [they] needed a book case?" The only consolation for such sacrifice, the magazine concluded, was that the tenant "undoubtedly has a highly eligible place from which to view processions."

When the scaffolding was removed in June 1902, the *New York Tribune* reported that "there is scarcely an hour when a staring wayfarer doesn't by his example collect a big crowd of other staring people. Sometimes a hundred or more, with heads bent backward until a general breakage of necks seems imminent, collect along the walk . . . and stay there until 'one of the finest' orders them to move on." The *Tribune* decided that it was, after all, a "remarkable" building and "a marvel of building construction." If not the tallest building in the city, the paper said, "it is the slenderest—as a bright girl expresses it, 'the most aquiline.'" But the *Tribune* also encouraged the prevailing fear for the safety of the building's inhabitants and passers-by in case it should fall; it determined that if the building crashed to the east "it would almost reach Madison Avenue."

The dangers were exaggerated by rumors that the Flatiron Building could be seen to sway in the wind. Since the corner was supposed to be one of the windiest in the city this was not hard to believe. The *Herald* sent reporters with wind gauges to make a scientific chart of the breezes, and quoted tenants as being fearful of the building's vibrations. The Fuller Company affirmed the strength of the building, citing its 3,680 tons of structural steel as evidence, but this did not prevent hundreds of people from reporting that they actually saw the building bend. The swirling breezes did not budge the building, but they did bring it a reputation Black certainly did not seek. Sir Philip Burne-Jones, an English artist who visited New York soon after the Flatiron was completed, described the phenomenon in *Dollars and Democracy*. "One vast horror," he wrote, "[it] is distinctly responsible for a new form of hurricane, which meets unsuspecting pedestrians as they reach the corner, causing them extreme discomfort. . . . When its effects first became noticeable, a little rude crowd of loafers and street Arabs used to congregate upon the curb to jeer and gloat over the distress of ladies whose skirts were blown into their eyes as they rounded the treacherous corner. Hanging about this particular spot soon became a recognized and punishable offense." The kind of problem Sir Philip described was graphically reported by the *Herald:* A young lady was the victim of a strong gust. After she had been "unwound from the lamp post," the *Herald* said, "and her hat had been rescued from under the heels of a cab horse, she was escorted to the lee side of the *Herald's* Twenty-third Street office. 'Well this is awful!' she exclaimed through her tears. 'I will never pass that hateful old Flatiron Building again. Somebody ought to arrest the man who built it.' "

Black was not arrested, nor did he enter the purgatory to which other outspoken critics assigned him. William Ordway Partridge, an artist, called the Flatiron "a monstrosity, a disgrace to our city, an outrage to our sense of the artistic and a menace to life." Other artists came to the building's defense, however, and Black had the satisfaction of seeing the building survive its critics and become the most painted, photographed, written about, and visited building in New York. John Sloan's *Dust Storm,* now at the Metropolitan Muscum of Art, carried some sense of the controversial air currents; Edward Steichen's photograph of the Flatiron by night was exhibited at the London Salon in 1905 and is considered one of the classics in its art form. Pictures of the building appeared in geography books and encyclopedias, and one on a postcard was, with that of the Brooklyn Bridge, the city's best-seller for years. O. Henry never failed to mention it in stories which brought his characters to Madison Square. The greatest accolade may well have been a poem, a rare tribute to a commercial building, written in 1903 by Sidney Allan, whom Amy Lowell, herself a fine poet, called "the most mysterious man in American literature." There was no mystery about Allan's feelings for the Flatiron Building; the poem ended with these lines:

> *Well may you smile over Gotham's vast domain*
> *As dawn greets your pillars with roseate flame,*
> *For future ages will proclaim*
> *Your beauty*
> *Boldly, without shame.*

With or without poetry, the Flatiron Building was an immediate commercial success, and a major impetus to skyscraper construction in New York. Black, who benefited from both the Flatiron and the new boom, did not even mind that the building was never identified as the Fuller Building. "The year that has just closed," wrote the *Real Estate Record and Builder's Guide* in its issue of January 3, 1903, "has been one of the most remarkable years in the history of New York real estate." Plans for ninety-three skyscrapers—arbitrarily defined as buildings of nine stories or more—had been filed during 1902 to be built at an estimated cost of $37,778,000. Altogether, plans had been filed for 811 buildings of all kinds, so that skyscrapers represented only 11 per cent of the total; nevertheless, the tall buildings accounted for 47 per cent of the projected expenditure for construction. More important for the city's growth, perhaps, was the location of the new buildings; sixty-three were to be built north of Fourteenth Street, and all ninety-three were to be either on Broadway or Fifth Avenue or within a few hundred yards of them. The prow of the Flatiron had indeed pointed the right way.

Black immediately understood the significance of this. Construction was but one phase of real estate, and the success he had made of that so far and the prospects for even greater gain were undeniable. Yet there was the nagging awareness that his talents could just as readily and profitably be applied to other branches of real estate—buying, selling, owning, operating and financing. In an era of oil, steel, beef, sugar and even bicycle trusts, Black conceived, and set about to establish, a real estate trust, or, as the press sometimes called it, "a skyscraper trust."

The United States Realty and Construction Company was formidable by any business standard, and quite the largest single organization in real estate. All of Black's skills, backed by his personality and reputation, were needed to bring it into being. For purposes of acquiring the

Flatiron Building, the Fuller Company had been reorganized and freshly capitalized at $15,000,000. Of this, $5,000,000 was in preferred stock, and although half the valuation of the $10,000,000 in common stock was attributed to "good will," Black had been able to attract a highly respectable board of directors, among them James Stillman, president of the National City Bank; Henry Morgenthau, whose son would be President Roosevelt's Secretary of the Treasury; and Hugh Grant, a former Tammany mayor with good political connections. Black's plan consisted merely of consolidating into one giant firm the country's five largest corporations then operating in the various branches of real estate. Stillman, who considered Black "the brightest young man in Wall Street," was easy to convince, and Black embarked on a whirlwind campaign. Within a month after the Flatiron was opened, rumors of the merger appeared in the trade press, and a month after that articles of incorporation were filed in Jersey City.

The companies brought into United States Realty, besides Black's, which by then was valued at $24,000,000, were the Central Realty Bond and Trust Company, of which Morgenthau was president, with a capital of $2,000,-000 and a surplus of $8,000,000; the Lawyers' Title Insurance Company, with $3,500,000 in capital and $4,500,000 in surplus; the New York Realty Corporation and the Alliance Realty Company, each with a capital of $3,000,000. The new company was capitalized at $66,000,000, $30,-000,000 of which was in preferred stock, the rest in common. The *New York Post* said skeptically, "One half of this capitalization is pure water and wind," but with a representative of J. P. Morgan on the board of directors, which also included Charles M. Schwab of U. S. Steel, Charles Francis Adams, Cornelius Vanderbilt and John W. (Bet a Million) Gates, such criticism was hardly noticed.

Black was made chairman of the board, while retaining his presidency of the Fuller Company, which was to be maintained as the construction branch of the new firm. Albert Flake and Robert Dowling, of the New York Realty Corporation, were to be in charge of the buying and selling of property.

If the names and the amount of money involved were not enough, the properties held by the new company would have quieted any cynic. Among its many buildings and parcels of land in the financial district and along Fifth Avenue and Broadway was the Broad Exchange building, then New York's largest office building; the Plaza Hotel, already one of the most exclusive in the city; and another triangular plot, this one at the corner of Seventh Avenue and Broadway, then known as Longacre Square, and soon to become Times Square. The *Architectural Record and Builders Guide*, worried about the possible unwieldiness of such a large corporation and what it considered inflated real estate values, nevertheless conceded that the new company's "strength presents an . . . imposing front. The properties the company will take over is the cream of New York real estate . . . If it can hold these properties long enough, there can be no doubt about the prosperity of the result."

Ushering in what the *World's Work* called "a new era in financing real estate," United States Realty moved boldly on a number of fronts. It bought land on which to build apartment houses, hotels, offices, loft buildings and stores. Its management branch brought economies to the operation of buildings the firm owned, and the construction company handled all the building contracts it could fulfill. As long as the city boomed, all was well with United States Realty. Black sold the triangle at Longacre Square to the *New York Times* and built another flatiron-shaped building for the newspaper there, which brought a change in the area's name and, eventually, its personality. He undertook the construction of a tremendous department store for R. H. Macy at Sixth Avenue and Thirty-fourth Street, a daring leap from the traditional Fourteenth Street shopping area. Due to opposing interpretations of what constituted a cubic foot—Black had contracted to put up the building at twenty cents a cubic foot—the Fuller Company lost money on the job. Black's experts had measured from the bottom of the foundation to the parapet wall; the Straus family, which owned Macy's, did not consider these parts of the space they had bought. Black instituted a lawsuit, which was expensive and dragged for five years. It had been a $4,800,000 contract, but Black eventually showed a loss on it. There were not many such losses, however, as new buildings—many now demolished, many still important New York landmarks—rose under the supervision of United States Realty. In time, the Pennsylvania and Commodore hotels, Pennsylvania Station, The United States Post Office across the street from it, and the Hippodrome, New York's largest theater, were built by the company.

Prospects for continued success were so bright that Black became more daring. He had always liked to gamble, and of his colleagues, was particularly fond of Gates. Once, at a game of baccarat, in which both men participated, Black came out $60,000 ahead after having been behind $55,000. This pleased him, of course, but he was most amused when he learned that a broker in the game reported a loss of $75,000. The gambling instinct led to the construction in 1905 of the Hippodrome, at Gates's suggestion, on the company's property at Forty-third Street and Sixth Avenue at a cost of $1,500,000. Although it was undoubtedly the most spectacular theater in America—with a seating capacity of 5,200, and lighted by 40,000 electric bulbs—under the management of two Coney Island showmen, Frederic Thompson and Elmer Dundy, it produced no profits. United States Realty later leased the theater to the Shuberts, and then to the Keith-Albee interests, who eventually bought it and made it profitable. Black's propensity for taking a chance annoyed some of his conservative associates, some of whom were already showing signs of unease at sitting on the same board with a gambler like Gates and a Tammany politician like Grant. Conflict did not come to a head, however, until real estate values dropped briefly in 1905, and the value of the company's stock with them.

The *Architectural Record and Builders Guide* brought some of the company's problems into the open. The trade paper was not concerned with the drop in stock prices— railroad and industrial stocks had fallen in the same period —but it was critical of "the exclusively speculative basis" on which United States Realty was conducting its business. The original idea of the company was sound, it said, and if "applied with good business judgment" would renew public confidence. In the company's board room, however, there was less talk of public confidence than of who would control the company. Black, who had faith in the long-term strength of United States Realty, had no doubts about where that control would go. As the stock dropped in price, he kept buying. When he had a substantial block he bought out Morgenthau's shares at a little above their market value, but at considerably less than they were to be worth later. Then, joining Stillman, Gates and Schwab, he took over the company. He named himself president and appointed a new board of directors and a new set of executives. Flake and Dowling were retained as vice-presidents, but not for long. When they left because of differences with Black, he changed the company name to United States

Realty and Improvement Corporation. This did not necessarily improve public confidence. Fuller Construction lost a few contracts because of the impression that it was the subsidiary of a gambling outfit—but it did open the way for Black to run a real estate trust in his own way.

By 1906, the real estate market in New York was booming again, justifying Black's confidence. Prices and stock values went up, and so did buildings. That year alone contracts were signed for $75,000,000 worth of building construction in Manhattan. No one knows precisely what share of this came to United States Realty, or to Black, but it had to be sizable. Starrett once estimated that from 1906 to 1923, the seventeen years in which he was president of the Fuller Company, the firm fulfilled building contracts worth $368,000,000, and that at one time it was handling 80 per cent of all building construction in New York. Construction aside, the rising real estate values would have vastly increased Black's equity in the company. When Black and his wife were divorced in 1905—the marriage had been marked by many separations and reconciliations —he gave her $6,000,000, which represented the increased value of the $2,500,000 her father had left her just five years earlier, and which Black had invested in his own enterprises. In addition, he made a settlement of $1,500,000 on her, "a very handsome amount," he told a reporter. It is highly unlikely that Black would have been so generous if he did not possess a considerable fortune himself.

The boom—and with it, Black's fortunes—was helped by an enthusiastic press. "New York City's real estate market is becoming more and more the concern of the entire nation and a constantly increasing volume of money is being attracted to it," *Moody's Magazine* reported in

March 1907. "It is also becoming more and more the favorite investment field of the largest capitalists and shrewdest financiers throughout the United States and even in Europe." The author deplored the notion that real estate was essentially a speculative area. He pointed out that the land value of the city in that year's assessment was close to $6,000,000,000, an increase of $400,000,000 over 1906, which in turn had an increase of $480,000,000 over 1905. His comparatives were spectacular. The value of New York real estate, he concluded, "is greater than the entire wealth of many states and even many foreign countries. It is 25 per cent more than the entire wealth of Holland, Spain, Sweden and Norway; 50 per cent more than Switzerland, Denmark or Portugal; it is one-third that of Italy; one-fourth that of Austria-Hungary; one-fifth that of Russia; one-seventh that of Germany; one-eighth that of France; one-tenth that of Great Britain and Ireland. It is indeed an imperial city in an empire state."

This kind of enthusiasm, repeated in other publications—including as conservative a one as the *Bankers' Magazine,* which found that New York real estate was one of the "few certainties" in the world of investment—also gave fresh impetus to the skyscraper race. The Singer Building—or the Singerhorn, as one writer named it—took the altitude lead in 1908 with forty-seven stories, but was almost immediately topped by the Metropolitan Life Insurance Company Tower. By the end of the first decade of the twentieth century, tall buildings dominated not only the city but nearly every discussion of it, especially by foreigners. These skyscrapers, *egratineurs de ciel, Himmelskratzer, grattacieli* and *rascacielos,* depending on the author's language, were deplored, admired, praised and condemned, depending on the author's reaction. H. G. Wells felt that "unlike St. Peter's great blue dome," New York skyscrapers had a sense of "immense incompleteness." Maxim Gorky, the Russian novelist, who was in the United States in 1906 to raise money for the Revolution, found them "dull, heavy piles" which gave the city the look of "a huge jaw with black, uneven teeth," sniffing "like a glutton suffering from overcorpulency." To Henry James the image was that of "extravagant pins in a cushion already over-planted." On the other side were the musician Charles Camille Saint-Saëns, who said the skyscrapers made a "fantastic and marvelous spectacle"; and the English poet Rupert Brooke, who thought that "their strength . . . of line and the lightness of their colour give a kind of classical feeling, classical, and yet not that of Europe . . . an existence and meaning of their own." American writers entered the debate, too. One of them called New York "the city of dreadful height" whose towers kept light and air from the streets, an effect both "malign and terrible." No longer, he said, was Madison Square a place "to which one could resort, whether in the morning or the afternoon of a bright day in winter, in the assurance that he might bask there in the sun."

All the discussions made building owners realize the publicity value of a tall structure bearing their name. This, more than anything else, inspired Frank W. Woolworth to undertake the construction of a building which, he said, "would advertise the Woolworth five and ten cent stores all over the world." He not only achieved this—with a building that held the title of world's tallest for nearly seventeen years—but gave the city a monument which, after fifty years, is still awe-inspiring. The sixty-story Gothic Wool-worth Building was designed by Cass Gilbert, one of the country's foremost architects, whose only instructions from his sponsor were to take inspiration from the Houses of Parliament in London, and to build tall. Woolworth had hired an engineer to measure the Metropolitan Tower. When he was informed that it was exactly 701 feet, three inches, he told Gilbert to top it by fifty feet, presumably a safe margin. Actually the Woolworth Building rose 792 feet, and cost Woolworth $13,500,000, which he paid in cash, making it the only building of such size ever to be built completely free of debt.

Dr. S. Parkes Cadman, a prominent clergyman, coined the term "Cathedral of Commerce" for the Woolworth Building. The exterior ornamentation was of an elaborateness that is rarely seen today—tourelles with gargoyles surround the tapering tower, and a cathedral-like effect is emphasized in the three-story-high arcade entrance. The lobby walls of matched golden marble from the Greek island of Skyros rise from floors of marble terrazzo and wainscoting of Italian marble. The vaulted ceilings are set with mosaic glass. Indirect lighting behind the lace-like marble cornices spread a soft cathedral-like glow over the lobby. Gilbert was as practical as he was aesthetic; anticipating the modern emphasis on natural light, he designed the building in a U-shape, so that every office was an outside one. The ceilings in many of them were as much as twenty feet high, and none were less than eleven feet, although in recent years tenants have hung lower ceilings and installed fluorescent lighting.

The publicity that Woolworth sought was guaranteed from the outset. President Woodrow Wilson pushed a button in the White House on April 24, 1913, and 80,000 light bulbs turned on simultaneously in the Woolworth Building. At that moment, Woolworth was the host to 900 guests at a dinner on the twenty-seventh floor to honor Cass Gilbert. Whether because of the publicity or its location—233 Broadway, overlooking City Hall Park—the building has always been fully tenanted. In 1962, forty-nine years after the building opened, twelve of the original tenants were still there. Until the Empire State Building was completed in 1931, the Woolworth Building observation tower attracted 300,000 visitors a year. This figure dropped to 250,000 a year until the start of World War II, when the tower was closed by order of the United States Navy because it provided too clear a view of ships in New York Harbor. In 1922 a Hollywood couple, as sensitive to publicity as Woolworth himself, got married in the observation tower and made the appropriate headlines. The tower was not reopened to the public after the war, a disappointment to couples who had visited it on their honeymoon and had sought it out again for sentimental reasons. It has been occupied in recent years by a medical center. A $7,000,000 modernization program has kept the Woolworth Building up to date. Twenty-four high-speed automatic elevators, a new power plant, air conditioning and brighter lights have been installed, so that the building, which is now the seventh tallest in the city, can compete in efficiency with its modern competitors.

Black was impressed with the Woolworth Building, although disappointed that the Fuller Company did not win the contract to build it, a fact which Starrett attributed to Gilbert's personal animosity. As far as Black was concerned, the new skyscraper was more evidence that New York's real estate boom was permanent, a fact he felt was sure to be reflected in the prosperity of United States Realty. He could even turn down chances for profit and not stop the continuing flow. Charles Rector, the famous restaurant proprietor, came to Black with a suggestion for a hotel on Times Square to be called the Claridge. In 1905, Black had constructed and helped finance for Rector a Chicago office building which, with a restaurant in the basement and a high rate of tenancy on the upper floors, had been very successful. Rector had repeated his restaurant success in New York, and had found substantial financial backing for his new plan. His figures allowed a sizeable profit for Black. But Black, whose instincts were generally sound, told Rector flatly that the scheme had no merit and that if he went through with it he would be "a hired man" before he died. Black turned Rector down, whereupon the restaurateur found another contractor, built his hotel, and died broke in someone else's employ.

Black could afford to skip some chances for profit. He was a wealthy man; by the mid-1920's, as the post–World War I real estate market reached its greatest heights, Black's personal fortune came to about $15,000,000. His value to the company was considerable, too. In April 1927 the board of United States Realty took out an insurance policy on his life for $1,000,000. This was such a substantial death benefit that the policy had to be divided between two companies. Furthermore, because of his financial acumen, Black was on the boards of a dozen important companies, including the National City Bank and the Missouri-Kansas-Texas Railroad.

With all his love for hard work, Black found time to relax, and seems to have done so with complete pleasure. With his first wife, he had made the fashionable round of Florida in the early spring, a visit to England and the Continent in the summer, and back to Saratoga by fall. He was married again in 1922—to Isabelle L. May, of a family prominent in Washington and Baltimore society—and although the locations changed, the forms of relaxation were much as they had been before. He had an apartment at the Plaza Hotel, of which United States Realty was the principal stockholder, where he maintained a fine art collection, especially rare tapestries and pottery. He also had a home at Lloyd Harbor, near Huntington, Long Island, and another at Newport, Rhode Island. Black made no secret of his affection for the Democratic Party nor of his distaste for the Eighteenth Amendment. In 1921 he was arrested in Miami when prohibition agents raided his private Pullman car and claimed to have found fifty-five cases of whiskey. Black's prominence and the fact—or at least it was claimed to be a fact by Florida officials—that this was the first raid on a private railroad car since the Volstead Act went into effect, brought national interest to the raid. The federal case against Black was dropped when a Negro porter testified that he put the liquor in the car without Black's knowledge or consent. And a few days later, a Dade County Criminal Court jury considered the problem for exactly three minutes and returned with a verdict of not guilty. Black had been able to prove that he had not been in the railroad car at the time the liquor was seized, and he said he had had no knowledge of its having been placed there. It is possible that the prosecution erred slightly; to secure its case against Black the prosecuting attorney had allowed each member of the jury to drink some of the seized stock of whiskey, ostensibly to determine whether it was an intoxicating beverage.

In the 1920's the money to support homes, art, trips and cases of bootleg whiskey came not so much from the dramatic construction of buildings like the Flatiron, as from the steady acquisition of profitable properties for their income, or, conversely, from the sale of those whose income was diminishing. Following this principle, Black and his associates in 1928 took over the Savoy Plaza, another luxury hotel of the class of the Plaza. They had earlier sold the Hippodrome for more than $5,000,000, and did not lack cash to carry on real estate operations at the stepped-up pace required by the activity of the boom years. The boom had brought competition; United States Realty, though

diversified, was no longer a trust in the sense that it had
been when it was created, and it was far from a monopoly.
Other groups had formed, following the principles established by Black, and if they were not yet quite so large as
United States Realty, they showed all signs of coming close.

Early in 1929, Black announced that United States
Realty would undertake a new method of financing real
estate. He carried the French plan and his own original
concept of real estate to their logical conclusions: mortgages would be eliminated altogether; preferred and common stock would be issued for the entire cost of a new
building, thus doing away with many traditional costs. A
new company, the U.S.R. Management Corporation, was
formed to handle the new style of operation. It was capitalized at $5,000,000, its stock held jointly by United States
Realty and National City Bank. The idea was well received,
the *New York Times* giving it a prominent column on its
financial pages. But it was never to be fully tried. When the
stock market crashed in October, buyers for real estate were
among the first to vanish. At about the same time, Black,
who had been ill for some time, was found unconscious in
an overflowing bathtub in his apartment at the Plaza. A
pulmotor crew, working over him for nine hours, saved his
life. There was no indication at the time that this was anything more than what Black's doctor announced, a fainting
spell brought on by excessively hot water. But the following
July 19, when Black was found dead at his Long Island
home, there was no question as to what had happened. He
had a bullet wound in his right temple, and a pistol in his
hand. He was sixty-six years old, in good physical health,
and had not, despite the usual flurry of rumors, suffered
heavily from the fall in stock prices. United States Realty
refuted such reports with a statement of its financial situation for the six months ending June 30, 1930. Net earnings

for that period were $3,396,719.95, a decrease of a little more than $400,000 from the same period in 1929, an excellent record for those panic-ridden months. Furthermore, as testimony to Black's skill in his profession, the companies' assets came close to $18,000,000, of which nearly $14,000,000 was in cash or on call; its liabilities amounted to $2,000,000, and the George A. Fuller Company had $32,000,000 worth of contracts to complete.

Black's will was more liberal than Astor's had been; after bequests to friends, family and employes amounting to $175,000, he asked that the rest—estimated at $5,000,-000—be put in trust for his second wife and his nephew, the son of his first wife's sister. If either died childless the money was to go to charities which "are kindly and wisely contributing to the relief of unfortunate men, women and children who are either sick or physically disabled." One clause would have endeared Black to that segment of the New York press which found Astor ungrateful to the city which made him wealthy: "As the beginning of the estate which goes into this trust was made in the city of Chicago, and its completion in the city of New York, I hope that my trustees will endeavor to distribute about forty per cent of the net income . . . in Chicago, and the residue . . . in New York."

Whatever provision Black made for New York at his death was already surpassed by what he had created while alive. The Fuller Company—today capitalized at slightly less than $10,000,000—is the largest building contractor in the country. In 1960 it constructed $193,000,000 worth of buildings in twenty-nine states. Although it has worked on missile bases, laboratories and factories—and during World War II developed the Quonset hut while building the naval air station at Quonset Point, Rhode Island—it is still primarily a builder of skyscrapers. Since 1938, when the

(219)

Fuller Company was separated from United States Realty, it has occasionally made a modest investment in building properties. This amounted to about $1,000,000 a few years ago, very small by modern standards, and by Black's. But its newest achievements in construction would have pleased Fuller, the company's founder, and Black, who brought it to New York and maturity. The United Nations Headquarters, Lever House, Manufacturers Trust Company, Seagram and Union Carbide buildings are dramatic additions to the city's skyline—as distinct from their contemporaries as the Flatiron Building, whose tradition they maintain, was from the buildings of its time.

Black's death came a few months after the skyscraper race entered its last phase. In 1929 the Bank of Manhattan Company Building at 40 Wall Street and the Chrysler Building at Lexington Avenue and Forty-second Street had started to rise simultaneously, each taller than the Woolworth Building. Even before they were completed former Governor Al Smith announced that he was the president of a company that would build the highest building in the world—to be called the Empire State—on the site of the old Waldorf-Astoria Hotel between Thirty-third and Thirty-fourth streets on Fifth Avenue. Announcements of additional "world's tallest" building were quite common in New York before the full extent of the stock market crash was felt. Fred F. French talked of a 1,100 foot building on the site of the Hippodrome. Abraham Lefcourt, who had started his working life as a bootblack and had $25,000,000 worth of buildings going up at one time, promised one just as tall at the corner of Broadway and Forty-ninth Street. Irwin S. and Henry I. Chanin, sons of Russian immigrants, had already built the fifty-five-story Chanin Building and were looking for more space to conquer. "Higher and higher go the skyscrapers which make New York the structural wonder of the world," the *New York Evening Post* said in December 1929, "and architects hint that the only obstacles preventing them from scaling the Heavenly heights are lack of somebody else's money to build with, and a sufficiently large available site."

By 1930 the only obstacle was lack of money, anybody's money, and of all the promised giants, only the Empire State Building, 1,250 feet high, had been completed. For one thing, its financial backers were extremely wealthy and respected men. Pierre S. Du Pont, chairman of the board of E. I. du Pont de Nemours; John J. Raskob, financier and chairman of the Democratic National Committee; Louis G. Kaufman, president of the Chatham Phoenix National Bank; and Ellis P. Earle, president of the Nipissing Mines Company, were able to advance the estimated $25,000,000 needed above a $27,000,000 mortgage from the Metropolitan Life Insurance Company. As a result no public stock issue was necessary. (In time, Raskob bought most of the equity held by the others and at his death in 1950 owned nearly 95 per cent of the stock in Empire State, Inc.) Besides having money and access to more, the directors of the Empire State Building got under way before the crash, when few people doubted that American prosperity and buildings would ever stop rising.

On October 1, 1929, Smith, on the payroll for $50,000 a year, and his associates took part in the traditional ground-breaking ceremonies—in this case, token demolition of the old Waldorf-Astoria—and the huge project was under way. The site, once a farm which had been a disputed battlefield between Colonial and British troops during the Revolution, had been bought by William B. Astor in 1827. It remained in the Astor family, first for lavish homes, and later for the Hotels Waldorf and Astoria which were combined to become New York's most fashionable hotel. In 1928, the Bethlehem Engineering Company bought the property, and a year later sold it to the Empire State syndicate. By then the area was a prime one for commercial construction. It was two blocks from Pennsylvania Station and nine from Grand Central. Smith, acknowledging the influence of his friend Fred F. French, declared that the building would solve rather than create traffic problems, if residential housing were built nearby alongside the two rivers. "The solution," he said, "is in the building near the business centers of residential districts. This has been attempted in Tudor City. . . . It is better for health to walk five or ten blocks in the morning than to take a chance of life and limb in the subways."

With this rationale to reinforce a number of others the building started to rise on April 7, 1930, when the first steel columns were set. Twenty-five weeks later, nearly two weeks ahead of schedule, the last of some 60,000 tons of steel had been topped out on the eighty-sixth floor, and a flag unfurled to mark the event. Stone setting and outside wall construction moved at the rate of a story a day, and in one ten-day period during that triumphant September, fourteen upper floors were set. An average of 2,500 workmen were employed during construction, although 4,000 were on the job during its busiest day, and the payroll at its peak reached $250,000 a week. On May 1, 1931, nineteen months after the first wreckers tore into the Waldorf-Astoria, the Empire State Building was formally opened.

The event was appropriately dramatic. At 11:30 A.M., President Herbert Hoover paused on his way to a Cabinet meeting in the White House to press a button which turned on the lights of the building in New York. Immediately after that, Smith led some 350 guests to the eighty-sixth floor, where, the *New York Times* reported the next day, they "viewed Manhattan Island and the metropolitan area from a new pinnacle. Few failed to exclaim at the smallness of man and his handiwork as seen from this great distance. They saw men and motor cars creeping like insects through the streets; they saw elevated trains that looked like toys. 'There's Central Park, no bigger than a football gridiron,' exclaimed one spectator." Following a buffet luncheon, Smith, Governor Franklin Roosevelt and Mayor James Walker spoke glowingly of the achievement. Proper acknowledgment was made of all who had contributed to the building—the work crews; the architects, Shreve, Lamb and Harmon; the builders, Starrett Brothers and Eken, headed by Paul Starrett who had left Henry Black to start his own firm. Roosevelt evoked hearty laughter when he asked Smith "to reserve for me an office in this building so that when I leave Albany I will have someplace to go."

As things turned out Roosevelt found more substantial office space, but had he needed it in the Empire State Building he would have had no trouble at all, even without a reservation. The 2,000,000 square feet were far from fully rented in the depression years. Vacancies of as much as a third of the space were normal, and the phrase "Empty State Building" was common. A popular joke was that the building would be filled only when it was towed out to sea. If tenants were rare, visitors were not. In its first thirty years, 22,500,000 people visited its observatories on the eighty-sixth and 102nd floors, among them Winston Churchill, Pope Pius XII and Nikita Khrushchev. On clear days suburban Connecticut is visible, even without the telescopes that are available. With the telescopes, Bridgeport, sixty-four miles away, can be seen.

Since the depression, however, the question of vacancies has been less serious. There were 900 tenants in 1961, employing 16,000 people. The tenants have brought a sizable income to the four sets of men who have owned the Empire State Building over the years. In December 1951, a year after Raskob's death, a syndicate headed by Roger L. Stevens, Alfred R. Glancy, and Ben Tobin paid $50,000,000 for the building, a record price for the purchase of a single structure. Actually, their cost came to $1,500,000 more, to cover legal fees and a premium to the Metropolitan Life Insurance Company for paying off the outstanding mortgage which then stood at $15,000,000. A 24 per cent interest in the new company, known as the Empire State Building Corporation, was held by Henry Crown, a Chicago industrialist. In the next three years he bought additional shares as they were made available, and in October 1954 he became sole owner. The building was by then an exceedingly lucrative property. It was assessed by the city at $45,000,000 (taxes were paid at the rate of $35,000 for each million dollars of assessed valuation) and showed an income of nearly $7,000,000.

By the time the Empire State Building was sold again, in 1961, some $10,000,000 had been spent on improvements, and its annual income was estimated at $11,000,-000. This naturally caused another record to be broken; the purchase price this time was $65,000,000, and the deal was one of the most complex in real estate history. Lawrence A. Wien, a lawyer and the owner of a number of properties around the country, including at one time the Desert Inn at Las Vegas, headed the Empire State Associates, which bought the building from Crown. Wien, who had once come close to buying the Chrysler Building, negotiated for three years before the Empire State sale was final. And when he was through, he was not really the owner of the Empire State Building after all, but the holder of a 114-year lease on which he would pay rent of $3,220,000 a year for the first thirty years, and then, over four twenty-one-year renewal periods, diminishing amounts to an eventual $1,610,000 annually. This arrangement, called a sale-and-leaseback deal, was made when Empire State Associates sold the building to the Prudential Insurance Company of America almost immediately upon buying it. Prudential had owned the land on which the building stood since 1951, when it paid the Stevens-Crown syndicate $17,000,000 for it. The syndicate had needed that money to close their own purchase, and were willing to pay Prudential $1,020,000 in annual rent to get it.

A state law which limits to $50,000,000 the investments of insurance companies in any one property prevented Prudential from buying the building directly from Crown when he had it up for sale. Instead, the insurance company bought it from Wien's group for $29,000,000—giving it a total investment of $46,000,000, well under the legal limit. Prudential's total income from leasing the land and the building now comes to 7 per cent of its investment; when it owned the land alone its return was 6 per cent. For Wien and his group, the plan required a total of $68,-000,000, the extra $3,000,000 being fees and commissions. Of this, $29,000,000 was promised on the resale to Prudential, and from $26,000,000 to $39,000,000 through the sale of shares to the public, the final amount to be determined by the size of a mortgage Wien would raise on the lease. Thus, for $39,000,000, Empire State Associates in effect bought the right to pay rent for, and manage, the Empire State Building in a way designed to increase its $11,000,000-a-year income.

Each sale of the Empire State Building was page one news, of course. Over the years the building has made headlines in other ways, some amusing, some tragic. Early in its history, five members of the Polish Olympic ski team raced up the stairway from the fifth to the 102nd floor in twenty-one minutes. The Czechoslovakian ski team, which was also in town, immediately offered to better the time, but the building management decided to end sporting events on its stairs before anyone got hurt. During an elevator operators' strike in 1945, though, a lunch counter proprietor, making no effort toward a speed mark, carried 150 sandwiches and a container of coffee to a brokerage office on the thirty-first floor. His enterprise was rewarded with a $75 tip. There have been a few successful suicide attempts, and several more tries; the building management now has a suicide-proof fence around the observation platform. On July 8, 1945, a B-25 bomber crashed into the north side of the building between the seventy-eighth and seventy-ninth floors. Ten people, including three men in the plane, were killed, and twenty-five injured. The accident occurred on a foggy Saturday morning; the toll on a weekday would undoubtedly have been much higher. Damage to the building itself was slight, a tribute to the solidity of its construction.

The intensity of feeling that skyscrapers once aroused has abated in recent years, especially since the competition for "world's tallest" seems to have ended. When the debate raged it divided architects, real estate men, journalists and ordinary citizens. The effect of skyscrapers on traffic, the economy, people's souls and the beauty of cities has been the subjects of books, newspaper and magazine articles, after-dinner speeches, and radio talks. But the debate is not altogether dead, because tall buildings continue to rise, and continue to present the same problems that they did in Louis Sullivan's day, and when the Flatiron, Woolworth and Empire State buildings were built. Before he died, Frank Lloyd Wright, who once saw so much promise in Sullivan's "proud and soaring thing," had come to consider the skyscraper "one of the most abominable of man's inventions." Le Corbusier, one of the world's outstanding architects, made his first visit to New York in 1935. He saw nothing wrong with skyscrapers if they were built far apart from each other "so that the city would have space and light and air and order." In that event, he said, they could be even taller than they were, vastly taller than the Empire State Building. Thus, perhaps, they would come close to the Sullivan-Wright concept.

On February 13, 1949, the *New York Times* carried a brief dispatch from San Francisco. A. McF. McSweeney, identified as a local architect, had submitted to the Mayor a proposal for a mile-high building, big enough, the story said, to house half the city's population, overcome the school shortage and provide underground parking for 80,000 automobiles. Its 440 stories would have 100,000 apartments for 400,000 people, 1,000 stores and shops, fifty schools, fifty movie houses, fifty night clubs, twenty churches, ten hospitals, ten gymnasiums, and 10,000 offices. Movement would be facilitated by 300 elevators and a twenty-foot wide walk circling the interior of the building from the 2,300- to the 4,300-foot level. McSweeney thought he could swing the project for between four and seven billion dollars.

"It would be a landmark," the architect told the mayor.

"Ninety-nine per cent of the people
pray for us."

8

The Levitts and Their Towns

In 1947, two years after the end of World War II, the United States was going through the worst housing shortage in its history. The absence of all but essential military construction during the war years and the pent-up demand of veterans for homes of their own combined to create a need for 5,000,000 dwellings. By all the traditional principles of capitalism this situation should have brought an increase in home construction, competition in price and quality to win a share of that incredibly large market, steady employment for labor, profits for builders, contractors and suppliers, and, of course, places to live for those who needed them. No such thing happened. In the first five months of 1947, *Fortune* reported, "the [housing] industry showed no appreciable gain over 1946 except in the price of its product, which advanced enormously." There had been excuses for 1946—shortages of raw and finished materials and government interference. In 1947, there were no excuses. "Materials are comparatively plentiful," *Fortune* said, "government regulations are only a vestige—and the industry is perilously close to falling on its face." Fortune's editors expressed no surprise at this. Housing, which the magazine called "the industry capitalism forgot," was also an industry with no memory of its own. It had met a similar, though smaller-scale, housing shortage after World War I by raising the cost of five-room houses 40 per cent in less than twelve months, and did not relate this to a subsequent two-thirds drop in demand. With all the signs indicating that postwar history was about to repeat itself, the housing industry was desperately in need of a thorough shaking up if the United States was ever to get the houses its citizens required.

By the time the country was aware that something drastic had to be done—the word "revolution" was freely used in the press—William Jaird Levitt, a Long Island builder and a man who has hardly ever been accused of modesty, had decided that he was superbly qualified to reshape the American housing industry. He did so in a number of remarkable ways, and the results—a curse or a blessing; either position is tenable—have been permanent, which is more than can be said for most revolutions. Levitt, in his corporate capacity as Levitt & Sons, Inc., simply adapted to housing some of the principles of mass production used by other large industries. The results were not any more attractive than the Model T Fords, with which his conceptions have often been compared, but they filled a known, definite need, which put Levitt one up on Henry Ford, who had to create a market for his product. For the price of $7,990, or a rental of $65 a month, Levitt produced by the hundreds, and later by the thousands, houses with two bedrooms, a living room, a bathroom, and a kitchen equipped with steel cabinets, sink, stove, refrigerator and washing machine. He laid the houses out in rows on small

(229)

lots, and carved streets in front of them; the result was a suburb in the tradition of the Van Sweringens and Shaker Heights, but the community Levitt created was a new kind of suburb, as revolutionary in its own way as the houses he created. "The little Levitt house," one critic wrote, "is American suburbia reduced to its logical absurdity . . . it can be excused only by a shortage that should never have existed and the inability of an entire industry to reform itself."

Whatever critics have had to say about Levitt and his houses, that shortage and that inability were present when he started to operate. The nature of the building industry at that time was summed up best by the editors of *Fortune* in their lead article in August 1947. "Any industry that functions as badly as the housebuilding business," they said, "must have some really distinguished ailment. It has often been called a monopoly, which it is not. Every town, village and hamlet in the U. S. has at least one house-builder who is beholden to no one except God and an unbelievably inefficient system for building houses. Currently there are at least 100,000 of these entrepreneurs. But while the housing industry is subject to no general monopoly control, neither is it competitive. The individual builder produces an individualized product tailored either to the whim of a particular customer, or, if he is a speculative builder, to the demand of a limited clientele. The price, more often than not, is cost plus what the market will bear. The builder has nothing in common with the wheatgrower, the classical exemplar of pure competition, who supplies a homogeneous commodity to a nationwide market; and he has nothing in common with the automobile manufacturer, who must survive in a constant struggle to improve quality, add new gadgets, forecast the public taste in fenders, and outdo competitors in merchandising skill. In the world of housebuilding the terms competition and monopoly have no meaning. . . . Recognition of the feudal character of the housing industry is essential for understanding its sorry performance in the past and assessing its chances for improvement."

The feudalism of house building, which Levitt set about to destroy, was based on its historic ties to small-scale operations. Before the war, 60 per cent of all builders had built only one house a year, and another 26 per cent had built two. Although postwar builders had increased their output, conditions had not changed much. Builders still had no recourse but to watch production methods become increasingly inefficient; complain, but do nothing, about the delays of subcontractors or the demands of labor unions; and pay increasingly high prices for the materials that went into their structures. "The search for reform in the housebuilding business," *Fortune* concluded, "becomes primarily a search for large-scale operations. Efficient house production requires firms big enough to mobilize capital and organize production in systematic, repetitive operations. They must be big enough to assume full managerial responsibility instead of dividing it with subcontractors; to oppose strength to strength in dealing with labor; to buy supplies in quantity; to counter the rapacity of the suppliers of building materials; and to take the responsibility for making a fair price to the customer." William Levitt, who had reached the same conclusion, said it more simply: "Everything that is wrong with U. S. housing—high prices, slow production, labor troubles, archaic building codes—can be licked by size."

Levitt's company already had the size when he undertook large-scale housing. Actually, it was not an especially risky undertaking; despite the sharp break with past practice, the manufacture of housing on a large scale was a national necessity. "The dice," Levitt later said, "were loaded. We had known all along we could mass-produce houses if there was a market for them and credit for builders. Now the market was there and the Government was ready with the backing. How could we lose?" Levitt and Sons, Inc., had strong financial resources and experience. It had come into being because Abraham Levitt, its founder, a Brooklyn lawyer, had to foreclose mortgages on some Long Island real estate in the late 1920's. When one piece of property thus acquired remained unsold, Levitt and his two sons decided to build a house on it. William and Alfred Levitt had left New York University before acquiring degrees. "I got itchy," William has said. "I wanted to make a lot of money. I wanted a big car and a lot of clothes." If Alfred had similar ambitions, he did not mention them; he simply told the dean the place couldn't teach him anything more. Alfred designed the house for his father, even though, as Abraham Levitt said, he "loved to draw, but he didn't know what a two-by-four was." William was the salesman, and he not only loved to sell, he knew how. The house sold at a profit, thereby establishing Levitt and Sons as builders. During the next four years the company sold 600 houses, most of them in the $12,000 to $20,000 class. Its greatest prewar effort was a $10,500,000 development called Strathmore-at-Manhasset, Long Island, a traditional collection of some 500 homes—ranging in price from $10,000 to $18,500—a clubhouse, swimming pool and shopping center. The Levitts prospered, and by Pearl Harbor had built 2,000 more houses. The Levitts were by then among the largest home builders in the East, but still some years away from putting their size to the task that William Levitt was to create.

Experience in low-cost mass building came with the war. Levitt and Sons built 2,350 rental units for the Navy at its Norfolk, Virginia, base. The techniques the Levitts mastered on that job convinced them that low-cost mass-production housing was possible. But, as nearly everyone else at that time was forced to do, they had to postpone their plans. In 1943, William Levitt entered the Seabees as a lieutenant (j.g.), where he may have picked up some further ideas about construction. He himself discounts the possibility. "That little branch of the Navy that had the pleasure of my company learned much more about building from me than I did from them," he told a reporter after the war. Whatever the case in wartime, soon after Levitt's return to civilian life in 1945 the housing industry was to learn much more about building from him than he did from it.

In 1946 the Levitts built in the New York area about a thousand versions of a two-story, five-and-a-half-room structure with cellar and garage, to sell for slightly under $10,000. This was still not the low-priced, mass-produced house they had in mind; as they built these houses, however, the Levitts started to acquire property near Hicksville, Long Island. The land they bought had been potato fields, which before the war were selling for some $300 an acre but were now priced at $3,500 an acre. Nevertheless, the Levitts bought more than a thousand acres, while "the potato farmers," William Levitt said, "got rich off us." By 1947, when the American housing crisis had aroused the concern, not only of *Fortune*, which happened to articulate it better than most, but of the rest of the press, the Congress and the White House, to say nothing of the millions of families living in crowded or substandard quarters the Levitts were ready to unfurl their revolutionary flag over those potato fields.

By then, Levitt and Sons, Inc. had made some organizational changes. William Levitt, its president, who preferred to be called Bill, had at forty a brash self-confidence that was to confound his competitors, most of whom called it arrogance. He is five feet, eight inches tall, but invariably refers to his height as "nearly six feet," an understandable enough stretching of truth in keeping with his chosen role as salesman; he has also referred to his company as "the General Motors of the housing industry." One observer said at the time that "his wavy hair and mournful, wide-open eyes make him look like a tired Marx Brother turned master of ceremonies in a run-down night club," and this was accurate enough, if only to indicate that his energy lay below the surface. Alfred Levitt was vice-president in charge of production, which in 1947 meant supervision of a staff of some sixty engineers, project supervisors and salesmen. Abraham Levitt was director of landscaping and community planning, or, as a contemporary put it, "vice-president in charge of grass seed." Whatever Abraham contributed at this stage, the Levitt plan would succeed or fail on how Bill and Alfred Levitt organized construction. Because of the great demand for houses, nobody seemed very concerned with the nature of the product; it was just assumed, and properly as it turned out, that the four-and-a-half-room house the Levitts were about to put on the market could not miss at its price. Building these houses on the scale the Levitts envisioned called for financial resources denied most builders. The Levitts, however, had all the money they needed. The profits they had accumulated before the war at Strathmore, during the war at Norfolk, and since the end of the war with their $10,000 houses gave them a substantial base. The Levitts have never made their finances public, and so no precise figure on their 1947 position is available, but it was large enough to warrant the Bank of Manhattan Company's extending the firm a $7,000,000 line of credit. With money in the bank, a thousand or so acres on Long Island, a house at $7,990, and

Bill Levitt as chief salesman, Levitt and Sons was well armed for its initial assault on traditional building methods and, more than incidentally, on the wide-open market for houses.

Levittown, the development at Hicksville, Long Island, which the Levitts started to build in mid-1947, was at first called Island Trees, but that name did not last long enough to be remembered by any but local historians. The family name was invoked as "a monument for posterity," Levitt once explained; there is little likelihood that the name will be changed again. Bill Levitt was, in his own way, kind to the families who came to Levittown. While it is true that his simplified Cape Cod cottage—Cape Coddage was an early and obvious pun—would have sold before the war for half the price he was getting, it was still the biggest bargain on the housing market, selling for at least $1500 less than anything comparable. To keep the price down and yet show a profit on each house—the best guess is $1,000, although this, too, is a Levitt secret—was the object of the Levittown builders.

A bargain for the buyer and a profit for the seller called for exceedingly close attention to cost of both material and labor, a job to which Alfred Levitt devoted himself with assiduous effort. He learned it so well that he dismayed not only the traditional builders but also the builders of prefabricated houses, who felt that the real housing revolution would come only when houses were actually mass-produced in factories. Alfred Levitt accepted some of the principles of prefabrication—lumber pre-cut to size, modular units and factory-built window frames, for example—but since a third to a half of the man-hours on a house went into work on the site, he did not consider the factory-made house entirely practical. "Many more man-hours are put into a prefabricated house," he told a Massachusetts Institute of Technology housing conference a few years ago, "than when certain good truths of prefabrication are applied on the site. . . . You cannot prefabricate the site preparation, the paving of roads, the installation of sewers and storm drainage systems, underground electric lines, the planting of parks and the building of the town hall and the installation of swimming pools, all of which are necessary in building a community. . . . The superficial shell [of a house] doesn't take many man-hours."

Levitt's idea was basically sound; except for improved machinery the techniques have not changed since 1947. Mass housing construction depended on, among other things, a huge inventory of materials—which the Levitt finances permitted, of course—prepared in advance to Levitt specifications and brought to the home site on clockwork schedule. It did not depend, as did traditional home-building, on skilled labor. Because the lumber was pre-cut, on-the-site carpenters did not even have to know how to handle a saw; they merely hammered nails. The Levitts had broken down housebuilding into twenty-six operations, and hired subcontractors to carry them out. Their own staff remained small, and for the most part supervised the subcontractors. In time, workers doing the same job over and over increased their skills and speed despite the essential monotony; that kind of work "is boring, it is bad," Alfred Levitt has said, "but the reward of the green stuff seems to alleviate the boredom of the work."

When materials and workers met, the resulting rhythm of construction, while not exactly musical, was a pleasant sound to the Levitts. Houses did go up fast, first at the rate of sixty during a forty-hour work week, then a hundred, and finally more than a hundred and fifty. Within a year, the Levitts had built 4,000 houses, within three years nearly 11,000, and by November 1951, when their last one on the Hicksville site went up, exactly 17,442, giving Levittown a population of 75,000, about the same as Stamford, Connecticut, which had taken three hundred years to attain that size. The Levitt process fascinated the press. A *Time* reporter caught its essential features as he followed the trucks from the Levitt warehouse one day. "Every 100 feet," he wrote, "the trucks stopped and dumped identical bundles of lumber, pipes, bricks, shingles and copper tubing—all as neatly packaged as loaves from a bakery. Near the bundles, giant machines with an endless chain of buckets ate into the earth, taking just thirteen minutes to dig a narrow, four-foot trench around a 25-by-32-foot rectangle. Then came more trucks, loaded with cement, and laid a four-inch foundation for a house in the rectangle. After the machines came the men. On nearby slabs already dry, they worked in crews of two and three, laying bricks, raising studs, nailing lath, painting, sheathing, shingling. Each crew did its special job, then hurried on to the next site. Under the skilled combination of men and machines, new houses rose faster than Jack ever built them; a new one was finished every fifteen minutes."

This kind of efficiency did not come to the Levitts problem-free. Each step of the process, beginning with raw materials and ending with the completed house, required an unorthodox solution. To reduce the cost of lumber, the Levitts bought timberlands on the West Coast and a mill, the Grizzly Park Lumber Company, at Blue Lake, California. Owning their own trees and lumber mill not only gave the Levitts a guaranteed supply during shortages, but a saving of upward of 30 per cent in the cost of wood alone; further savings were obtained by having the lumber cut to the size needed by Levittown and shipped directly there. Since appliance manufacturers had never sold their products directly to home builders, but to distributors who sold them to wholesalers, who sold them to retailers—each taking a profit—the Levitts established their own wholesale supply house. With the North Shore Supply Company they eliminated one mark-up in price. They also decided that it was cheaper to make their own nails and concrete blocks than to buy them ready-made, and eventually they were making enough to sell to other builders. The Levitt system of subcontracting was as unprecedented as their purchasing methods. Plumbing, shingling, carpentering, cementing crews were hired by negotiation, not bidding. "My father always taught me," Bill Levitt said, "when you talk to a builder keep your hands in your pockets." Levitt improved on his father's advice by insisting that his own staff supervise the subcontracted work.

The men who performed the work itself gave the Levitts their major headaches. Building trades unions had over the years developed a series of practices and taboos which had raised the cost of housing. Many made sense, if only to maintain a decent income for workers in a seasonal and fluctuating industry; many were simply archaic habits or out and out feather-bedding devices. The Levitts bypassed the problem by not hiring union labor, and by using labor-saving equipment such as paint sprayers and automatic trowels, which union workers refused to handle. Although Bill Levitt has said, "I am not against unions. I just think we can build houses faster without them," the unions reacted as expected. Once the Levitt plant was picketed, at other times boycotts were tried, but efforts to unionize the Levitts failed, probably because they paid the prevailing wage scale, and all but guaranteed the kind of annual income that had been the unions' goal.

(238)

Whatever traditional builders or union leaders thought of the Levitt building methods, the finished houses at Levittown stood row on row to mock them. The home owners or renters, mostly war veterans and their families, had no sympathy for anyone trying to balk the Levitts. They were in homes of their own, most of them for the first time in their lives. If the original Levitt houses were small and, except for the five variations in exteriors, identical to those of their neighbors, this was still infinitely preferable to crowded city apartments. The sixty-by-hundred-foot lots on which the houses stood were already landscaped when the tenants moved in, and all they had to do was see that the lawn was mowed once a week in the summer (neglected lawns were mowed by Levitt employees and a bill sent to the laggard resident). By 1950 there were not only parks and playgrounds, but swimming pools and shopping centers as well. Levittown offered a new, and in many respects strange, way of life for its inhabitants. "Everyone is so young," one of them said, "that sometimes it's hard to re-member how to get along with older people." Outsiders were critical, snobbish, or both about Levittown. One Long Island dowager used to take her friends on rides through Levittown in a chauffeur-driven car to show "what Levitt has done for the poor people." One Levittown housewife reported that "whenever I tell people outside where I live I get the same old freeze. Some of them think that everyone who lives in Levittown is on relief." But there was little criticism within the community. A veteran who had come to Levittown from a one-room apartment said, "Getting into this house was like being emancipated." Bill Levitt, who preferred to deal in hyperbole, liked to say that "in Levittown 99 per cent of the people pray for us."

More to the point than the power of prayer was the political power of Levittown residents. Bill Levitt knew

(239)

that without the veterans, and the government's eagerness to help them get housing, there would have been no Levitt building revolution. Government-guaranteed mortgages made it easy for veterans to buy with little or no money down and thirty years to pay, which in turn made it easy for large builders to finance home construction. Veterans were also useful to Levitt beyond their basic role as customers. Once, when he wanted a revision in a local building code, he paid for a series of advertisements announcing a meeting for veterans who needed housing. To the hundreds who appeared he cited the building code as one reason for the housing lack, and in a short time the code was amended. Levitt acknowledged this debt to the veterans in a practical way. When Congress removed a veteran-priority clause from a housing bill, Levitt announced that veterans still came first at Levittown. "Too bad there aren't more men like Levitt & Sons," a veteran's wife wrote a Long Island paper. "I hope they make a whopper of a profit." If, as Eric Larrabee wrote in *Harper's Magazine*, Bill Levitt sometimes had a "dramatic air, as of one who had just turned a khaki handkerchief into the American flag," he could be forgiven. After all, he had provided housing where there had been none.

The Levitt Cape Cod house itself was no thing of beauty, which architects were quick to point out. Competitors talked about inferior work, green lumber and poor masonry, but these charges were simply untrue; the Levitt savings beyond those inherent in the construction methods did not derive from that kind of corner cutting. They came by omitting cellars, for instance; the houses were built on concrete slabs into which pipes for radiant heating were embedded. They came from making walls of rockboard instead of plaster, and the floors of asphalt tile instead of hardwood. The Levitts made a virtue of these changes by pointing out that they were part of the departure from tradition which made low-cost housing possible. For the most part, though, Levitt advertising stressed the extras, not inexpensive substitutes. The Bendix washing machine, which retailed at $229 and was included as standard equipment, was easily worth twice that in publicity and sales appeal. "A dream house," Bill Levitt once wrote for a General Electric advertisement, "is a house the buyer and his family will want to live in a long time . . . an electric kitchen-laundry is the one big item that gives the homeowner all the advantages and conveniences that make his home truly livable." Although the fully equipped kitchen remained an important sales point, Bill Levitt moved on to more striking extras when he introduced his 1950-model house to Levittown. It was of ranch-style design, but, of special interest to prospective buyers, it came equipped with a television set—and sold for the same price as the earlier models. Although there was a general easing in the housing shortage and sharper competition from builders who were imitating many of the Levitt methods, the 1950 houses were quickly sold.

Despite the model changes at Levittown (there had been one in 1949 and the last one was in 1951), the houses were still in large clusters of sameness which, with their proximity, caused some critics to say that they formed the nucleus for the "slum of the future." In 1962, fifteen years after the Levitts started their development, there were fewer indications that Levittown was headed for the slums than at any time in its history. Part of this is due to the original concept. Like the Van Sweringens, the Levitts eschewed the gridiron street pattern. The curvilinear streets were not only more attractive, they added a safety factor; four-way intersections were kept to a minimum. The landscaping for each house gave residents a base from which to apply their own horticultural imagination. The

Levitts' insistence that the houses be set back from the street at varying distances reduced the monotonous effect of row houses. Although there must have been at the start for many veterans a sense of the barracks they had left behind, this effect has vanished as trees and shrubs have grown and as individual owners have altered the outside appearance of their homes. Far from decreasing in value, the Levittown houses have over the years brought comparatively high prices when resold. The $7,990 Cape Cod cottages and the later ranch-style houses have brought from $10,000 to $12,000, and, depending upon internal and external improvements, as much as $20,000; these are obviously not slum prices.

Levittown's potential as a slum has rarely been discussed in recent years. Instead there has been an increasing tendency by social scientists to worry about what Levittown —and by extension all the other postwar package suburbs —does to its inhabitants. This speculation started early for Levittown, since it was the pioneer on the new suburban frontier. "A community that, by nature, is limited to families of the same generation from the same financial bracket, is potentially a monster," an early observer wrote in 1948. "The community that Bill Levitt has fastened onto the Long Island soil is of the most class-stratifying sort possible." Criticism of the way Americans live is not particularly new, and it was not strange that after the war the suburbs should have been the subject of studies, novels, plays and movies. "In the days of Lincoln Steffens and later," David Riesman wrote in an essay entitled "The Suburban Sadness," "people emphasized the 'shame of the cities,' and in the Twenties major novelists emphasized the constraints of small-town and occasionally of small-suburban life. Today, the comparable worry, in the books dealing with the suburbs, is conformity: writers point to the uniformity of the ranch style, the everpresent television antennae, the lamp in the picture-window (which usually provides a view of the nearly treeless street, the cars and someone else's picture window). Observers have been struck by a kind of massification of men in Levittown and other housing developments such as was once postulated for the endless residential blocks of the cities created by the industrial revolution."

Whereas criticism of this sort in the past has often offended its targets—most small-town residents were not amused by *Main Street* or *Winesburg, Ohio*—a good many suburbanites today seem to enjoy the analyses. In *The Organization Man*, William H. Whyte, Jr., noticed this phenomenon in studies he had made of the new package suburbs, which he called "not merely great conglomerations of mass housing [but] . . . a new social institution." The residents, he wrote, are well aware of their communal way of life, and "are of many minds how to describe it. Sometimes they lean to analogies like the frontier, or the early colonial settlements. Other times they are a little wry: 'sorority house with kids,' a projection of dormitory life into adulthood, or, slightly better, a lay version of Army-post life. But no matter how sharp the coinages—'a womb with a view,' 'a Russia, only with money'—it is a way of life they find suited to their wants, their needs, and their times. They are not unwitting pawns; educated to be more aware of social trends than their forebears, they discuss their situations with considerable sophistication; at times, the way they casually toss out words like 'permissive' and 'kid-centered,' it almost seems as if everyone was his own resident sociologist."

Oddly enough, although Levittown, New York, once symbolized the "homogenized" suburb at its worst—in 1950, few of its 40,000 residents were older than thirty-five and less than 900 of its 8,000 children were more than seven—it has escaped the harshest of the recent criticism. "The Levittowns," wrote William M. Dobriner of Hofstra College in *The Suburban Community*, "with their fusion of working-class and middle-class elements, do not fit the generalizations founded on research in the upper-middle-class suburbs. Life styles on a single Levittown street may range from those of a second generation, working class, ex-Brooklynite of Italian 'extraction' to those of a struggling young executive of 'The Organization,' to those of a medical intern from an 'upper upper' New England family who is completing his residence at a local hospital. . . . The Levittowns . . . are characterized by a considerably greater class spectrum and consequently its life styles almost defy generalization." Dobriner, a resident of Levittown at the time he wrote in 1958, reported a definite change in the community over the years. Where there had once been "intensive neighboring" based on sharing the new experience of founding a neighborhood, "as families moved away and new ones took their place, the early solidarity and spontaneous cliquing gave way to greater formality and social insulation." Levittown, he said, had turned into a great "horizontalized" apartment house, with much the same features of anonymity and groupings found in the vertical apartment houses in the city.

It is likely that the social scientists will continue to assess Levittown, although one has suggested that "the final judgment . . . will come from an analysis of the children produced [there], since these offspring are the only homogeneous element present in places like Levittown." Whatever that final judgment may be, future historians may find it noteworthy, or at least footnote worthy, that the creators of Levittown did not see their development as leading to a new way in American life, but as returning to an old one.

As chief salesman, Bill Levitt revived the American notion
—all but dead during the depression—that one of the major
goals of life was a home of one's own on ground of one's
own. It is ironic that what may once have been an expression of individualism has now become a symbol of conformity. But the Levitts cannot be blamed for that. To break
down the archaic structure of the building industry meant
using the techniques of mass production. Succeeding in
this—a considerable achievement by any measure—also
meant accepting the major drawback of mass production,
which too often is monotony and mediocrity, whether in
homes, automobiles or frozen foods.

The Levitts were conscious of, although not particularly disturbed by, the monotony they had established on
Long Island. They are pragmatic men, and building houses
quickly and cheaply was their prime consideration. In 1951,
though, when the Levitts announced a new project—another Levittown, this time in Bucks County, Pennsylvania
—Alfred Levitt added that "this will be the least monotonous mass-housing group ever planned in America." The
new city, which eventually contained more than 17,000
homes, was also, the Levitts said, to be "the most perfectly
planned community in America." Making the usual allowances for Levitt exaggeration, Levittown, Pennsylvania,
was planned as a significant and bold step toward consoli-
dating the revolution in house building. It would apply the
Levitt techniques to high-priced houses as well as low-
priced ones. In Levittown, Pennsylvania, the price range
was to be from $10,000 to $18,000 a house, which would
require standards of quality superior to those on Long Island. The Levitts, who felt that they had been improving
their product since they first introduced it, had no doubts

that Levittown II, as *House and Home* called it, would confirm their company's position as the nation's leading home builder.

By the fall of 1952, when Levittown II had progressed far enough for an appraisal to be made, reaction to it could not have been better phrased if the Levitts had written the notices themselves. *House and Home* sent reporters and photographers to the scene of the new city and concluded that "nothing like it has ever happened before. This is the free enterprise system at its lustiest." *Fortune* said that "a good case can be made for the proposition that the best thing that has happened to the housing industry in this century is Levitt & Sons, Inc., builders, of Manhasset, Long Island." Good things had happened to the Levitts, too; in five years the company had built houses worth some $170,-000,000 and was now in a position to start a development worth $200,000,000. In addition to the corporation's huge profits, Bill and Alfred Levitt were each drawing salaries of $150,000 a year, and father Abraham $60,000; from the California timber forests and other sources the brothers drew another $150,000 each; and in 1950 they sold the last 4,028 rental houses at Levittown I to a company for $5,150,000 beyond their mortgage values. The Levitts also had the satisfaction of knowing that their influence was felt wherever houses were being built. Three years after they set their houses on radiantly heated concrete slabs, 25 per cent of all new American houses had been built on slabs. After the Levitts put the kitchen of their 1949 model in the front of the house and the living room in the back, thousands of home builders made the same switch. Throughout the country, as developments mushroomed around cities, the houses in them bore startling resemblance to the Levitt prototypes on Long Island.

Flattering as the imitations were, the Levitts were not

disposed to rest on past performance. By the time they invaded the Pennsylvania countryside they had made many improvements in their building techniques and had found ways to provide more housing per dollar. When most new houses were selling for $12 to $15 a square foot, Levitt houses were selling for $10, a remarkable figure in view of increased costs. What is more, their houses were generally acknowledged to have "better exterior design, better interior design, more mechanical improvements, and more all-around merchandise appeal" than any other commercial houses of their price. With this kind of reputation the Levitts knew they could sell their houses; the question in Pennsylvania was whether they could sell the idea of their city. It presented problems that had never come up on Long Island. "In Levittown I," said *House and Home,* "the Levitts didn't know their own strength. They bought land in relatively small parcels and gradually built a town. Of necessity the town grew irregularly, streets were sometimes a maze, commercial areas were located by chance." Levittown II had to be designed down to the last of its 250,000 trees and shrubs. Although fewer houses were involved than at Levittown I, the new project was more intricate, and decidedly more ambitious than the first.

The new city was an outgrowth of the industrial expansion of Bucks County. United States Steel Corporation had built its new Fairless Works in Morrisville, three miles from the Levittown site, and predictions were that new industries would bring more than 100,000 workers into the area. To provide for the home buyers among them, the Levitts had divided their 5,000 acres into eight master blocks, each about one square mile, a fifty-five-acre shopping center, and special areas for light industry. Each master block was to have a school, churches, recreation areas and a swimming pool. The blocks themselves were to be further divided into three or four "neighborhoods" of 400 to 600 families each.

Through roads were built to keep heavy traffic away from the houses, and for the houses themselves to be within walking distance of the schools. In addition to the $20,000,-000 shopping center, which was to have a special building for doctors, dentists and lawyers, each neighborhood was to have small groups of food, drug and service stores. Throughout, the landscaping skills of Abraham Levitt were to create the sense of a city that had grown naturally; about $8,000,000, an average of $500 per house, had been allocated for shade trees, fruit trees and evergreens. Each lot would contain six four-foot-high evergreens, one apple, one peach and one pear tree, and a grape vine. "The magnificence of father's planting is not to be put in words," Alfred said of this arrangement. The planting was also considered good business. "In the Thirties," Alfred recalled, "father was the one who had the foresight to realize that by intelligent landscaping the normal depreciation of our houses could be offset." The remarkable planning of a brand-new community was most evident in the Levitt building operation itself. When it got under way, the flow of materials to each lot was so smooth that eight pounds of yellow nails were in front of every seventh house on time; every seventh house was faced with yellow siding.

Despite their acute foresight, in what a television commentator called "the biggest planned community since the Continental Congress invited L'Enfant to plan Washington, D. C.," the Levitts could not plan for every contingency. Housing codes and regulations are strictly interpreted in Pennsylvania; as a result, Bill Levitt estimated that the cost per house there came to $500 more than had been anticipated. A rule on shingles forced the Levitts to increase by 25 per cent the manpower and materials needed to finish a roof. A state agency insisted that concrete slabs be cured for twenty-eight days. Since the Levitts were turning out forty a day this would have called for an inventory of 1,120 slabs. After a number of heated discussions, the agency reduced the period to fourteen days, and finally agreed on seven. Organized labor harassed Levitt briefly, just as it had on Long Island. A picket line, set up across the main entrance of the development, was manned by 300 workers from the Buildings Trades Council of Philadelphia. Their complaints were familiar to the Levitts; they were not using union labor, skilled mechanics were performing jobs which cut across craft lines and thus were violating union rules, and many workers were paid on a piece-work instead of an hourly basis. The Levitts responded by getting a county court injunction against the pickets. When the pickets continued to march in the face of this, the governor called on the state police to "provide whatever assistance is needed" to preserve order. There was no violence, and eventually the pickets dispersed; the Levitts continued as always to build houses without union labor.

One matter the Levitts had neglected in their meticulous planning did not become a problem until Levittown II was all but completed. It involved housing for Negroes, and when it erupted in 1957 it did so with all the ugliness usually associated with desegregation conflicts in the South. Bill Levitt had never made any secret of how he stood on the question of housing for Negroes in his development; it was simply that he was a builder, not a social reformer. On Long Island the original contracts had read, "No dwelling shall be used or occupied by members of other than the Caucasian race, but the employment and maintenance of other than Caucasian domestic servants shall be permitted." Until 1948 such clauses were not illegal, even when government funds, as represented by the Federal

Housing Agency, were involved. It had been the F.H.A.'s policy to reject mortgages involving "incompatible racial elements." When the Supreme Court ruled against racial covenants, the F.H.A. changed its policy. In time, and with some friction, Negroes had bought homes in Levittown, New York, although not more than three families were known to be there as late as 1958. Bill Levitt himself has said that "the plain fact is that most whites prefer not to live in mixed communities. This attitude may be wrong morally, and some day it may change. I hope it will." Hopes aside, Levitt had no intention of encouraging the change. He could not insert a racial covenant in Pennsylvania leases, but there was never any question that Levittown II was to be a white community. A reporter who stopped at a Levittown office in 1952 to apply for a house told the salesman, "There's something I want to ask you about that's very important to me." The salesman was reassuring. "You mean the talk that's going around about colored people living here?" he asked. "Listen, this is the point of sale— strictly between you and me—and believe me, we sell to whites only, mister."

Five years later, Levittown, Pennsylvania, had its first Negro family, and the kind of national attention surburban communities dislike. The house that William E. Myers, Jr., a refrigeration engineer, bought at 43 Deepgreen Lane in the Dogwood Hollow section of Levittown, had belonged originally to Irvin Mandel, who paid $12,000 for it in 1953. Before Mandel moved out in 1955 he had added a third bedroom and a garage. With the Levitts still building houses—with added features, and often smaller down payments—used houses were not selling well in Levittown II. Finally, in April 1957, Mandel found his buyer; Myers, whose wife was expecting a third child, needed a larger house than the one he was living in at Bloomsdale Gardens, an integrated community not far from Levittown. Mandel and Myers settled at $12,150, with Myers paying $3,150 in cash and taking over Mandel's mortgage. On August 11 the Myers family moved in, and started to clean up their new house. The next day rumors began to spread in Dogwood Hollow; the Negroes on Deepgreen Lane were not a painter and a maid, as some people said, but new residents. The next morning, a crowd began to gather in front of the Myers home. By early evening the street was filled with cars, by ten a mob had formed on the sidewalk. Screamed insults filled the night air, and at midnight two rocks shattered the Myerses' picture window. "The most perfectly planned community in America" was in trouble.

For eight nights the howling mob surrounded the Myers house. Township police and state troopers tried to keep the crowds under control, and after a fashion maintained order. They could not, of course, control the surliness or the comments from the mob. "He's probably a nice guy," said one of the neighbors, "but every time I look at him I see $2,000 drop off the value of my house." Inside their home the beleaguered Myers family remained as calm as possible under the circumstances. As soon as the trouble started Mr. and Mrs. Myers had sent their older children to stay with Mr. Myers' parents, keeping their five-week-old daughter with them. They were not completely alone. The Myerses' next-door neighbors, Mr. and Mrs. Lew Wechsler, were sympathetic, and stayed with them much of the time. On the eighth night of the siege, a rock knocked a local policeman unconscious; only then did the state troopers disperse the mob. This was not the end of the harassment for the Myers family, however. A Levittown Betterment Committee was formed by James E. Newell, a native of Durham, North Carolina, to keep up the campaign against the Myers family; at one point its executive committee voted to seek

(251)

help from the Ku Klux Klan. Outside help hardly seemed necessary. A cross was set on fire on the Wechsler lawn and another outside the home of a Quaker family which had also been friendly to the Negroes. During the day, members of the Betterment Committee walked dogs whom they called "Nigger" in loud voices down Deepgreen Lane. Telephone threats came to the Myerses throughout the day and into the early morning hours, a pharmacist would not deliver medicine to them because his driver was frightened, tradesmen who did serve them were threatened with boycotts, their fire insurance was canceled because of the risk, and, despite the police guard, a red-painted KKK was painted on the Wechsler house.

Myers continued to work through this ordeal, while white friends took turns in his house with his wife and children. Soon a Citizens' Committee for Levittown, headed by the Reverend Ray L. Harwick, an Evangelical and Reformed minister, formed in opposition to the anti-Myers group. "I heard the hate forces talk," Harwick said, "and it was very frightening. There was so much hate there was no question that somebody had to do something. I couldn't look the other way." Harwick's group helped rally support for the Myers family, but the opposition was still strong. A vacant house behind the Myers house became the headquarters for the anti-Negro group. A Confederate flag was raised from its roof and "Old Man River" was repeatedly and loudly played on a phonograph. At this point Myers turned to State Attorney General Thomas D. McBride, who got the Bucks County Court to issue an injunction to prevent further harassment. Only then did the open expressions against the Myers family stop. Since that time, the Myers family has been permitted to live, if not altogether happily, at least quietly. "We will be good neighbors," Myers said, "and I hope those around us will be the same." The follow-

(252)

ing June another Negro family moved into Levittown. There were no incidents. Levittown had returned to suburban calm.

Racial strife in Levittown was not the way the Levitts would have chosen to celebrate the tenth anniversary of their housing revolution. It was, however, the only bad publicity associated with their name in that period, and except for some who blamed the mob scenes around the Myers house on the Levitts' white-only sales policy, nobody held them responsible for the actions of excitable home owners. In 1958, Levitt and Sons was still "the best known name in homebuilding," and continued to dominate the industry. That year, the Levitts were working on the last group of houses in Levittown, Pennsylvania, and were planning Levittown, New Jersey. The announcement of Levittown III brought the inevitable joke that the Levitts would not be happy until they had a Levittown in every state, and the fact that they inspired humor was as good a sign of the Levitts' success as the sale of their houses.

Levittown III, projected at 15,000 houses, lies between Camden and Trenton not far from the Delaware River. Twelve years after the war, costs had risen, and home buyers were looking for more space than they had in the past; four-bedroom houses were in great demand as families got larger. Levitt houses were selling for more than they had in the past, but when measured by the builder's yardstick of square feet per dollar they were actually cheaper than the houses on Long Island. As usual, Bill Levitt also managed to offer the extras which gave his salesmen an advantage over their competitors. The biggest extra at Levittown III was probably Levitt's best-selling device since the Bendix washing machine; he was in effect giving away a school with every purchase. He proposed to build a school building—which would also double as a community building—in each self-contained neighborhood. This, as every prospective home buyer knew—or was told by Levitt salesmen—would free residents of the inevitable taxes for new school construction. As Levitt explained it, he was going to build "millions of dollars worth" of public schools and "turn them over to the school board lock, stock and barrel." The school would be at the center of each Levitt neighborhood of 1,200 to 1,500 homes, an idea which had not been fully realized in Levittown II. Around it, Levitt planned the by now expected amenities of his cities—swimming pool, park, playground. Most of what Levitt had in mind was possible because Levittown III was within the single township of Willingboro, whose officials accepted as the town building code the minimum standards of the F.H.A. This gave Levitt a freedom he had not had in the past, when he was often hampered by a wide variety of local building codes, many of which he considered antiquated, if not downright discouraging to his kind of home building.

Levittown III, which had over 5,000 homes in 1962, is the last of the city-size communities the Levitts have undertaken. In October 1960, Belair, Maryland, outside Washington, D. C., was opened to the public; when completed it will contain 4,500 houses. The following year the Levitts opened Strathmore, at Matawan in New Jersey, a few miles south of Staten Island, New York; it called for 1,300 houses. If Bill Levitt surprised the trade by cutting the size of his projects, he also surprised the public by discontinuing the Levittown designation. There were good reasons for both decisions. Belair was a name with a fine tradition and was almost a synonym for Maryland thoroughbred horses; Nashua and Gallant Fox had been developed at Belair Farm. Perpetuation of its name had more publicity value than a repetition of Levittown. New Jersey was another matter; a second Levittown in the same state would have been troublesome, so Levitt revived the name that he, his brother and his father had used in their largest prewar development on Long Island. The reduction in the size of the new developments resulted from a decision by Levitt to spread his total production over a wider geographical area. He wanted to build, he said, "Anywhere and everywhere there is substantial demand, available land, and the opportunity to make money."

In 1962 it was evident that "anywhere and everywhere" was not limited to the United States, as it was most likely interpreted. That year, Bill Levitt started construction of two apartment house developments in Paris—one of 200 units at the Rue de la Croix-Livert and Rue de la Courbe, south of the Eiffel Tower, and another of 180 units on the Rue de Versailles in St. Cloud, just outside the city. At the same time he opened negotiations with the French government for permission to build a housing development on land just beyond Paris. Because of his construction methods, he told the French, he had to build a minimum of 1,000 houses to get the most economical results. The developments would, of course, have schools, shopping centers and playgrounds as well as park areas. As for the houses, they would be almost identical to those Levitt had been building in the United States and would naturally come with a fully equipped kitchen. Levitt, the *New York Times* said, "believes that home buyer tastes do not differ from country to country." Acting on that principle, Levitt was also studying the possibility of suburban development near Bordeaux, Lyons and Marseilles as well as in northern Italy, West Germany and England.

If all these plans are carried out, and in view of the Levitt record there is no reason to doubt that they will be, they would represent the greatest American commercial triumph abroad since Coca-Cola. The housing shortage in much of Western Europe is so monumental that Levitt may well face less resistance than the soft drink which was once equated with American imperialism and led to charges that Europe was being cocacolonized. A Europe that has already accepted supermarkets, snack bars and frozen foods is probably ready for the package suburb. The only sacrifice Levitt may have to make is in pride of authorship. Frenchmen are not likely to take kindly to Levittown-sur-Seine, Germans to Levittown-am-Rhein, or Englishmen to Levittown-by-the-Thames.

"I'd rather be alive at 18 per cent than dead at the prime rate."

9

William Zeckendorf's
Many-Splendored Cities

The failure of history to accommodate itself into neat packages—few people believe that it really repeats itself, for example—makes it all the more remarkable that the story of American real estate does begin with A, for Astor, John Jacob, and is currently at Z, for Zeckendorf, William, and, to tie it nicely, that Z leapfrogged to the head of the class because of his adroit direction in the twentieth century of properties which A had carefully assembled in the nineteenth. The strange circumstance of a non-Astor's involvement in the Astor Estate was a result of World War II, which, among other dislocations, took Vincent Astor, the great-great-grandson of John Jacob, from his properties in New York to duty as a commander in the United States Navy. Because of an old friendship with a man named Eliot Cross, Astor turned the management of his $50,000,000 portfolio over to the real estate firm of Webb & Knapp, of which Cross was a founding member and Zeckendorf its newest associate. What with Cross being ill and the firm's three other senior members off to the war, it fell to Zeckendorf to handle the Astor properties. In 1946, after four years of supervision, Zeckendorf returned the package with its value increased somewhere between $5,000,000 and $15,000,000; the variation exists because the lower estimate comes from conservative sources, the higher from Zeckendorf. In either case, the sum is tidy, and would certainly have pleased John Jacob himself. Aside from the $1,-500,000 in fees which Webb & Knapp received for its services, Zeckendorf benefited from the publicity which accrued when his name was linked with that of Astor nearly every time a deal was made. Since some hundred and fifty deals were consummated in the course of his stewardship, Zeckendorf came in for considerable public exposure and gained a reputation for superior intelligence in the handling of property. This, when added to his considerable talent and his flair for the imaginative and headline-provoking deal, very quickly made him just about the best-known name in American real estate. He still is, and despite failures as monumental as his successes, he is undeniably the spiritual heir of John Jacob Astor.

As far as anyone can tell Zeckendorf carries his historical responsibility lightly, since he is invariably engrossed in the deal, or deals, at hand. These use up nearly all of his waking hours, because Zeckendorf is apparently most at ease when deals are the most complicated; many of his are beyond the ken of his business contemporaries, let alone laymen. In fact, some of Zeckendorf's associates believe that he prefers an intricate deal with a small profit to a simple one with a large profit, but some of his profit figures bely this. What is more likely is that he enjoys complicating a transaction in order to get greater profit out of it; in the course of doing this he behaves in much the same way a grand master in chess does, planning his forthcoming moves, weighing his opponent's possibilities, and simultaneously keeping the whole chess board clearly in mind. Zeckendorf once explained the moves to checkmate in what was for him a relatively routine game. "We had a property in Detroit that cost $100,000," he told *Life*. "It didn't look like it was going to make any money. So we swapped it for another piece in Brooklyn and a second one in Camden, N. J., and took on a $60,000 mortgage. We exchanged the mortgage for a building in Rockland, Mass. Then we sold that for $60,000. We still weren't getting anywhere. So I gave the Camden property and $80,000 for a piece in Trenton, N. J. We raised a $100,000 mortgage on that and about the same time sold the Brooklyn piece for $77,000. Then we got out of the Trenton deal for $30,000 and a building on 161st Street, Manhattan, and sold that for $20,000 and finally we had the Detroit turkey off our hands and $50,000 in the bank. Simple."

This simple transaction can be dated by students of Zeckendorf's career as belonging to his early, or pre-million, period, which ended when he finished his chore for Astor and embarked on buying sprees on behalf of Webb & Knapp itself. Although Zeckendorf completed a number of important transactions within a short period in 1946 and 1947, the one which brought him the greatest pleasure and fame, although not the greatest profit, was assembling the East Side New York properties which are today the site of the United Nations. In his autobiography in Who's Who he lists "purchaser of land of new United Nations site, N. Y. City" as the achievement for which he seemingly would most like to be remembered. Sentiment aside, it was an amazing performance by any standards. The land east of First Avenue from Forty-second Street to Forty-ninth Street was the slaughterhouse district of New York. Fred F. French built

Tudor City opposite some of the abattoirs, and came as close as he could to them without running the risk of the stench pervading every apartment. For years, especially after French's pioneering and the growth of the Grand Central area into an important business district, real estate men looked longingly at the land under the slaughterhouses. Long before 1946 they had become a standing joke, a symbol of the unattainable in New York. Zeckendorf recalled being told early in his career that the slaughterhouses would never be sold because it was unlikely that the city would ever again give a franchise for that kind of building use, and Swift and Wilson, the meat packers, did not want to leave Manhattan. This did not prevent dealers from offering the property from time to time, finding willing buyers, hoping to convince the packers to sell, but always being unable to deliver.

Early in 1946 Zeckendorf received a call from a broker who offered him the slaughterhouses. Having wasted enough time on that problem before, Zeckendorf referred the man to an associate. Some years later Zeckendorf recalled with considerable clarity the chain of events which followed that visit. The man to whom he sent the broker stopped at Zeckendorf's desk.

"I presume you gave him the usual brushoff," Zeckendorf said.

"Yes, sure, nothing to it," his associate said. "By the way, he said he was related to the Swifts."

"Are you sure?" Zeckendorf asked. "Let's get him back here."

The broker returned, and when bluntly asked what made him think he could deliver the slaughterhouses replied that "my daughter is the sole heir to the Swift fortune and I think I can do it." Whereupon Zeckendorf opened negotiations with the time-honored question: "What do you want for them?" Swift and Wilson, the broker explained, had pooled their properties and were willing to sell their total holdings in one package for $17 a square foot. This price, which would bring the total sales figure to $6,000,-000, was decidedly disproportionate to the land just beyond the slaughterhouses, which could be bought for $5 and less a square foot. Zeckendorf told the broker so, but merely received the reply, "I know it's a ridiculous price but that is what they want."

Confronted with a price which left no room for bargaining, Zeckendorf retired for thought and consultation with his partners, in the course of which he developed a line of reasoning which goes a long way toward explaining his standing among real estate men: he thought of the value of the area without the slaughterhouses. "Here is the greatest opportunity that I have ever seen in my life," he later recalled telling his partners, "and I never expect to see one like it again. Regardless of whether the properties are selling for $5 per foot, $1 per foot, half a dollar per foot, around this area that they want $17 per foot for, that has nothing to do with it. The only reason they are selling for $4 a foot or $5 a foot is because the slaughterhouses are here. If you can think in *pro forma* terms of X, the slaughterhouses, there is no excuse for the $5 land and there is no excuse for the $17 land. The whole thing is worth $50. By eliminating the abomination you can pull the whole thing up by its own bootstraps." This, Zeckendorf later told an audience at the Harvard School of Design, was "a very simple rule of real estate economics. It was so centrally located, with the site and size and dimensions of the property such that there were limitless potentials. Regardless of whether you could see them all the way through to the end at first view, you knew that they were there. 'Therefore,' I said, 'I advocate buying the property for $17 a foot.' Which we did. We also bought the $5 land. We bought some land for less, some for as little as $1 a foot."

The accumulation of the land bordering the slaughter-houses was not quite so simple as Zeckendorf made out. He paid a million-dollar deposit for the slaughterhouses and tried to keep that deal and the purchases which followed secret, so that prices would not rise. Secrecy was difficult, even though Zeckendorf used brokers never before employed by Webb & Knapp to do most of the negotiating, and at one point took off for a month in South America just to keep his own role from being discovered. Although he picked up many parcels at bargain prices—seventy-five separate deals were made, including one that took an agent to Rio de Janeiro—Zeckendorf did have to meet some stiff demands; in retrospect even these were bargains. "There was one fellow, an Italian," Zeckendorf recalled, "who had put his life savings into a purchase for $10,000 of the only outstanding property on the east side of First Avenue that did not belong to the slaughterhouses. That was the northeast corner of Forty-second Street. Fifty by one hundred— $10,000. That is $2 per foot. We sent the broker over to buy the property, and his wife said she wouldn't sell it for less than $12,000. We okayed that, but the broker came back and said, 'Wife wants thirteen!' I said, 'Buy it.' This little dialogue went on between the broker and wife until finally we paid her $100,000." Zeckendorf had no regrets. When he recalled this incident several years later, he concluded the account with, "And that piece of real estate today would be worth a minimum of $500,000. A minimum! It would be a bargain at that price."

Having gathered his bargains, Zeckendorf proceeded to announce plans for the property which, even more than the acquisition itself, indicated the kind of imagination—or sense of publicity values—he could apply to property. His starting point was the same as French's: New York's traffic. The city, said Zeckendorf, "is choking to death." To let it breathe, Zeckendorf outlined plans for something he called X City, a name which by itself intrigued headline writers, and may have evolved from his earlier equation in which he permitted X to equal the slaughterhouses. X City was to rise on a forty-foot foundation on which were to be built a fifty-seven-story office building, four forty-story office buildings, three thirty-story apartment houses, a convention hall to seat 6,000, a 6,000-room hotel, an opera house *and* a concert hall, a yacht basin on the river, a helicopter landing field on rooftops, and parking space beneath the city for 5,000 cars. Zeckendorf budgeted X City at $150,000,000, and sat back to wait for the tenants to come flocking. There was more publicity than tenants, although the project was considerably more modest than an earlier plan of Zeckendorf's to convert 144 square blocks on the West Side into one vast rooftop airport at a cost of $3,-000,000,000. Newspapers and magazines displayed Zeckendorf's plans—he did own the land for X City, which made it a decidedly more likely prospect than his earlier proposal —and Zeckendorf himself became as familiar a figure in the press as a major league baseball player.

X City was never realized, however; it gave way to a good cause and even better publicity. A few months after Zeckendorf released his plans, he read in the papers at breakfast that the United Nations site selection committee had decided to pick Philadelphia as its home because Flushing Meadows, which New York had offered, was unsuitable; that the residents of the Westchester-Greenwich suburban area, which the committee liked, had been unreceptive; and the Russians had said no "first-class" diplomat would go to San Francisco. This news nettled Zeckendorf, who was born in Illinois and, like many non-natives, had become a

New York chauvinist once he made his home there. He turned from his paper to Mrs. Zeckendorf and announced, "I'm going to put those birds on a platform." She asked, "What birds on what platform?" To which Zeckendorf replied, "Those U.N. birds on the platform on the East River." He promptly called Mayor O'Dwyer and, after being assured that His Honor did want the United Nations in the city, said, "Put this down. I'll offer you seventeen acres of land on the East River from Forty-second Street north at any price the United Nations wish to pay. That will be their new home."

O'Dwyer passed the offer along to the site committee, among whose members were Wallace K. Harrison, who had designed X City, and Nelson Rockefeller, later governor of New York. Rockefeller was impressed and called his father John D. Rockefeller, Jr., with the suggestion that the family buy the site and donate it to the U.N. Five days after Zeckendorf had seen the newspaper item, and one day before the committee was officially to have selected Philadelphia, the elder Rockefeller told his son to take an option on X City. Zeckendorf gave the Rockefellers a thirty-day option to buy more than two-thirds of his land for $8,500,000. Eight days after that the United Nations approved the site, and the Rockefellers bought it at Zeckendorf's price and presented it to the U.N. Zeckendorf's profit was about $2,-000,000, a modest figure when compared to what he might have made if he had carried out even part of the X City plan. "My profit was practically nothing," he said later. "If I hadn't sold the land to Rockefeller as a quixotic gesture, I'd have made thirty million on it. Well, twenty, anyway."

Eventually Zeckendorf made $3,000,000 more, but in a way that did not please him. He still owned five acres around the U.N., when the city decided to develop a proper

approach to the new buildings. It was Zeckendorf's notion
that the city should condemn six blocks, from the north side
of Forty-sixth Street to the south side of Forty-ninth Street
between First Avenue and Third Avenue, and sell them to
him for $13,500,000, which represented 20 per cent more
than their assessed valuation. He would then donate to the
city the two blocks between Forty-seventh and Forty-
eighth streets, which could be turned into a great boulevard
1,600 feet long and 320 feet wide, more than twice the
width of Park Avenue, New York's widest street. As for
himself, he would develop the four freshly acquired blocks
plus the acreage he already held in a manner befitting
the United Nations; the United Nations would benefit, the
city would benefit, Zeckendorf would benefit, and even the
people who owned the property to be condemned would
benefit, since, as Zeckendorf said, "they would have gotten
more than they ever dreamed of getting at 120 per cent of
assessed value." This broad, philanthropic view was received with much less enthusiasm than Zeckendorf's offer
of land for the U.N. Robert Moses, whose many state and
municipal jobs included that of New York City Construction
Coordinator, had a plan of his own, and also felt that con-
demning private property in order to sell it to another private owner was a bad policy. Residents of the area which
would have been demolished wrote stirring letters to the
newspapers and often got stirring replies from Zeckendorf. "We do not seek either profit or glory," he wrote in answer to one from Dorothy Thompson, the journalist.
Eventually the city's Board of Estimate rejected Zeckendorf's plan, even after he had sold his own acreage for $3,-
000,000 so that he could no longer be accused of acting
for profit *or* glory. Looking back on it, Zeckendorf described
the abortive venture as "a pipsqueak deal." It was certainly

not what he had visualized for himself or New York when he first planned to erase the slaughterhouse district of New York.

Zeckendorf was forty-one years old when he did the United Nations, the Rockefellers and the city of New York a favor. He had already been in real estate more than half his life. Unlike Astor, he did not come into it with a fortune made in other fields. His family's beginnings, however, do provide a coincidence to strengthen the historical continuity. Zeckendorf's paternal grandfather arrived in the United States in 1848, the year Astor died, and with four brothers opened a general store in Santa Fe, and later moved it to Tucson. Although the business became successful, Zeckendorf's father decided to reverse Horace Greeley's dictum and see what the East had to offer. On the Zeckendorfs' way to New York they stopped at Paris, Illinois, where William was born on June 30, 1905. Two years later the family was living on Long Island, and twelve years later, on Manhattan. Zeckendorf's father sold, and later manufactured, low-priced shoes; this gave the family a modest income. William Zeckendorf went to the city's public schools, and at seventeen enrolled at New York University, which he left after three years. (Considering the academic careers of William and Alfred Levitt and Zeckendorf, a case could almost be made that success in post–World War II real estate depended on *not* getting a degree at New York University.)

At the age of twenty, and with no qualifications, Zeckendorf was hired by Samuel Borchard, a maternal uncle, to manage an office building at 32 Broadway for a salary of $25 a week. Zeckendorf knew nothing about building management, but was aware that the more office space he filled the happier his uncle would be. With several of his former college classmates, hired on a commission basis, Zeckendorf raced through lower New York seeking tenants, often, to the dismay of other building managers, in offices where they were seemingly content. In a few months of active soliciting, Zeckendorf had nearly filled his uncle's building, and had increased its income by $200,000 a year. After a brief period under Borchard's tutelage, Zeckendorf decided to break family ties and seek his fortune elsewhere. On the basis of his accomplishment at 32 Broadway, he convinced Leonard S. Gans, the New York broker, that he was a first-rate salesman. Gans hired Zeckendorf, but it was a year before he made his first sale; after that his income soared. In 1929, Zeckendorf made $43,000 in commissions; in 1930, the year Gans made him a partner in the firm, his commission on a single transaction was $21,000. "He was a great salesman, but full of crazy ideas," Gans later said of Zeckendorf, "and I had to be careful which clients I let him handle. He'd scare some of them to death. And he always loved complicated deals. I won't say he went out of his way to complicate them, but he always looked for the trickiest ones he could find. Still, we were one of the few brokerage firms that made money right through the depression, and one reason was that Bill never knew when he was licked."

In 1938, Zeckendorf left Gans to join Webb & Knapp, a conservative firm which specialized in building management. The company had been started in 1922 by W. Seward Webb, Robert C. Knapp and Eliot and John Cross as 385 Madison Avenue, Inc., for the address of the building in which its offices were located; the name was changed in 1933. Knapp died not long after, and Webb and John Cross retired in 1936. Eliot Cross brought in new associates on an equal-membership basis, but the essential dignity of the operation was unaffected. In 1937, however, Cross met Zeckendorf, who had acted as broker for Webb & Knapp on a building it bought on Lexington Avenue, and a year after that asked him to join the firm, also as an equal member. This gave Zeckendorf a quarter interest in the company, which as cash value was tantamount to practically nothing, and a salary of $9,000 a year. Although Zeckendorf was averaging twice that with Gans, he recognized the prestige value of the Webb & Knapp reputation. This insight was more than amply confirmed when the company was awarded the Astor properties to manage, at which point Zeckendorf was ready to remake Webb & Knapp into his own image.

Some of Zeckendorf's detractors have said that his success with the Astor portfolio was due more to a rising real estate market than to his own skill, and although there may be some truth in this it does not do justice to his accomplishments. About one-third of Astor's real estate was showing no profit at all, "a messed up portfolio," a Webb & Knapp man called it. "My first conclusion after examining it," Zeckendorf said later, "was to have a fire sale of the Commander's junk, and to re-invest the proceeds in long-term leases with guaranteed rents and percentage clauses as a hedge against inflation." Zeckendorf did not hold a fire sale, but he did a few things that John Jacob might not have liked; he mortgaged some of the properties, and he bought outside New York City. "We used the prestige of the Astor name to convince people they were getting bargains," Zeckendorf has said. "We let 'em buy for a little cash and a couple of first and second mortgages. Then we sold the mortgages. We used the money to pick up some nice 100 per cent retail locations all over the country, mortgaged those and bought some more." Despite the breaks with family tradition, Vincent Astor was pleased with what Zeckendorf had done for him in his absence. He considered the $1,500,000 he paid in fees a reasonable sum for his improved position; and even that figure was sharply reduced when Webb & Knapp bought from Astor a property which it had bought for him a few years earlier, and gave him a million-dollar profit on the transaction.

The Astor fees permitted Webb & Knapp to begin operating on its own account in ways that the founders of the company could not have foreseen. From a net worth of minus $127,000 in 1942, the company rose sharply. By 1946 properties under its control were valued at some $50,-000,000, and by 1954 at about $250,000,000, at which point Webb & Knapp's net worth was estimated at more than $75,000,000. By then Webb & Knapp had dealt in more than half the states in the union, and Zeckendorf had fallen into the banker's habit of dropping the zeros in the millions; he would have called the last three amounts simply fifty, two-fifty and seventy-five. The millions went into a highly diversified group of properties, including, at one time or another, gas stations, oil tankers, a night club, supermarkets, a cemetery and the municipal jail of Boise, Idaho. One of Zeckendorf's first transactions was to buy for $8,000,000 nearly a mile of the waterfront of Hoboken, New Jersey, which included nine piers and the Hoboken Manufacturers Railroad with nine miles of track. Less than a year later Zeckendorf sold half of his purchase for slightly less than he had paid for all of it. The money Zeckendorf brought to Webb & Knapp not only made him the most prominent member of the firm, it soon permitted him to take over the company. Cross had retired in 1946, and in 1949 Zeckendorf bought out the last two members Cross had brought in by paying them $3,000,000 in cash and $3,000,000 more in real estate. *Fortune* once estimated that he made more than $25,000,000 for the shareholder-members of Webb & Knapp.

Webb's former associates became millionaires as a result of the kind of imagination Zeckendorf applied to the slaughterhouses of the Upper East Side. Once a broker offered Zeckendorf an old riding academy which ran between Sixty-sixth and Sixty-seventh streets just west of Central Park in New York. The asking price was $700,000, which Zeckendorf considered too high, since the 40,000 square feet of property was not large enough for an investment in an apartment house, and the academy building itself looked completely useless. A few weeks later Zeckendorf was caught in a traffic jam in front of the building, and decided he might as well use the lost time for a quick examination of its interior. "I noted that the main building, the riding arena, was ninety-two by two hundred feet with a great high vaulted ceiling and no interior columns," he has since recalled. "I said to myself, here is a perfect place for a television studio. . . . I called the broker and we bought the property at his price, $700,000 with twenty per cent cash, balance on purchase money mortgage. We circularized all the radio companies immediately, offering the property for television purposes, and to our dismay received letters from all declining the proposal. This put us in the horse business. We bought 150 horses and went into the market to buy hay and sell manure, running a regular monthly loss of $3500 to $4500. This went on for almost a year, when one day the phone rang and a rather uncertain voice announced that he was Mr. E. J. Noble . . . the owner of the American Broadcasting Company. . . . He said, "Some time ago you suggested that we buy your barn for a TV station. Perhaps we'd better have a look at it." In short order, Zeckendorf leased the riding academy to A.B.C. and later sold it outright at a profit of $600,000. Several months later, Noble invited Zeckendorf to join the board of A.B.C., because as he explained, "You're the first man to make money out of TV."

Despite the horses, the riding academy sale was less complicated than one Zeckendorf completed on the block between Thirty-third and Thirty-fourth streets, strategically located between Macy's and Gimbels. The site consisted of a number of nondescript buildings, among them a hotel, a theater and a city-owned firehouse. As he had done in the slaughterhouse district, Zeckendorf imagined the site with the buildings removed. What swam into his vision then was a twenty-five-story building with a tremendous store on its ground floor which would be a short cut for shoppers between Macy's and Gimbels, and which would benefit by this flow of money-laden traffic. Little by little, Zeckendorf bought the properties on the block, but he realized that nothing could come of his vision unless he also had the firehouse. The city informed him that it could not be sold except by auction to the highest bidder, and besides, the firehouse, even though fifty years old, was still in serviceable condition. Zeckendorf considered this a proper challenge, and sent his lawyers looking into the city statutes. This search revealed that there was nothing to prevent the city from exchanging one property for another of equal or greater value. Zeckendorf also discovered that the city maintained another firehouse at Twenty-ninth Street. Would it not be more efficient and a boon to traffic conditions, Zeckendorf asked the city officials, if they had a brand-new firehouse on Thirty-first Street, where he owned property of just the right size, to replace the two old ones? The city agreed, and Zeckendorf built a new firehouse for $375,000 which he turned over to the city in exchange for the one he wanted in the first place. That done, Zeckendorf signed F. W. Woolworth to a lease for a store to occupy the strategic space. It is the largest store in the company's chain, and at last reports was doing precisely the kind of business Zeckendorf had predicted when the Herald

Square Hotel, the Savoy Theater and the New York Fire Department occupied the area.

Making something out of nothing, or a great deal out of very little, is the Zeckendorf hallmark. He himself, having acquired gourmet tastes in the course of his rise to fame and wealth, is inclined to use food analogies to describe his successes. "I make grapefruit out of lemons," he said once. Another time he suggested, "I make bananas out of peanuts." In more serious moments, he says, "What I like to do is recognize a great piece of land and conceive a suitable edifice for it." Whatever the form of expression, there is no doubt that many transformations have taken place under his guidance. He is, as *Fortune* said in 1954, "a gifted man. He has a mind of unusual caliber in intuition, rough calculating ability, and resourcefulness; and an imagination that can take fire without appreciable loss of discipline." Beyond this, he is an exceedingly hard worker, with an incredible memory which permits him to know everything of importance, not only about every Webb & Knapp property, but about every major property in Manhattan and a good many in other cities as well. When he does not already know the value of a property, he is quick at appraisal. Once, the owner of what was then McCreery's department store on Thirty-fourth Street, between Fifth and Sixth avenues, dropped in on Zeckendorf and asked what he would pay for it. Zeckendorf considered the question for a few minutes, and announced a price of $5,-500,000. This was within 4 per cent of the building's book value, and that afternoon the deal was closed at Zeckendorf's figure. A month later, Zeckendorf had leased the building to Ohrbach's, a department store which was eager to leave its location at Union Square, at a price which would bring Webb & Knapp a $2,000,000 profit.

By 1952, when Webb & Knapp issued its stock to the public for the first time, Zeckendorf had made a profound impact on American real estate. The major change in his own life was his occupancy of an office which cost $500,-000 on top of the Webb & Knapp Building on Madison Avenue. The suite is a duplex. Its top floor is cylindrically shaped, like a huge barrel on end, has oak paneling on its inside and teakwood on its outside, is soundproof, and has dials which permit the overhead lights to be changed to suit the mood of the occupant. For some time to come that mood was to be high-spirited. Webb & Knapp bought and sold, developed and redeveloped, and became increasingly wealthy. The spectacular deals made newspaper copy, but dozens of others were known only to the trade; both kinds brought profits—and more clients with more deals.

Zeckendorf's reputation was such that in 1953, when money was difficult to raise for most investors, he was able to find the backing to pay $52,000,000 for the Chrysler Building, the Chrysler Building East and the Graybar Building, a transaction which was announced in agreeably large headlines. Despite a closing session which lasted three days and employed the talents of forty-five lawyers, thirty bankers and twenty-two businessmen, the Chrysler-Graybar deal was not as complicated as some which Zeckendorf made in the same period. The most significant, though unpublicized, of these involved a building at 2 Park Avenue. Having understood how property values increase with the proper application of demolition followed by development, Zeckendorf also understood that the many parts of a developed property were worth more when dealt with separately than when treated as a whole. In a building, for instance, the separate parts would include the land on which it stands, the building itself, the rental income, the interest on the mortgage. Each of these, Zeckendorf decided, carried risks, tax consequences and potential profits in varying degrees. One position might appeal to one kind of investor, a second to another, and so on.

In practice, 2 Park Avenue resulted in the kind of deal on which Zeckendorf thrives. He had calculated the building to be worth $10,000,000, of which Webb & Knapp owned a 40 per cent interest. He assumed he could sell the building outright for $9,500,000. On the other hand, the property produced a net of about $1,000,000 a year, with a potential of $750,000 more. So Zeckendorf sold an operating lease on the building for $5,000,000. The purchasers of that lease—they paid $1,500,000 in cash and gave Zeckendorf a mortgage for the rest—were entitled, for a rental of $600,000 a year, to manage the building and collect its rents. In short, for their outlay of $1,500,000 they would have a profit each year of at least $400,000, and a chance for more, less the interest payments on the mortgage, a decidedly attractive investment. This done, Zeckendorf mortgaged the land and building for $6,750,000 and followed this with a second mortgage of $2,250,000. He now had $14,000,000 in cash and mortgages for a building he was once ready to sell for $9,500,000. He was paying out nearly $500,000 in interest on his first and second mortgages, but he was also receiving $600,000 plus mortgage interest from the holder of the operating lease. It ended even more happily than that, because when Zeckendorf was ready to buy the Chrysler and Graybar buildings he used the $2,250,000 in cash and the $3,500,000 leaseholder's mortgage as collateral. With that and a $40,000,000 mortgage from Equitable Life Assurance Society, Zeckendorf had virtually all he needed to become the major stockholder in three of New York's most important office buildings.

(274)

Although Zeckendorf deserves full credit for his conception of the split-up technique, its success derived, as much as anything else, from the nation's tax laws. Annual depreciation of a building is tax deductible; until 1958 such depreciation could be deducted by a leaseholder during the life of a lease. Since leases were usually written for twenty-one-year periods, annual deductions of close to 5 per cent were common, and higher ones were possible during the early years of a lease under the so-called "accelerated depreciation" provision of the law. As a result, returns on the cash investment in buildings were frequently tax-free or close to it. This helped make real estate an attractive investment for individuals in the higher tax brackets, and these people, when money was abundant, were just the kind of customers who sought out Zeckendorf. And for them, and Webb & Knapp, Zeckendorf would apply the split-up technique and variations of it to show a profit for all. He had become so adept that one of his competitors once felt moved to say, "Zeckendorf's got the greatest real estate brain that ever hit this country."

As Webb & Knapp grew in wealth and prestige, Zeckendorf occasionally took time out to theorize about the development of cities, which is what he felt was his *raison d'être* in real estate. In an article entitled "Cities Versus Suburbs, A Struggle for Survival," which he wrote for the *Atlantic Monthly* in July 1952, Zeckendorf, to no one's great surprise, plunked strongly for the cities. "Satellite towns, which are the product of decentralization, are parasites," he wrote. "The high cost of maintenance of the central core that supports the whole metropolitan area is borne by the city, but the revenues and benefits go to the towns at the periphery. . . . Every satellite town saps off the buying power, the taxing power, and the vital factors that make for a cohesive, comprehensive, healthy city. This is just as though the United States suddenly lost the taxing power of California and New York . . . but continued with the central bureaucracy and cost of maintenance of the Army and Navy, and so on." Zeckendorf's solution for saving the cities from the suburbs was revolutionary: "The satellite communities should be forced into the large city and taxed to make them a contributing part of the whole community." The test as to whether a suburb was truly independent was simply, "Can this community survive financially, socially, and economically without the benefits from the large city?" If most of a suburb's income came from the earnings of its residents in the city, for instance, "then the city should have the right to incorporate the town." The results of this would be a rebirth of the cities, Zeckendorf said, to the increased happiness of both urban and suburban dwellers.

Despite Zeckendorf's high standing as an urban developer, his idea did not catch on, and is not likely to be carried out in Zeckendorf's lifetime. In time, although most of his activities were essentially urban, Zeckendorf bowed to the inevitable and made some suburban moves himself. When he did, they were gigantic. The most impressive one that has actually been realized is on the site of Roosevelt Field, twenty miles from Manhattan, where Charles Lindbergh, Clarence Chamberlain, Wiley Post, Harold Gatty and Douglas "Wrong Way" Corrigan once took off on glorious flights. The field had been closed since 1951, by which time it was practically surrounded by housing developments. This state of affairs appealed to Zeckendorf in spite of his prejudices against suburbia. Roosevelt's 370 acres, he decided, were the ideal site for a shopping center—announced as the world's largest—and for offices and factories. Zeckendorf estimated that the whole thing could be put together for $60,000,000, and proceeded to convince the blue-chip companies of the logic of the location. The potential market consisted of 1,300,000 people within a ten-mile radius, and the best estimates were that the total would go to 1,600,000 by 1960. Despite these rosy figures, Zeckendorf had to make terms so favorable to R. H. Macy & Co. that it is not likely he showed a profit in the space the department store took. But with Macy's, Zeckendorf had no trouble finding other retail clients. The same loss-leader approach brought him excellent industrial clients. American Bosch, Pepsi-Cola, Sperry Rand, Graybar Electric and others signed up for Roosevelt Field space. Zeckendorf's first invasion of the suburbs was as dramatic as his conquest of the cities.

Unlike his performance in the city, however, Zeckendorf did not run together a string of suburban successes. It was not that his suburban ideas lacked the flair and imagination he brought to other projects; not even his severest critics could belittle his concepts. In some cases money became tight just when he needed it most; often he was so busy putting the beginning, middle or finishing touches on other deals that he could not see his suburban plans through. It is also likely that his commitment to city development was so great and his feelings against suburbia so strong that failure was built in when he got beyond a city's lines. Very little has happened to 5,000 acres between Fort Worth and Dallas, Texas, or to 32,000 acres along the Mississippi River between New Orleans and Baton Rouge, which he planned as industrial and housing developments, although it would be foolish to predict that nothing will ever come of them. Except for the purchase of some 380 acres in the Baychester section of the Bronx, and plans for a $65,-000,000 housing project on Staten Island, neither of which is exactly suburban, Zeckendorf has returned to the centers of cities, where he is obviously most at home. Part of the Baychester property has been made into an amusement area called Freedomland, which has been far from successful, but this could be a holding operation until such time as Zeckendorf can develop it into something fitting its size and location. In 1961, even with Freedomland's losses, *Business Week* said that Baychester, which cost Zeckendorf $5,900,-000, "some day may become Zeckendorf's crown jewel."

Whatever happens to Freedomland, or to any of the other suburban or near-suburban ventures at which Zeckendorf has tried his hand, it is doubtful if he will wander far from the city in the future. In 1958, he returned to his thesis about suburbia in an article for the *Yale Review*, and although he repeated his earlier suggestion that the cities take over the suburbs they supported, he also added a new solution to the conflict. "We can solve the problem of the exodus to the suburbs by making the city a better place to live in," he wrote. "So far as I am concerned, modern urban redevelopment is based on the principle that man has achieved his highest cultural development in the urban area and that there is nothing wrong with the city that cannot be cured by eliminating its sick areas and importing something of the countryside." He foresaw buildings taller and slimmer than those in existence, "gracious spires surrounded by quiet green areas." Scattered among them would be "single-family houses of two or three stories and row houses designed specifically for urban living. These town houses will have private gardens and garages; in some places they will be built around a central park. This city of the future will be a place where families can raise children in a quiet and safe atmosphere. . . . This pattern of urban living will offer many of the amenities of suburbia without its drawbacks." This was not necessarily a sour grapes attitude. Zeckendorf had been on record a long time about where he stood on cities versus suburbs.

Zeckendorf had never forsaken the cities, of course, even while probing the suburbs. He had continued to acquire properties for management or development and was able to announce from time to time one spectacular project or another. And even when they did not come off there was a quality about them that was in the bold tradition of X City, which did, after all, lead to the United Nations: a grandeur in concept, a majestic clutch of buildings to embrace a wide area of human activity, and, of course, a seemingly noble indifference to cost. At a time when many unimaginative office buildings were going up all over the United States, Zeckendorf did contribute, as an otherwise critical observer commented, "to the gaiety of nations." One grand scheme was for a $200,000,000 Palace of Progress, to be the world's largest office building (with 154,000,000 cubic feet, compared to the Pentagon's 84,000,000), to contain a permanent world's fair and a merchandise mart, and to be built over New York's Pennsylvania Station. When that project died for lack of financial backing, after Webb & Knapp, by Zeckendorf's estimate, had spent $1,000,000 on plans, studies and models, a new one was immediately announced. This was for a $500,000,000 Atomic City, which would include most of the ideas that were to have gone into the Palace of Progress, plus a hotel, a helicopter field and a Television City, to be built on the Upper West Side, above the freight yards of the New York Central and Pennsylvania railroads. In announcing the demise of the Palace of Progress and the birth of the Atomic City early in 1956, Zeckendorf seemed to be aware for the first time in his career that he had to overcome a certain amount of skepticism. "We're dead serious in everything we propose," he said, in the nearest he had ever come to an attitude of defense. "We never announce a project without every intention of doing it. But you have to realize these things take time. We can't do them overnight. We don't have the time or the money."

Yet, as *Business Week* pointed out, "The trouble with this is that the scales are becoming increasingly weighted with giant schemes on which the firm is working while completions remain comparatively few. In the case of the . . . announcement . . . involving the $500,000,000 plan, the press paid far less attention than it had to the earlier $200,000,000 one." The magazine found Zeckendorf's position wanting on several counts. "Webb & Knapp's cash position," *Business Week* said, "is less than $5,000,-000; it has 20,000,000 shares of common stock already outstanding . . . two classes for preference stock, one of which is publicly held; almost $8,000,000 in debentures; $102,000,000 in encumbrances ('substantially all of the land, buildings, leaseholds, tankers and equipment are pledged to secure mortgages') according to the latest annual report. Life insurance policies with a face value of $3,200,000 on the lives of officers and other individuals have been pledged to secure notes." This, the magazine suggested, was not economically sound. It also implied that Zeckendorf's big schemes were generated for their publicity value alone and made a point of the fact that "his firm keeps a vice-president in charge of public relations—one of the few real estate companies to do so—and retains another outside firm for several of the big projects."

Until the *Business Week* article there had been very little open criticism of Zeckendorf's methods or achievements. Public expressions that fell short of praise had been limited to raising the question as to how far he could go, or what would happen if the inflationary spiral should curve downward. Zeckendorf was especially sensitive about the charges that he was seeking publicity for its own sake or for personal aggrandizement. Publicity, he told *Business Week,* was "to establish credibility. We are traveling uncharted seas. Credibility on one of our major plans is established by being positive. If we were in the least bit tentative or were, ourselves, doubting Thomases we'd never put the deal across. Also our big plans usually go against building codes, and when you do that you're in politics. By firing the public imagination on our projects, we hope to have the politicians, always sensitive to public opinion, swing behind us. Finally, though we never announce a plan just to get the reaction, we do get a lot of help from banking, real estate and governmental sources. Everything that was criticized about the Palace of Progress has been solved in Atomic City." The magazine had the last word in this debate. "Officers of Webb & Knapp," it wrote, "insist the aura of publicity surrounding the firm brings in the bread and butter business and saves the company the expense of hunting it up. As Zeckendorf declares, it also lends credibility to the schemes. The question can't help arising, however, following such a raft of publicity as accompanied the Palace of Progress, whether the opposite effect is beginning to take place."

The opposite effect was indeed beginning to take place, a variation on Gresham's law in which incompleted projects were driving out completed ones, at least in the public mind. Zeckendorf, like many of his predecessors in New York real estate, wanted to sponsor the world's tallest building. He had plans drawn for one to soar a hundred stories over Grand Central Terminal, several hundred feet taller than the Empire State Building. His imagination had even conceived of an open latticework tower in which glass elevators would carry sightseers to the top, putting it one up on the Empire State, but also contrary to the city's building codes. The building was built, but not under Zeckendorf's supervision, and without the glass elevators. Instead, the Pan-American Building, the largest office building in New York and second only to the Pentagon in the world, was started under the auspices of the late Erwin S. Wolfson, a builder whose dreams were as grand as, if less varied than, Zeckendorf's. The building will rise fifty-nine stories, making it less than *the* tallest in the city, but all its other statistics are Zeckendorfian: 10,000 telephones, 2,000 gallons of water used every minute, electricity enough to supply 10,000 homes, 200,000 pounds of steam an hour for heat, hot water and power to drive the compressors for the air-conditioning system.

With the world's tallest building and the world's largest office building tantalizingly beyond his reach, Zeckendorf moved in one more direction, and an almost entirely new one as far as New York was concerned. He decided to build the first hotel in the city since the Waldorf-Astoria went up in 1931. It was to be, in Zeckendorf's words, "The Greatest Hotel Ever Built," and it was to be called the Zeckendorf. Its forty-eight stories would contain 2,000 luxury rooms, ten banquet halls, fifteen private dining rooms, and shops and offices on the Sixth Avenue block front just north of Rockefeller Center. It was undeniably a Zeckendorf conception, from birth to death. As late as 1949 the site consisted of a number of small holdings on Fifty-first and Fifty-second streets and Sixth Avenue—bars, seedy night clubs, brownstones and a restaurant called Toots Shor's, which was not only doing a fine business but held a lease that was good until 1967. Encouraged by the New York building boom, which was just getting under way, and sensing that the site's proximity to Rockefeller Center gave it a special value, speculators started buying plots as they became available. Within four years prices went from $50,-

ooo for a seventy-foot frontage to $250,000 and more. In 1953 the Equitable Life Assurance Society of the United States decided that this was a desirable location for a new office building and assigned a man to pick up the separate parcels. After a year, Equitable had acquired almost what it wanted; those who had bought the small plots on speculation had made their profits and moved on, but there was one holdout—Toots Shor, the owner of the restaurant of the same name. Equitable had paid $1,000,000 for the property which he leased, but Shor still had a lease, and obviously knew its value.

By 1956, Equitable still did not have the Shor lease—the generally accepted rumor at the time was that the two could not get together on the difference between $1,000,-000, which Equitable would pay, and $1,500,000, which Shor wanted—and costs were going up on acquiring the necessary plots. In 1957, after trying to bring Rockefeller Center itself into its plans, Equitable decided to give up on the office building. At this point Zeckendorf decided that Equitable's problems were a ready-made opportunity for him. His information on the situation was so good that he had a talk with Toots Shor before he even talked to the people at Equitable. He did not do any better with Shor than his predecessors—"He and his son, Bill, Jr., offered me $1,-000,000," Shor said later. "I turned it down. Then they went up to $1,200,000 or $1,300,000. I still said no"—but Zeckendorf decided to proceed anyhow. In May 1958 he had an option to buy the land from Equitable, and until October to raise the money and, since just about everything depended on it, to buy Shor's lease. With neither of these possibilities in sight, Zeckendorf already had his vision of the hotel he wanted.

The complicated negotiations which followed were in the by now accepted Zeckendorf pattern. He borrowed

$17,500,000 from the Chase Manhattan Bank with which to pay Equitable for the land and Shor for the lease. This done, he sold the land to Prudential Insurance Company, and leased it back from them. For this, Prudential was also to lend Zeckendorf $27,500,000 toward construction—if he could raise the rest of his costs. He paid Shor $1,500,000, and with that problem behind him, announced his plans for the Zeckendorf Hotel—from Gracie Mansion, the residence of the Mayor of New York and a favorite announcement site for Zeckendorf's New York projects. Then, at the actual site, posing for photographers wearing a builder's metal hat and wielding a pneumatic drill, he proclaimed that excavation was under way. It was, and for something like $2,500,-000 Zeckendorf was soon the owner of a hole fifty feet deep, 250 feet wide and 450 feet long. At this point the digging stopped; Zeckendorf lacked the $35,000,000 or $40,000,-000—because of rising costs, some guesses were as high as $50,000,000—essential to complete the hotel.

Now Zeckendorf sought money, if not frantically, at least determinedly, and at the same time had to parry increasingly embarrassing questions as to why work had ceased on Sixth Avenue. Block-high signs still called attention to the forthcoming hotel, but Walter Winchell, a columnist normally preoccupied with the vagaries of members of the entertainment world, called it "Zeckendorf's Folly," and the *New York Herald Tribune* referred to it as "the city's most conspicuous hole in the ground." For a while Zeckendorf's office blamed the delay on a slowdown on steel deliveries, which few people really believed. Zeckendorf went, as did Equitable before him, to Rockefeller Center, Inc., which had indicated that it was in favor of a hotel on the site. The answer was no, and "they gave us reasons not comprehensible to us," Zeckendorf said. Perhaps the only people who know why they said no are the officers of

Rockefeller Center, and they have never revealed it. The most reasonable explanation is that the essentially conservative Rockefeller Center did not want to become involved with the essentially radical Zeckendorf. Zeckendorf turned to hotel proprietors—Laurence Tisch, the Sheraton chain, the Hiltons—but they were just as disappointing. Costs were too high for a hotel to be profitable. Zeckendorf blamed himself for this. "It was our fault," he said. "We could have changed the design. It was an expensive one at $30,000 a room." At last, in the spring of 1960 Zeckendorf accepted the fact that the money was not going to be available, not even after he announced that he had rented all of the building's office space and had booked banquets and conventions well into the hotel's first year of operation.

By mid-1960 Zeckendorf's problem was reduced to finding buyers for his hole in the ground. Reverting to an earlier metaphor, he said that "offers came our way in a hurry. Everybody likes a fire sale." Unlike real fire sales, where scorched or smoky merchandise goes at bargain prices, Zeckendorf's sale gave him a profit, in this case $2,-500,000. However pleasing the sum, it could not have brought Zeckendorf the satisfaction that "The Greatest Hotel Ever Built" would have. Furthermore, the purchasers of his lease had no intention of building a hotel on his site at all, but decided instead on a forty-three-story office building. The buyers, Uris Buildings Corporation, the largest builders in the city, already had plans for a hotel project under way a few blocks north, where land was cheaper and the prospects for profits therefore better. In this they found agreement from Hilton Hotels Corporation and Rockefeller Center, Inc. And to compound the irony, Rockefeller Center joined on an equal-ownership basis with Uris to put up the office building—which will be called the Sperry Rand Building for its major occupant—on what was to have been the site of the Zeckendorf. "We saw the economics of it," said a spokesman for Rockefeller Center, Inc.

About the time that Zeckendorf was getting rid of his hole on Sixth Avenue, the economics of his operation was given a thoroughgoing review by *Fortune,* the tenor of which was clearly indicated in the title, "Man in a $100-Million Jam." It was, in a way, an answer to the question raised by *Business Week* in 1956. "During prosperous 1959 and early 1960, when Zeckendorf should have been securely entrenched in the economy," *Fortune* wrote, "he found himself in the most critical straits of his whole career. Webb & Knapp, which has never paid a dividend on its common stock, lost $9,700,000 (before tax credit) in 1958, and made only a little in 1959. Owing to Zeckendorf's headlong expansion, his short-term debt at the end of 1959 mounted to $104,000,000, or around forty per cent of his total liabilities, and his year's interest payments and other expenses connected with his short-term debt alone came to a staggering $10,700,000. Zeckendorf has been obliged to pay some creditors, whom he affectionately calls 'my Shylock moneylenders,' twenty per cent or more; and to meet his bills and due notes, he is engaging, amid rumors of crisis upon crisis, in the biggest sell-off of properties in his company's history." The trouble, the magazine said, was that Zeckendorf "is a creative artist who gets more of a kick out of making heroically complex deals that may pay off handsomely tomorrow than he does out of making millions of routine dollars today."

This was not the whole problem, of course. Operating and administrative expenses had gone up sharply; Zeckendorf was paying more than he ever had for interest, taxes, running expenses, depreciation and amortization of leasehold costs and leasehold rentals themselves. For a number of years he had been selling properties and leasing them back. Normally this was sound practice; it provided him with cash, and also gave him an annual income. But in time, in order to get a high price for his property he had to pay disproportionately high rentals for the leasehold. In 1956, leaseholds brought Webb & Knapp a profit of $2,300,000; in 1957 they showed a loss of $1,500,000 and in 1958 a loss of $2,400,000. This was not particularly disturbing to Zeckendorf, who felt that the potential earning power of the leasehold properties was very great. Nevertheless, he was paying $14,100,000 in rentals in 1958, an exceedingly high gamble on the future. Administrative expenses included nearly $1,000,000 in salaries for Webb & Knapp officers, despite Zeckendorf's cutting of his own from $140,000 to $115,000 a year; another $1,500,000 for other employes; $1,000,000 for miscellaneous expenses; and $750,000 for an architectural and design department.

Zeckendorf undertook in 1959 to put his house in order, but without jeopardizing his stake in the future. In addition to cutting administrative expenses, Zeckendorf sold a number of properties outright. He had once said that at Webb & Knapp "Everything's for sale—at a price," but had managed to hold on by leasebacks to a good deal of what he sold. Now, sales were final. The Mile High Center building in Denver, Colorado, the Graybar and Chrysler leaseholds, and the Airlines Building in New York were among the buildings Zeckendorf had to let go. One sale, because it involved land of the kind that could support a project in the old Zeckendorf manner, may have been more painful than most. It was 12,000 acres in Los Angeles called Mountain Park, of which Zeckendorf had once said, "Here's an empire that will sell for upwards of $25,000,000." He had paid $2,500,000 for it in 1947, and by 1958 it was on the Webb & Knapp books with an appraised value of

$11,500,000. But in 1960, Zeckendorf sold it for $8,500,-000 plus 15 per cent of the profits that would come from its development. This was considerably less than his book value, of course, but Zeckendorf thought the deal was a good one "when you take the profit-sharing feature into account." The nagging thought remained, though, that had he been able to hold on to it and develop it in his own way, Mountain Park would have stood a good chance of attaining the empire status Zeckendorf had assigned to it.

Zeckendorf, while thoroughly aware of his problems, had faith not only in the future of American real estate, but more specifically in that part of it which was controlled by Webb & Knapp. "If we work out our problems," he said, "we'll be one of the greatest companies in the world." *Fortune's* solution for Zeckendorf was one that the magazine did not itself totally approve. "The time has come," it said, "for him to deviate into a more conventional style of operating—to improvise less and plan more—and to undertake half the deals he now gets into. Most of his properties are well chosen for the long pull, but even so there is the possibility that the real estate business is attracting so much capital and increasing its 'values' so swiftly that supply may well overtake demand. If William Zeckendorf survives and changes his tactics, the real estate world will be measurably less exciting. The spectacle of a man daily risking vast sums, gaily thumbing his nose at what he calls dodos, sharing the wealth he creates with syndicators and moneylenders, and generally acting the part of an economic *enfant terrible* is an exhilarating one in a world where businessmen sometimes take one another too seriously. Zeckendorf, however, has become an important enough part of business to take it seriously. If he doesn't, this irrepressible, freewheeling entrepreneur who has done so much for the real estate business can end up by doing it incalculable harm."

Zeckendorf had no intention of repressing himself, of doing the real estate business harm, or of going broke. He still liked the big deals, and did not shy from them any more than he ever had, and he still dropped the zeros when discussing millions, as if somehow that habit made the gambles less risky. "Any businessman can tell you that two and two make four," he once said, "but even though he knows equally well that two million and two million make four million, the mere magnitude of the figures deters him from looking at them squarely. Instead, he trembles with fright." Even when friendly critics like *Fortune* took to worrying about him in print, Zeckendorf continued to look at figures squarely, and at the possibilities of developing the land those figures could buy. In 1961, not long after the *Fortune* article appeared, he closed a deal whereby in partnership with the Aluminum Company of America he bought for $43,000,000 some 260 acres of West Los Angeles land owned by Twentieth Century–Fox Film Corporation. Eighty acres were to be leased back to Fox, the other hundred and eighty to be developed into the largest privately financed urban development in the United States, a $500,000,000 Century City.

If at first look at the headlines this plan sounded much like the other "cities" Zeckendorf had projected, there was actually a good deal more behind it, and its chances of success are good, if only because Alcoa is bearing the major share of the financing. Zeckendorf had been negotiating for the Fox properties off and on for four years. He had originally promised to purchase the land for $56,000,000 to be paid over ten years, and had actually gone to Hollywood in May 1959 for a ground-breaking ceremony with Spyros P.

Skouras, president of Twentieth Century–Fox. At that time Skouras, who had paid less than $2,000,000 for the land, had made a little joke appropriate to such an occasion by suggesting that Zeckendorf had done him in because the land was worth three times the sales price. Zeckendorf, equally at home with this kind of humor, informed Skouras that the total outlay by the United States for the Louisiana Purchase, the Gadsden Purchase, Alaska and the Virgin Islands amounted to less than what he was paying. Despite the humor, that deal did not go through because Zeckendorf could not raise the money. In 1960, Zeckendorf with Alcoa's backing reopened negotiations, but this time his offer was $43,000,000; to justify the reduced price, he offered to pay in cash instead of over ten years and to lease back eighty acres to the movie company. Fox stockholders approved the new deal—besides the appeal of immediate cash, there was the likelihood that the acreage it was leasing back would rise in value once Century City was a reality. And for Zeckendorf there was the promise he always saw in developing a city from the ground up, the profits which would accrue thereby—and the satisfaction of a properly complicated deal properly completed.

Zeckendorf also had strong resources in an area that had always seemed to escape public notice, despite his constant reference to them. His bread-and-butter operations were always there, delivering comparatively small but steady profits which helped make big deals possible, and which in turn came his way because of his reputation for the big deals. By 1960, Zeckendorf was the country's foremost developer of urban housing. Under a program popularly known as Title I because it was the first provision of the National Housing Act of 1949, Zeckendorf was replacing slums in New York, Chicago and Washington, D. C., with middle-income and luxury housing, and furthermore, in an atmosphere marked elsewhere by scandal, had never had his own honesty challenged by so much as a rumor. Title I was authorization for cities to acquire slum areas by condemnation, relocate tenants, clear the land and sell it to private builders for redevelopment at what it was estimated the land without the buildings was worth. The federal government was to pay two-thirds of the difference between the cost of the land to the city and what the city received for it. In addition, because of tax laws, depreciation write-offs and F.H.A. allowances, redevelopers stood a good chance to make a healthy return on their investment, and even have their money back within a short while. Theoretically, this should have brought builders and developers into the program by the hundreds; actually, because of political bottlenecks, physical problems, especially in relocation, and the costs of advance planning, the program was slow to get going. When it did, one of the foremost Title I advocates and activists was Zeckendorf. He liked the idea of a small equity compared to gross project cost, what he called "maximum leverage," and, of course, he liked the chance it gave him to return to his theories about rebuilding cities at their core.

For a while, Title I was referred to in Washington as the "Zeckendorf Relief Bill," because he had more projects going under its terms than any builder in the country. He had not entered the program early enough to be justifiably so identified, and might never have been involved except for a major housing scandal in New York City. Robert Moses, who was in charge of the city's slum-clearance program, had awarded an area bounded by Amsterdam Avenue, Central Park West, and Ninety-seventh and Hundredth streets to a builder before the area had been cleared and its occupants relocated. The builder, operating under the name of Manhattantown, Inc., had paid about $1,000,-

ooo down on a price of a little more than $3,000,000 for the land the city had condemned for $16,000,000. Manhattantown, Inc., never seemed to get around to relocating the slum tenants, but collected rents from them instead. This went on for five years, until the story broke in the press and the city had to act; among other things, Manhattantown, Inc., had neglected to pay taxes on the property it was milking, and furthermore had not made a single move toward redevelopment.

At this point Zeckendorf offered to take Manhattantown off the city's hands. He paid $1,300,000, and, in contrast to the previous holders of the land, proceeded at once to redevelop it. Park West Village, the name he gave to the project, now houses more than 2,000 families, and Zeckendorf is working on a number of others in New York City, including one called Lincoln Towers, which is in the vicinity of the new cultural center and will eventually have apartments for 4,000 families. If his glamorous projects excited popular imagination, his simple but successful attempts to provide housing where inadequate housing existed before have brought him a new kind of popularity, and he thrives on this public esteem as much as he did on the headlines. Letters with phrases like "we are familiar with many of your projects throughout the country, and we wish to learn whether any of our projects here . . . would be of interest to you," were especially pleasing. As Zeckendorf's activities in Title I increased, the adjective "flamboyant" seemed to be used less often in connection with his name, and even a good many people who were skeptical of his accomplishments were beginning to feel that he might work his way out of the financial problems he had amassed.

Another important bread-and-butter supplier for Webb & Knapp is the Canadian operation Zeckendorf started in 1955. By 1961 it was Canada's largest real estate developer,

with more than $200,000,000 in projects completed or un-
der way. Among them was the Place Ville Marie, an $88,-
000,000 project in Montreal on land owned by the Canadian
Railways System. Besides a forty-two-story Royal Bank of
Canada Building, Zeckendorf put up other office buildings,
a 1,500-car garage, a shopping promenade and several
theaters on a seven-acre lot. If it is not quite as grand as
some of the American cities he has projected, it is nevertheless complete and doing business. He has also built
shopping centers in several Canadian cities, started an industrial park in Vancouver, taken control of a Canadian construction and development company, and in 1962 was preparing a $100,000 master plan to remake sixty acres of
downtown Edmonton.

The Canadian experience not only brought profit to
Zeckendorf—the American Webb & Knapp owns 55 per
cent of Webb & Knapp (Canada)—but led in December
1961 to a solution to his major financial problems, the short-
term debts that *Fortune* was so worried about. British real
estate men who had joined with him in financing the Place
Ville Marie project now became his partners in his American projects. They brought what Zeckendorf needed most,
immediate cash, $43,750,000 of it, and for that sum be-
came equal partners in a new company, the Zeckendorf
Property Corporation. *Business Week*, which had first
asked whither Zeckendorf was drifting, now proclaimed
that "the archetype of the New York real estate promoter
pulled off the supreme coup of his career." The new
money, the magazine said, would pay off nearly $40,000,-
000 in loans on which Webb & Knapp was paying 20 per
cent interest. "It was a close thing. As recently as two weeks
ago, seasoned real estate analysts on Wall Street were saying that 'it couldn't be done.' But Zeckendorf did it, and
Webb & Knapp—which one banker who was involved in

the financing says was 'unbelievably close to the wall'—
has gained a new lease on life."

The British company, the Second Covent Garden
Property Co., Ltd., of London, took a half-interest in thirteen of Webb & Knapp's urban redevelopment properties,
including the 380 acres in the Bronx which now contain
Freedomland; Park West Village; Lincoln Towers; Kips Bay
Plaza, a 1,120-apartment unit development in New York
City; the shopping center at Roosevelt Field; and the company's part of Century City, among others. If this seemed a
high price to pay to rid himself of pressing and expensive
obligations, Zeckendorf did not say so. He once said he
would "rather be alive at 18 per cent than dead at the
prime rate," but it was also apparent that he would rather
be alive as a partner than dead at 18 per cent. *Business
Week* speculated that the "biggest price" Zeckendorf paid
for the new partnership was that "over the next few years at
least, he will have to subordinate his own flamboyant personality and restless imagination to the judgment of more
conservative men."

This does not seem likely, unless there is a sudden
change in character to which there have so far been no
clues. Chances are that Zeckendorf will still make the su-
perlative gesture, by himself or in partnership, and that it
will have its effect on a city, either in the United States or
Canada. Less than six months after he had formed Zeckendorf Property Corporation, he still managed to act in the old
style. He bought the Savoy Hilton Hotel, once the Savoy
Plaza, on Fifth Avenue at Fifty-ninth Street. It was his
ninth hotel in the city, the others being the Astor, Manhattan, Commodore, Drake, Taft, Stanhope, Chatham and
Gotham. He did not have the world's greatest hotel, but
with the new acquisition he could announce, and no one

could deny, that he was "the largest owner of hotel facilities in New York City, with a total of 7,000 rooms." For a man who likes superlatives, it was probably a decent interim announcement; at least, until he is ready to make the next one.

Notes and Acknowledgments

We are especially indebted to Jerry Korn for invaluable editorial suggestions, and to Henry Schlanger, whose painstaking and creative research was the basis for everything in this book. Neither of them is responsible for any errors, or for any of the conclusions we reached. The following list of sources is by no means complete; it is an attempt to summarize the most important books, magazines, newspapers and documents consulted in the course of writing the book.

CHAPTER I. JOHN JACOB ASTOR AND THE PASTURES OF MANHATTAN

All appraisals of Astor's career must start with Kenneth Wiggins Porter's two-volume *John Jacob Astor, Business Man* (1931), a monumental piece of research. Its document-filled appendices were especially useful. *The Life of John Jacob Astor*, by James Parton (1865), was the first full-length biography of Astor. It has special interest because the author had access to people who knew Astor. *John Jacob Astor, Landlord of New York*, by Arthur Howden Smith (1929), does not add a great deal to Parton. Harvey O'Connor in his *The Astors* (1941) provides an excellent profile of John Jacob, despite its brevity; the rest of the book is the fascinating history of the Astor family until the outbreak of World War II. Other good short biographies are in Gustavus Myers' *History of the Great American Fortunes* (1910), *McClure's Magazine*, April 1905, and *Fortune*, October 1933.

CHAPTER II. THE LAND GAMBLERS: VICTIMS AND VISIONARIES

The only full-length history of American land speculation is *The Great American Land Bubble*, by A. M. Sakolski (1932).

Scholars have looked into various aspects of the subject, however. Among these, "The Homestead Law in an Incongruous Land System," *American Historical Review*, July 1936, and "The Role of the Land Speculator in Western Development," *The Pennsylvania Magazine of History and Biography*, July 1942, both by Paul W. Gates, were most informative. *Western Expansion*, by Ray Allen Billington (1960), one of the best histories of the American movement to the West, helps put the land speculation in perspective.

Jay Cooke, Financier of the Civil War, by Ellis Paxson Oberholtzer (1907), is an uncritical biography, but its pages are crammed with documentary detail. Henrietta M. Larson's *Jay Cooke, Private Banker* (1936) is scholarly and objective. Cooke's career is also discussed by Matthew Josephson in *The Robber Barons* (1934), but the best sources for Cooke's venture into railroads and land are in the historical studies compiled by scholars. Among these, "Some Colonization Projects of the Northern Pacific Railroad" by Harold F. Peterson, *Minnesota History*, June 1929; "Early Minnesota Railroads and the Quest for Settlers" by the same author, *Minnesota History*, March 1932; and "Jay Cooke and Minnesota: The Formative Years of the Northern Pacific Railroad," a Ph.D. dissertation by John L. Hansberger, University of Minnesota, 1956, were the most valuable. "Charles Dickens' Visit to Illinois" by J. F. Snyder, *The Journal of the Illinois State Historical Society*, October 1910, is a good account of a little-known incident in the life of the author. *Duluth and St. Louis County, Minnesota*, a collection of early letters and papers edited by Walter van Brunt for the Minnesota Historical Society (1921), was also helpful.

CHAPTER III. THE VAN SWERINGEN BROTHERS AND THE DISCOVERY OF SUBURBIA

By the time the Vans were considered proper subjects for newspaper and magazine articles, the main interest was in their railroad holdings; their accomplishments in Shaker Heights and Cleveland were hardly noted. To reconstruct that part of the story we have relied on the Cleveland newspapers—*News, Press* and *Plain Dealer*—and architectural publications. "The Glory of Shaker Village," by F. A. Cushing Smith, *American Landscape Architect*, was one of the first magazine articles on the suburb. *Smooth Is the Road*, a history of the Chesapeake and Ohio Railroad, by Joseph F. Doherty, provided some biographical material on the Vans, as well as information on the beginnings of Shaker Heights. *The North Union Story*, by Mary Lou Conlin, a pamphlet published by the Shaker Historical Society, tells the history of the sect, and something of their land before the Vans bought it. Much unpublished material was provided by Shaker Heights officials. The market research was conducted by *House and Garden* in 1961 as part of a series of "community profiles of upper-level suburbia."

Lords of Creation, by Frederick Lewis Allen (1935), tells part of the story of the Vans after they started to acquire railroads; Ferdinand Pecora's *Wall Street Under Oath* adds some pertinent details, as do the transcripts of many Congressional hearings. John T. Flynn summed up a good deal of the testimony in his scathing article, "The Betrayal of Cleveland," *Harper's*, January 1934.

CHAPTER IV. FLAGLER, FLORIDA AND FANTASY

The best history of Florida's East Coast is *Florida's Golden Sands*, by Alfred Jackson Hanna and Kathryn Abbey Hanna (1950). Flagler himself was the subject of a book entitled *Florida's Flagler*, by Sidney Walter Martin, University of Georgia Press (1949). Matthew Josephson's account of the rise of Rockefeller and the creation of Standard Oil in *The Robber Barons* was also useful. Cleveland Amory's *The Last Resorts* (1952) contained many anecdotes about Palm Beach, Colonel Bradley, and social life during and after the Flagler period. The Florida boom of the twenties has been covered in a number of books and articles, among the best of which are *Boom in Paradise*, by T. H. Weigall (1932), and *Miami, U.S.A.*, by Helen Muir (1953). None, however, can compare with the delightful account by Alva Johnston, who in *The Legendary Mizners* (1953) went beyond biography and caught the whole spirit of the time and places in which the brothers operated. The quotation from Ben Hecht is from his autobiography, *A Child of the Century* (1955).

CHAPTER V. ABRAHAM KAZAN VS. THE SLUMS OF NEW YORK

Slums and housing reform have had a fascination for social historians for years. One of the most impressively documented works on these subjects is James Ford's two-volume *Slums and Housing* (1936). Robert Bremner's *From the Depths*

(1956) is a fine supplement to Ford. The two books are not only scholarly but colorful as well; they make clear why the articles of the early muckrakers like Ray Stannard Baker and Charles Edward Russell and the books of Jacob Riis had to be written.

The story of the Amalgamated cooperatives is found in the files of the union itself, in its newspaper, *The Advance*, and in the *Amalgamated Co-operator*, which was the house newspaper. Histories of the union, especially *The Amalgamated Clothing Workers of America*, by Charles E. Zaretz (1934), and another book with the same title by Earl D. Strong (1940), contain references to the union's role in cooperative housing. *The Monthly Labor Review*, published by the United States Bureau of Labor Statistics, carried articles about Amalgamated housing from time to time. *Survey Graphic's* article in February 1948, "The House: A Success Story," was based on interviews with residents of the Bronx project. By far the best account, although a modest one, was written by Kazan himself in his report to the union on the thirtieth anniversary of the Bronx houses. In recent years Kazan and his housing projects have been the subject of magazine and newspaper articles, the best of which have been "Homes, Not Just Housing," by Margaret Hickey, in *The Ladies Home Journal*, December 1958, and *"A Decent Place to Live,"* by Bill Chambless in *Minutes*, October 1959. Current issues of *Co-Op Contact*, published by the United Housing Foundation, added recent details.

CHAPTER VI. THE WHITE-COLLAR CITIES OF FRED F. FRENCH

French's career is outlined in the morgues of the New York newspapers—especially those of the *Times* and the *Herald Tribune*—which gave him and his projects considerable coverage, and in his own speeches, the most important of which were reprinted in the *Real Estate Record and Builders Guide*, a trade paper. French's financing methods were discussed in a series of articles in *Architectural Forum*, May, July and August 1929, entitled "Wall Street Enters the Building Field" by John Taylor Boyd, Jr. Albert Mayer's critique of Knickerbocker Village appeared in *Architecture*, January 1935. "The RFC Subsidizes Fred F. French," by Henry J. Rosner, *The Nation*, April 19, 1933 was critical of the government's role in Knickerbocker Village.

CHAPTER VII. HARRY BLACK, THE MAN WHO BUILT SKY-
SCRAPERS

The most important skyscrapers were always newsworthy,
so that contemporary accounts have been the basis for much of
this chapter; the *New York Times* and the *Herald Tribune*,
among the papers, and *The New Yorker, New York Times Magazine, The Literary Digest* and *Fortune,* among the magazines,
were the most useful. Trade publications like *Architectural
Record, Real Estate Record and Builders Guide* and *The Bankers' Magazine* were also informative. Francisco Mujica's *History
of the Skyscraper* (1930) has a good account of the early arguments pro and con skyscrapers. The quotation from Frank
Lloyd Wright is in "The Tyranny of Skyscrapers," *Creative Art,*
May 1931, which reprinted it from his *Modern Architecture.*
The stories of the Flatiron, Woolworth and Empire State buildings are almost part of American folklore by now. Grace M.
Mayer's charming *Once Upon a City* (1958) provided colorful
pictures and text on changing New York.

Black was the subject of many short articles during his
lifetime and a long obituary at his death, but many of the most
important details come from *Changing the Skyline* (1938), Paul
Starrett's reminiscences of his years in the building industry.
The financial aspects of Black's life were fully covered in the
trade press. "Building's No. 1 Contractor" by David B. Carlson,
Architectural Forum, April 1961, reported on the modern
phase of the Fuller Construction Company.

CHAPTER VIII. THE LEVITTS AND THEIR TOWNS

The activities of the Levitts have been thoroughly reported
in the trade press, and from time to time in the general press.
In addition to articles about them in *Fortune* and *House and
Home,* they have been the subjects of feature stories in *Time,
Life, Look* and *Business Week.* "The Six Thousand Houses
That Levitt Built," by Eric Larrabee, *Harper's,* September 1948,
was the first to question whether the results of the Levitt building methods were necessarily beneficial. Since then the social
scientists have studied suburban communities as if they were so
many Indian tribes. William H. Whyte describes some of the
results in *The Organization Man* (1956). Other studies may be
found in a fine collection, *The Suburban Community* (1955),

edited by William M. Dobriner, in which the Riesman article appears. Our account of the segregation fight in Levittown, Pa., is based on newspaper and magazine stories.

CHAPTER IX. WILLIAM ZECKENDORF'S MANY-SPLENDORED CITIES

Zeckendorf has so dominated the urban real estate picture since World War II that every one of his major announcements has made headlines. His career has also been the subject of a *New Yorker* Profile ("Big Operator," by E. J. Kahn, December 8 and 15, 1951) and of lengthy articles in *Life* ("The Man Who Wants to Build New York Over" by Robert Sellmer, October 28, 1946), *Look, Fortune, Architectural Forum, House and Home* and *Business Week.* "Man in a $100-Million Jam" by Gilbert Burck, *Fortune,* July 1960, is the best recent analysis of Webb & Knapp and of Zeckendorf's finances. Zeckendorf's own version of some of the deals he managed often tells the story best. His talks to students at the Harvard School of Design were published in the *Atlantic Monthly,* under the titles "New Cities for Old" and "Baked Buildings," in the issues of November and December 1951. "Cities versus Suburbs" appeared in the *Atlantic,* July 1952, and "Fluid Suburbia" in *Yale Review,* September 1958. Daniel M. Friedenburg's "The Coming Bust in the Real Estate Boom," *Harper's,* June 1961, is an informative, if critical, article on current urban building.

ABOUT THE AUTHORS

EUGENE RACHLIS was born in Roxbury, Massachusetts, and educated in the Boston public schools and at Boston University. He joined the Washington Bureau of International News Service in 1941. Before and after service in World War II, he was Washington correspondent for the *Chicago Sun*. He has been a writer for *Changing Times;* information officer for the Marshall Plan mission to The Netherlands; director of operations in Paris for the Marshall Plan information program in Europe; staff editor for the *New York Times Magazine;* associate editor of *Collier's;* and managing editor of the *Woman's Home Companion*. He was co-author of *Peter Stuyvesant and His New York*, published by Random House in 1959; has written a number of books for young people, including *The Story of the U. S. Coast Guard, The Voyages of Henry Hudson* (both Landmark Books) and *Indians of the Plains;* and has published many articles. Mr. Rachlis' own experiences as a landlord are limited to three-quarters of an acre on Shelter Island, New York.

JOHN E. MARQUSEE is Vice Chairman of the Board and Chief Executive Officer of United Improvement & Investing Corp., a diversified real estate company, as well as chairman of the executive committee of two other publicly held real estate companies with which his company is closely affiliated. He is also a former president of the New York State Association of Home Builders. Mr. Marqusee began his career as a builder and developer in Westchester County, New York. With his partner, he has since organized the syndication of properties valued at more than $72,000,000. A graduate of Cornell University, Mr. Marqusee has a law degree from New York University. With his wife and five children, he lives in Scarsdale, New York.